Jeffrey T. Fritz

Sams Teach Yourself
ASP.NET Core

in 24 Hours

SAMS 800 East 96th Street, Indianapolis, Indiana, 46240 USA

Sams Teach Yourself ASP.NET Core in 24 Hours

ISBN-13: 978-0-672-33766-6

ISBN-10: 0-672-33766-5

Library of Congress Control Number: 2017955882

1   17

Trademarks

Warning and Disclaimer

Special Sales

Editor-in-Chief
Mark Taub

Senior Acquisitions Editor
Trina MacDonald

Development Editor
Mark Renfrow

Managing Editor
Sandra Schroeder

Project Editor
Mandie Frank

Copy Editor
Kitty Wilson

Indexer
Lisa Stumpf

Proofreader
Abby Manheim

Technical Editor
Javier Lozano

Editorial Assistant
Courtney Martin

Designer
Chuti Prasertsith

Compositor
codeMantra

Contents at a Glance

Table of Contents

About the Author

Jeffrey T. Fritz is a long time web developer with ASP, ASP.NET, and now ASP.NET Core. He loves the challenge of building web applications that look amazing while at the same time performing like an installed application. The browser is his bane and his best friend, as he has built applications that work with every browser going back as far as Internet Explorer 4.

Jeff is a senior program manager on the .NET team responsible for the creation of the ASP.NET Core and .NET Core frameworks, and has taught several thousands of developers how to build better applications with Microsoft's ASP.NET frameworks. Previously, he was a developer advocate for Telerik where he specialized in their AJAX Control Toolkit. Jeff's proposals and designs led to the development of dozens of controls that many developers use daily. Jeff holds a bachelor of science degree in Management Sciences and Information Systems from the Pennsylvania State University.

An avid social media contributor, Jeff would love to hear from you on Twitter at @csharpfritz and you can follow his current coding adventures on his blog at www.jeffreyfritz.com

Dedication

For Mom and Dad: A teacher and a technologist who taught me to love teaching about software development. Thank you for your encouragement to pursue my dreams; otherwise, I'd be a chemist lurking in a lab somewhere.

To my wonderful wife, Becky, and my daughters: Daddy's done writing the book. Thank you for your patience in putting up with my long hours of writing. Let's take a vacation.

Acknowledgments

We would like to thank the contributions of the following folks for their work on this book:

The ASP.NET Core team at Microsoft, for innovating and building such a cool framework that we all enjoy working with and who made this book possible.

Trina MacDonald, my acquisitions editor who helped me get the materials together for this book and deliver them effectively to the rest of the team.

Javier Lozano, my technical editor, who answered my goofy questions when I would write samples and needed to verify that they made sense and stayed on track with the pace and tone of the book.

Mandie Frank for giving us that last push to review and ensure that all of the contents, word documents, and images landed in the correct places for this book. Thank you for your effort to make our content read and look great.

We Want to Hear from You!

As the reader of this book, *you* are our most important critic and commentator. We value your opinion and want to know what we're doing right, what we could do better, what areas you'd like to see us publish in, and any other words of wisdom you're willing to pass our way.

We welcome your comments. You can email or write to let us know what you did or didn't like about this book—as well as what we can do to make our books better.

Please note that we cannot help you with technical problems related to the topic of this book.

When you write, please be sure to include this book's title and author as well as your name and email address. We will carefully review your comments and share them with the author and editors who worked on the book.

Email: feedback@samspublishing.com

Mail: Sams Publishing
ATTN: Reader Feedback
         800 East 96th Street
         Indianapolis, IN 46240 USA

Reader Services

Register your copy of *Sams Teach Yourself ASP.NET Core in 24 Hours* at informit.com for convenient access to downloads, updates, and corrections as they become available. To start the registration process, go to informit.com/register and log in or create an account*. Enter the product ISBN, 9780672337666, and click Submit. Once the process is complete, you will find any available bonus content under Registered Products.

*Be sure to check the box that you would like to hear from us in order to receive exclusive discounts on future editions of this product.

Introduction

The World Wide Web has been around for more than 20 years, and it's safe to say that it's here to stay. During this time, Microsoft has produced one of the most effective and productive frameworks for building and deploying websites: the Active Server Pages (ASP) framework. Through the evolution of ASP into ASP.NET, this framework has grown and changed to meet the needs of the ever-evolving web. The latest incarnation of ASP, ASP.NET Core, addresses many of the needs of modern web developers who want to build portable high-performance applications that can run on any operating system. This book teaches you how to build your first web application with ASP.NET Core and run it from Microsoft Azure.

A very productive development team can build custom easy-to-maintain web applications with ASP.NET Core. In this book, you'll learn how to get your first application running in minutes with the ASP.NET Core framework. With the open source licensing for ASP.NET Core, you can even enhance the framework in any way that your project needs, and you can contribute those changes to the team so that everyone can benefit.

By the end of this 24-hour book, you will have created your own travel management application and deployed it to Azure using Azure App Service. You will learn how to use modern JavaScript frameworks like Angular 4 with ASP.NET Core in order to create more compelling and interactive applications. Along the way, you will learn many tips and tricks to help improve your development experience, whether you are working on a Mac, Linux, or Windows machine.

Who Should Read This Book

This book is written for anyone who wants to build websites and applications easily, without having to reinvent the basic components of a website each time they write a new application.

If you know a little bit of C# and HTML, then this book will get you on your way with ASP.NET Core. Even if you don't know much of the C# language, this book will make it easy for you to pick it up and be productive.

The HTML, CSS, and JavaScript demonstrated in this book is elementary. It is intended to be approachable, not to show a beautiful user interface. The focus is on delivering value without making intimidating use of browser or web technologies that are not central to the ASP.NET Core development experience.

How This Book Is Organized

ASP.NET Core is a framework with significant depth, and 24 hours is not enough time to learn every nuance of the technology. This book covers the basics as well as some intermediate topics to get you writing applications as quickly as possible. The framework features and knowledge you will learn in a 24-hour day with this book will be invaluable to your future web development projects. The following breakdown contains the details of what you will learn in each of the hours:

▶ In Hour 1, "Introducing ASP.NET Core," you'll learn about the history of this web framework and what makes it a significant player in the technical community. You'll also learn about the sample project you will build throughout the book.

▶ In Hour 2, "Setting Up Your Work Environment for ASP.NET Core," you'll start configuring your machine to be able to write ASP.NET Core code. You will learn how to choose between the various versions of Visual Studio and how you can use your favorite text editor if you don't want to use Visual Studio at all. You'll also be introduced to the `dotnet` command-line tool.

▶ In Hour 3, "Exploring the New Project Templates," you will build your first website, using the templates that come with Visual Studio and the `dotnet` command-line tool. You will learn about the file structure of an ASP.NET Core project and how to work with the templates.

▶ In Hour 4, "Defining ASP.NET Core Configuration," you will learn about the various project configuration options and how to automate tasks for an application's build process. You'll also be introduced to NuGet and how you can add features to your application from the free repository at NuGet.org.

▶ In Hour 5, "Configuring the Service with the `Startup` Class," you'll learn about the `Startup` class and how it controls the flow of requests from browsers into an application.

▶ In Hour 6, "Configuring Your Application," your application will grow to start reading project configuration information from disk, environment variables, and secret data locations. You will also learn about how ASP.NET Core manages the application environment and how you can take advantage of that to keep developer-facing features out of a production environment.

▶ In Hour 7, "Accessing Your Data with Entity Framework Core," you'll start to connect your web application to the SQLite database. You'll learn how to build a database using .NET code and manage the data in the database by using Entity Framework Core.

▶ In Hour 8, "Introducing the MVC Architecture," you will learn about the basic MVC architecture concepts and structures that you will use throughout your application. This concept-focused hour will have you thinking more about how to structure your code than writing code.

- In Hour 9, "Building Your First Controller," builds on the concepts in the previous hour and will help you start constructing code to present information to your application users.

- In Hour 10, "Beginning MVC: Writing Your First View," you'll learn how to start formatting information in your application as HTML, the formatting language of the web.

- In Hour 11, "Scaffolding User Interfaces," you'll take a slight step back from Hour 10 to try out tools in Visual Studio that generate simple HTML formatting for you. You'll learn how to take advantage of these starting points and build your application quickly.

- In Hour 12, "Writing Data from a Controller," you'll start putting together the pieces from Hour 7 together with the previous three hours and write code that allows a browser to work with the content of your database.

- In Hour 13, "Writing Web API Methods," you'll write APIs for machines and other software to be able to interact with your application.

- In Hour 14, "Introducing Reusable User Interface Components," you'll look into simplifying some of the code that you have written to format the application using tag helpers and view components. You will learn how easy it is to reuse code that you have written throughout your application.

- In Hour 15, "npm and bower: Client-Side Package Managers," you'll step outside the ASP. NET Core ecosystem and learn how these community projects are enabled by ASP.NET Core and how you can consume the web components built and shared by their communities.

- In Hour 16, "Introducing Angular," you'll learn about the Angular JavaScript framework and why it is so popular. You will work for the next few hours on Angular and experience what makes it so efficient and productive for web developers.

- In Hour 17, "Connecting Angular to ASP.NET Core," you'll start using Angular to fetch and present data from your ASPTravlerz application. By the end of the hour, you will have a full Angular application that is able to read and write data using the API features written in Hour 13.

- In Hour 18, "Routing Angular Requests Around ASP.NET Core," you'll start working with the routing features of Angular and ASP.NET Core to control the web page addresses and navigation formats of the links in your application.

- In Hour 19, "Running Angular on the Server," you'll take what you learned about Angular in Hours 16, 17, and 18 and integrate it tightly with the ASP.NET Core project using the SpaServices features of ASP.NET Core.

- In Hour 20, "Authenticating Your Users," you'll learn how to enable visitors to log in to your application and the various configurations you can apply to your application to store and manage user credentials.

▶ In Hour 21, "Granting Access to Users," you'll learn about protecting features and components of your application from unwanted user access. You'll create security roles and policies that allow you to control who can access components of the application.

▶ In Hour 22, "Deploying to Production," you'll learn about using the `dotnet publish` command to deploy your application to Windows and Linux servers. You will also spend some time learning how easy it is to deploy to the Microsoft Azure cloud service.

▶ Hour 23, "Working with Docker Containers," introduces the virtual container concept and how you can use this unit of delivery to make building and deploying your application simple.

▶ In Hour 24, "Looking to the Future and .NET Standard," you'll learn about the planned features of ASP.NET Core, where to keep up to date with these features, and the new concepts introduced by .NET Standard.

Conventions Used in This Book

This book uses several conventions to make it easier for you to understand what is being explained.

Try It Yourself

The Try It Yourself activities provide hands-on opportunities to actively experience and engage in the topics covered. These hands-on activities provide an opportunity to learn by doing, which is the best way to learn ASP.NET Core.

Notes

Notes provide extra tidbits of information. The contain supplemental content or expand the information given in the nearby text.

Tips

Tips provide extra information that can be useful when you are coding. This information can range from tips on how to better use a program to certain things you might want to change in the code. Tips identify handy tricks or expert advice that will help you along the way.

Cautions

Cautions warn you when an action you might take could have dire consequences. This cautionary text warns you of potential hazards and provides advance warning of outcomes you want to avoid.

Code Listings

Code listings provide sample snippets of code that relate to the topic at hand. You'll be able to examine the sample code to get a feel for how your code should be written.

In this book, formal code listings are always surrounded by two lines to show where the code starts and where it ends. The text surrounding the listing explains where this code should be placed if that isn't clear from the code itself.

Downloading the Code and Resources

The code for this application can be found online at https://github.com/csharpfritz/AspTravlerz. The repository is structured with separate folders for each hour of this book. If you get stuck in a Workshop or Try It Yourself section, you can refer to this code for help. All of the code is commented and easy to follow.

HOUR 1
Introducing ASP.NET Core

What You'll Learn in This Hour:

▶ What is ASP.NET?

▶ Why should you program with ASP.NET Core?

▶ The significant changes in ASP.NET Core from previous versions, and why they are important

▶ Assumptions in this book

▶ Introduction to the sample project

In this hour you're going to learn what ASP.NET is, what makes it the preferred web programming environment for many developers, and what major changes have been made in the new ASP.NET Core framework. This lesson reviews the assumptions that are made in this book and wraps up with an introduction to the sample project you will build as you proceed through 24 hours of learning about ASP.NET Core.

NOTE

ASP Is over 20 Years Old!

This isn't the first version of ASP.NET. The fundamental architecture of the ASP framework was first released in December 1996 by Microsoft as Active Server Pages 1.0. In 2002, Microsoft updated the framework with a new development model and support for the VB.NET and C#.NET programming languages.

What Is ASP.NET?

ASP.NET is the Microsoft.NET implementation of the Active Server Pages architecture and concepts for web developers by Microsoft. Originally deployed as part of Windows servers with web hosting capabilities for enterprises, the framework grew over 12 years and through six versions to the most recent release, ASP.NET Core. The Microsoft.NET versions over time are displayed in Figure 1.1.

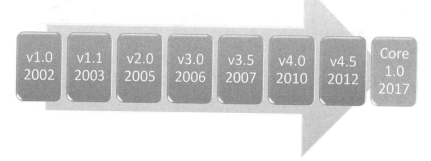

FIGURE 1.1
ASP.NET versions over time.

Development Frameworks

Throughout the history of ASP.NET, a series of child frameworks evolved from Microsoft to better support developers' needs. These frameworks supplemented the initial Web Forms style of programming to introduce new web programming paradigms that developers needed as web technologies evolved. The frameworks supported by all versions of ASP.NET are described in Table 1.1

TABLE 1.1   ASP.NET Development Frameworks

Framework Name	First Version	Description
Web Forms	1.0	A framework that allowed page-centric design with stateful concepts like postback and viewstate. The user interface was delivered as a set of controls that generate HTML.
AJAX	3.5	A framework that introduced JavaScript extensions for controls to provide immediate interactions with a browser.
MVC	3.5sp1	The Model-View-Controller paradigm, which no longer used postback, viewstate, or controls.
Dynamic Data	3.5sp1	A data-driven framework that generated content and layouts based on data presented from databases.
Web API	4.5	A RESTful service endpoint that was delivered using HTTP standard verbs and a controller architecture.
SignalR	4.5.1	A real-time push-enabled communications framework that allowed clients to subscribe to notifications from a hosted web service.

These frameworks have delivered significant value to developers and have enabled them to build customized solutions quickly and productively with very little ceremony. With the initial release of the latest version of ASP.NET, only a chosen few of these frameworks are available, and if history gives us a hint about the future, then it's safe to assume that there will be many new development frameworks to come.

Why Should You Program in ASP.NET?

Many developers new to the ASP.NET ecosystem wonder why they should program in ASP.NET. The answers are many and vary, depending on your project team's specific needs:

▶ If you're a Microsoft Windows developer, and you are expecting to deliver an application that needs to run from a Windows environment, you'll find that ASP.NET is a great solution that continues the support you are already receiving from Microsoft.

▶ If you need a productive web application environment so that you can get started quickly and build simple applications with little development knowledge and want to be productive quickly, you will find that ASP.NET and Visual Studio have tools to get you started developing your first web application quickly.

▶ If you are a developer who needs modern web capabilities and a set of prescribed tools that augment those capabilities to enable team collaboration, source control, and agile methodologies, you will find that ASP.NET with Visual Studio is an excellent choice.

▶ If you are tired of the drama with community-owned open source web frameworks and need tools with a top software vendor supporting them and also an open source pedigree that means you can make modifications and submit changes, ASP.NET is an excellent choice for you.

Significant Changes in ASP.NET Core

The new version of ASP.NET has diverged from the ordinal numbers of previous releases. Typically, the major version number of software changes when there are significant breaking changes in the software. In the case of ASP.NET, Microsoft could have named it ASP.NET 10, as there have been many significant changes over prior versions, but the team wanted to make it clear that this version is a significant break from previous ASP.NETs. Thus, Core 1.0 was announced and landed as a complete rewrite of previous releases with the following strategic pillars in mind:

▶ **Lean and composable**—The framework should not be a 250 MB install that is required on every machine that develops and hosts applications.

▶ **Modular**—You should be able to choose just the parts of the framework that you want to install and run with your application.

▶ **Open source**—All development of ASP.NET by Microsoft is publicly visible, and Microsoft accepts submissions from the community.

▶ **Fast development cycle**—Previous framework versions were only released with a new Visual Studio version, but now new versions will be available as updates to NuGet packages on NuGet.org.

▶ **Choose your own editor**—ASP.NET is no longer tied to just Visual Studio, and its tools now allow you to write code with your favorite text editor and deliver the same web application experience to your customers.

▶ **Cross-platform**—No longer is ASP.NET tied to development and deployment on Windows only. Support is provided for development and deployment on Windows, Mac, and Linux.

The following sections dig into each of these pillars and discuss how they are implemented in ASP.NET Core.

Lean and Composable

The web application framework has broken away from the rest of the Microsoft.NET Common Language Runtime (CLR). The CLR is the base collection of libraries provided by Microsoft that you can use to build web applications.

In prior versions of ASP.NET, the CLR contained everything to build desktop, phone, and web applications. These are very different formats, and each of these formats needs different tools and software. Splitting off the ASP.NET implementation from the base CLR means that developers can leave behind components that are normally used to write phone or desktop applications when they are writing server-side web applications.

Modular

With the .NET Framework and CLR of old, you needed to install a complete version of the CLR on a computer. With ASP.NET Core, the framework is delivered as a NuGet package, which is a bundle of software that you can retrieve from a central repository and make available for application development on a workstation. These packages can be chosen and assembled as needed, and they are completely isolated from each project or application that is running on a computer.

Previously, you needed to install the .NET Framework on a machine, and all applications would use the same framework. With ASP.NET Core, you can deploy your own version of the framework that is custom tailored to your application without fear of it interfering with other applications running on the same machine.

Open Source

Since 2012, open source has almost become a requirement of any software vendor. With security issues introduced by governments and nefarious organizations, it has become imperative that development of software development technologies exists in the open so that everyone can review and easily inspect what is going on "under the covers." This level of transparency provides the ultimate security for the framework that your application is running on because you can easily inspect how the framework operates.

The framework source code is licensed under the Apache v2 license, and the copy the ASP.NET team is distributing can be found at https://raw.githubusercontent.com/aspnet/Home/dev/LICENSE.txt. This license grants you the ability to distribute copies of the source code, access Microsoft's patents used as part of the source code, and modify the source code for public and private use. There are no requirements to return to the public any modifications that you make to the source code.

TIP

Source Code Has Always Been Available

The source code for the .NET Framework has always been available. It was originally published in 2002 as the Rotor project, and you could download and use the .NET Framework source code for free, but you could not republish it or submit changes to it. It's still available today at http://sourceof.net.

ASP.NET was written primarily by Microsoft but is supported by a nonprofit organization called the .NET Foundation, which supports open source projects in the .NET community and fosters collaboration between developers and communities. Some of the .NET Foundation's projects are listed in the word cloud shown in Figure 1.2. More details about the .NET Foundation can be found on their web site, at www.dotnetfoundation.org

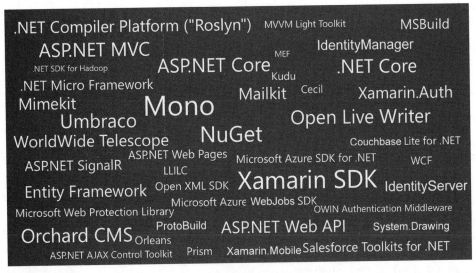

FIGURE 1.2
A word-cloud showing some of the .NET community projects sponsored by the .NET Foundation.

If you have advanced features that are not built into the original framework that was delivered to you, it is very easy to get a copy of the source code to ASP.NET and make the modifications you need and use that version instead of the "in the box" version that was delivered to you by Microsoft. As an example, a government organization might have very strict security standards with custom encryption algorithms. Engineers in that organization might be able to modify the source code to use their custom security algorithms and deploy those customized versions for use in their organization.

You can now find the source code to ASP.NET on GitHub, at http://github.com/aspnet/home. There are lots of people working there at all hours of every day, talking about and building the ASP.NET frameworks and tools.

Fast Development Cycle

The fast development cycle goes hand-in-hand with the modular nature of the framework. With the deployment of framework resources as NuGet packages, new versions can be deployed more quickly, and they can be consumed by developers who monitor the NuGet.org service for package updates. Using semantic versioning capabilities in the references of an ASP.NET project, developers can easily decide whether they want to accept minor fixes to a component or install major changes.

Choose Your Own Editor

This is a big deal: No longer is Microsoft tied to selling you a Visual Studio version to build with its web framework. ASP.NET Core comes with a collection of command-line tools that you can use with your favorite text editor to compile and deploy a real working web application. In addition, Microsoft is supporting developer community members who are building add-ons to help give text editors rich source code editing capabilities.

The command-line tools Microsoft provides are not half-baked tools that only developers on Mac and Linux will use. Every ASP.NET application is built with the same tools, and even Visual Studio uses these same tools. The difference with Visual Studio is that Microsoft put a nice graphical user interface in front of the command-line experience. For many developers who prefer the command line, this change has been a very welcome one.

Cross-Platform Capable

When cross-platform capability was announced, some technologists' minds melted. Microsoft is making a development technology for full development use on Mac and Linux. No longer are you required to buy Windows or a Windows Server license to run your web applications. Web operators who enjoy running server daemons on Linux can manage and support ASP.NET applications running on their favorite flavor of Linux with the same fidelity and support from Microsoft that they would receive if they were on Windows.

This is not your parents' Microsoft.

MVC and WebAPI

Previous versions of ASP.NET provided access to the Web Forms framework. Starting with ASP.NET Core, the preferred development framework is a combination of the ASP.NET MVC and WebAPI frameworks. This is not a direct upgrade but a "concept compatible" update that adds the same features you are already familiar with. This rewrite of MVC and WebAPI provides simpler syntax and use. You'll learn more about how to start programming in this model during Hours 8, "Introducing the MVC Architecture," through 13, "Writing Web API Methods."

Introducing the CoreCLR

One of the biggest changes that was made to accommodate a number of the pillars listed earlier in this chapter is the new CoreCLR. This new cross-platform-capable common language runtime supports delivery of binary components as packages and modular delivery to servers. It is not a requirement to develop with this framework, and you can still write your software on Windows with the full "desktop-capable" CLR if you like. However, if you develop with the full CLR, those applications can only be deployed to Windows servers.

The CoreCLR is a rewrite of the CLR based on work that was started by the Silverlight runtime. The CoreCLR combined with an operating system–specific loader and runtime makes cross-platform development possible.

Assumptions and Definitions in This Book

The aim of this book is to get you familiar with ASP.NET Core; it is not focused on teaching you how to write HTML or C#. This book assumes that you know enough HTML, CSS, JavaScript, and C# to get started.

Although this book uses Windows and Visual Studio 2017 as the primary source for screenshots and demonstrations, it does not assume that you are developing software or working on Windows. Hours 2, "Setting Up Your Work Environment for ASP.NET Core," and 3, "Exploring the New Project Templates," get you up and running with ASP.NET technologies no matter whether you are working with Windows, Mac, or Linux. All the source code and samples provided have been tested and proven to work on all three environments unless noted.

Introducing the Sample Project

In this book, you will explore the features and capabilities of ASP.NET Core with an ongoing sample project. The project you will be building is a travel planner web application that will allow you to capture important information about a travel itinerary and make it available as a mobile-capable website. Phones, tablets, and desktop-based browsers should all be able to work with this web application.

You will start simple with the ASPTravlerz company (so named because all cool startups drop a few letters and add a Z) and slowly build a functional web application that runs and feels great on all browsers. At the end of the book you will deploy the application to the Microsoft Azure hosting service so that you can always reach your travel information no matter where you are in the world.

▼ TRY IT YOURSELF

Check Out the Sample Project Online

The sample ASPTravlerz project source code is available online and a sample instance of the completed project is available. Follow these steps:

1. Navigate to https://github.com/csharpfritz/AspTravlerz to find the complete source code with tags for each completed hour of this book.

2. You can see the sample project completed and running on the author's domain, hosted from Microsoft Azure, at https://asptravlerz.jeffreyfritz.com.

Summary

This hour reviews the changes and updates that were made to the ASP.NET frameworks for ASP.NET Core. You have learned why these significant changes from previous versions of ASP.NET are important. With a quick review of where ASP.NET came from, you now have your sights set on a sample project and getting your workstation ready to build web applications with ASP.NET Core, starting in Hour 2.

Q&A

Q. Can I migrate my existing ASP.NET applications to ASP.NET Core?

A. Microsoft does not recommend that you attempt such an upgrade because the entire framework has been rewritten from scratch. You are welcome to go through the process, but Microsoft is not explicitly supporting a migration strategy.

Q. Can I run a Web Forms application in ASP.NET Core?

A. At this time, there is no support for Web Forms in the ASP.NET Core framework stack. However, the entire framework is open source, and there is plenty of opportunity for developers to build out their own versions of Web Forms projects if they want to.

Q. Is ASP.NET Core *really* open source?

A. Yes, and with no strings attached. All of Microsoft's development for the ASP.NET product is open source and available on GitHub. Microsoft is accepting patches from external vendors, active community members, and developers like you. You will always be able to download any version of the source, compile what you need, and develop against it.

Q. My organization does not allow open source products. Why should I trust ASP.NET Core?

A. Microsoft holds all contributions to the same standards to which it holds its own code. While you have the opportunity to download and work with the code directly, you can be assured that Microsoft will issue binary patches and provide support to all binary releases that it issues with the same diligence as with previous ASP.NET versions. This is a benefit for you!

Workshop

The workshop contains quiz questions and exercises to help you solidify your understanding of the material covered. Try to answer all questions before looking at the "Answers" that follow.

Quiz

1. Under what open source license is ASP.NET licensed?

2. What is CoreCLR?

3. What are packages?

4. Do you have to use tools made by Microsoft to write ASP.NET Core applications?

Answers

1. Apache License 2.0

2. CoreCLR is the new cross-platform-capable common language runtime. It can be deployed as a series of packages in a modular fashion to machines without having applications installing conflicting versions of the runtime.

3. Packages are the unit of distribution for ASP.NET Core components. Binary versions of libraries are bundled together and made available from NuGet.org for your use.

4. No. You can use any editor. In addition, the same command-line tools that a Microsoft tool would use to build an application are available to you.

Exercise

Explore the ASP.NET team's resources on the web to learn more about the framework and to keep an eye on how it evolves:

www.asp.net—The ASP.NET framework home page

www.github.com/aspnet/home—The ASP.NET source code home page

https://blogs.msdn.microsoft.com/webdev—The ASP.NET team blog, which provides announcements, interesting articles, and links to training videos

HOUR 2
Setting Up Your Work Environment for ASP.NET Core

Four Versions of Visual Studio: Where Do I Start?

It's no secret that the premier way to work with writing .NET code is to use the flagship tool Visual Studio.NET for ASP.NET Core. To do so, you need to install Visual Studio 2017, but there are now four different versions available. How do you choose the version that's most appropriate for you and your project team? Table 2.1 lists the versions and the trade-offs you make in choosing one over another. (For a more detailed comparison, from Microsoft, see https://www.visualstudio.com/vs/compare.)

TABLE 2.1 Available Visual Studio Versions

Version	Description
Enterprise	Includes all the features of the Professional edition, plus advanced load testing tools and advanced architecture capabilities. Also includes $150/month of Microsoft Azure credits.
Professional	Includes all the features of the Community edition plus powerful developer productivity features like Codelens. This edition includes team collaboration tools like team rooms and project management charts.

Version	Description
Community	Includes simulators for Windows, Windows Phone, and Android. Also provides basic unit-testing tools, integrated source control, refactoring capabilities, and Blend for user interface design. Supports development frameworks for Windows, Windows Store, Universal Windows Apps, ASP.NET, SQL Server, Apache Cordova, C++, Python, and Node.js.
Code	Provides a text editor with source control, syntax highlighting capabilities, and a built-in debugger for ASP.NET Core and Node.js.

One of the key features that all versions of Visual Studio provide is called IntelliSense, Microsoft's code completion help. As you type keywords in the text editor of any version of Visual Studio, suggestions are immediately presented, along with help text and hints to aid in your programming work.

Of course, as you choose an edition of Visual Studio near the top of Table 2.1, you pay a higher monetary cost. At the bottom, Visual Studio Code is completely free, and it's available for Windows, Mac, and Linux.

Community edition is available only on Windows 7, Windows 8.x, and Windows 10. Microsoft makes this version free for individuals working on open source projects, students, and those participating in academic research. To protect this version and make it available to nonprofit or commercial organizations, Microsoft limits licensing to organizations with fewer than 250 PCs or less than $1 million USD in annual revenue.

The Professional and Enterprise versions are available only on Windows and are typically purchased with an MSDN subscription that delivers a collection of additional Microsoft software applications and tools. With these subscriptions, you also get a fixed amount of Microsoft Azure service credit each month. At the time of this writing, the credit is $50 with the Professional edition and $150 with the Enterprise edition.

Finally, there is a way for startup companies to get a completely free copy of Visual Studio: Join Microsoft BizSpark. BizSpark is a program that Microsoft uses to encourage startup companies and companies participating in startup accelerators to use premium Microsoft solutions. For more information about BizSpark and the forms to sign up, visit www.microsoft.com/bizspark/.

You can download an installer for Visual Studio Community from www.visualstudio.com, and you can get a copy of Visual Studio Code from code.visualstudio.com.

Installation Options and the Tools That Are Installed

When installing Community, Professional, or Enterprise versions of Visual Studio, you must choose to install the .NET Core Cross-Platform Development workload in order to get access to the ASP.NET Core capabilities in the tool (see Figure 2.1).

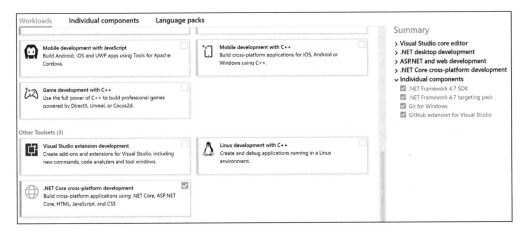

FIGURE 2.1
Visual Studio installation options.

In addition to the Visual Studio editor, several external tools are installed with Visual Studio. These tools are deposited by default in the C:\Program Files (x86)\Microsoft Visual Studio\2017\Enterprise\Web\External folder:

▶ Git

▶ nodejs

▶ npm

▶ bower

▶ Grunt

▶ Gulpjs

With these tools installed, you have everything you need to build a modern web application with Visual Studio.

Installing Visual Studio with Chocolatey

On Windows, you can automate the installation of Visual Studio by using the Chocolatey package manager tool. Chocolatey is a command-line tool that helps install software in an unattended manner from a central repository. Instructions for installing the latest version of Chocolatey are kept at www.chocolatey.org. The recommended way to install Chocolatey is to follow these steps:

1. Locate the command prompt on your Start menu.

2. Right-click the command prompt icon and choose Run as Administrator. (You need to do this because you are installing software and will need access to the registry.)

3. In the command prompt window that appears, execute the following command:

```
@powershell -NoProfile -ExecutionPolicy Bypass -Command "iex ((new-object
net.webclient).DownloadString('https://chocolatey.org/install.ps1'))" && SET
PATH=%PATH%;%ALLUSERSPROFILE%\chocolatey\bin
```

Once you have Chocolatey configured, you can run the choco command from the command line. You can install Visual Studio Community with the following command:

```
choco install visualstudio2017community
```

You can install Visual Studio Code with the following command:

```
choco install visualstudiocode
```

Both of these commands can be scripted, and additional parameters can be passed to further automate the installation process. This is a great technique that can be used to speed up the construction of virtual machines you use for development.

Installing Development Tools on Non-Windows Operating Systems

Here's where things start to go off the standard Microsoft path. Installing tools and building software in an environment that isn't Windows is a brand-new endeavor for the .NET team, but they've done a great job providing options that are fully supported on Mac and Linux.

Installing Visual Studio Code and ASP.NET on Mac OSX Yosemite

Mac OSX Yosemite is the current version of OSX that is supported by the Visual Studio Code project. You can install Visual Studio Code by following these steps:

1. Download the Mac version of Visual Studio Code from code.visualstudio.com.

2. Double-click the VSCode-osx.zip file that is delivered to your machine to expand its contents.

3. Drag the Visual Studio Code.app file to the Applications folder to make it available on your Launchpad.

If you want to run Visual Studio Code from the terminal, append the following to your ~/.bash_profile:

```
code () { VSCODE_CWD="$PWD" open -n -b "com.microsoft.VSCode" --args $* ;}
```

With this configuration, you can type code . to begin editing the project in your current folder location.

However, unlike with the Windows installation of Visual Studio, this does not install the ASP.NET runtime or the .NET compilers. This installation only adds the text editor and the nodejs command-line tool so that you can add additional features for web development.

You need to take several steps to install the runtimes and command-line tools needed to run Visual Studio Code and start writing ASP.NET Core applications on a Mac:

1. Install Homebrew (if you don't already have it) with the following command in a terminal window:

```
ruby -e "$(curl -fsSL
https://raw.githubusercontent.com/Homebrew/install/master/install)"
```

2. Add the OpenSSL package to your workstation with the following commands:

```
brew update
brew install openssl
mkdir -p /usr/local/lib
ln -s /usr/local/opt/openssl/lib/libcrypto.1.0.0.dylib /usr/local/lib/
ln -s /usr/local/opt/openssl/lib/libssl.1.0.0.dylib /usr/local/lib/
```

3. Install the .NET Core SDK from the Microsoft website, at https://www.microsoft.com/net/core#macos.

You should now be able to run the dotnet command in any terminal window and get some help text to get you started, as shown in Figure 2.2.

```
C:\>dotnet --help
.NET Command Line Tools (1.0.4)
Usage: dotnet [host-options] [command] [arguments] [common-options]

Arguments:
  [command]              The command to execute
  [arguments]            Arguments to pass to the command
  [host-options]         Options specific to dotnet (host)
  [common-options]       Options common to all commands

Common options:
  -v|--verbose           Enable verbose output
  -h|--help              Show help

Host options (passed before the command):
  -d|--diagnostics       Enable diagnostic output
  --version              Display .NET CLI Version Number
  --info                 Display .NET CLI Info

Commands:
  new           Initialize .NET projects.
  restore       Restore dependencies specified in the .NET project.
  build         Builds a .NET project.
  publish       Publishes a .NET project for deployment (including the runtime).
  run           Compiles and immediately executes a .NET project.
  test          Runs unit tests using the test runner specified in the project.
  pack          Creates a NuGet package.
  migrate       Migrates a project.json based project to a msbuild based project.
  clean         Clean build output(s).
  sln           Modify solution (SLN) files.

Project modification commands:
  add           Add items to the project
  remove        Remove items from the project
  list          List items in the project

Advanced Commands:
  nuget         Provides additional NuGet commands.
  msbuild       Runs Microsoft Build Engine (MSBuild).
  vstest        Runs Microsoft Test Execution Command Line Tool.

C:\>
```

FIGURE 2.2
dotnet command-line tool output when called with the --help command.

You'll learn more about the dotnet command-line tool later this hour.

Configuring a Linux Workstation for ASP.NET Core Development

Configuring a Linux workstation is really interesting and may require some minor changes on your part, depending on how your Linux machine is configured. Linux has many varieties and no real standard installation configuration. The following instructions have been tested and verified to work with Ubuntu 16.04, Mint 18, and some Debian distribution versions:

1. To configure the `apt-get` tool to connect to and download the .NET command-line tools for Linux, open a terminal window and execute the following at the command prompt:

```
sudo sh -c 'echo "deb [arch=amd64] https://apt-mo.trafficmanager.net/repos/
dotnet-release/ xenial main" > /etc/apt/sources.list.d/dotnetdev.list'
sudo apt-key adv --keyserver hkp://keyserver.ubuntu.com:80 --recv-keys
417A0893
sudo apt-get update
```

2. Get the `dotnet` package:

```
sudo apt-get install dotnet-dev-1.0.4
```

If everything completed properly, you should be able to run the `dotnet --help` command at a terminal and get the same help text shown with the Mac installation.

Adding ASP.NET Core Capabilities to Your Favorite Text Editor

What if you're already happy with a text editor, and you don't want to waste your time loading up some Visual Studio version? Maybe you don't like all that integrated development nonsense that Microsoft adds to its tools, and you just want to focus on editing text. A group of .NET developers who don't work for Microsoft put together an add-on called Omnisharp for some of the most popular editors available.

Omnisharp runs a service in the background that compiles and analyzes the code you are writing in your text editor and provides IntelliSense code suggestions for you as you type. These suggestions are delivered from a compiler, so they are based on what your project looks like and what your available references look like. You can find Omnisharp at www.omnisharp.net and install it to work with editors like Atom, Brackets, Emacs, Sublime Text, and even Vim. Figure 2.3 shows Omnisharp running inside Sublime Text.

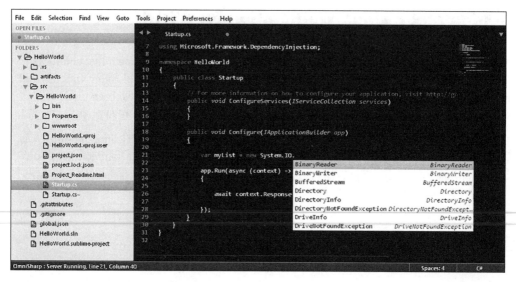

FIGURE 2.3
Omnisharp autocomplete functionality inside the Sublime Text editor.

Introducing the dotnet Command-Line Tool

Throughout the history of .NET development, there has been only one way to develop applications: Use Visual Studio on Windows. What if you don't want to use Visual Studio or Visual Studio for Mac? Never fear, Microsoft has you covered; in environments without Visual Studio, you can use the dotnet command-line tool to create, configure, and update NuGet packages and run your project. If you are a developer in Mac and Linux environments, you probably already know and love other command-line compilers, like gcc, javac, ruby, rake, npm, and node. You can now add dotnet to that list.

The dotnet command line tool is present and runs on all three platforms, even on Windows with Visual Studio. This is the really cool part: Visual Studio 2015 (and later Visual Studio versions), Visual Studio for Mac, and Visual Studio Code simply automate calls into the dotnet command-line tool. There is no "backdoor functionality" that only comes with Visual Studio that the developers on Linux and Mac will not have. That parity between the development environments is a valuable addition that Microsoft has delivered as it has given up having a dominating position on Windows only.

The following sections take a closer look at the functionality of the commands supports by the dotnet tool.

dotnet new

The new command generates a new project based on a template name submitted as the first argument. Running `dotnet new` without a template name triggers a report of the available templates from which you can choose. Figure 2.4 shows the list of templates reported by `dotnet new`.

```
Templates                    Short Name         Language        Tags
--------------------------------------------------------------------------------
Console Application          console            [C#], F#        Common/Console
Class library               classlib           [C#], F#        Common/Library
Unit Test Project           mstest             [C#], F#        Test/MSTest
xUnit Test Project          xunit              [C#], F#        Test/xUnit
ASP.NET Core Empty          web                [C#]            Web/Empty
ASP.NET Core Web App        mvc                [C#], F#        Web/MVC
ASP.NET Core Web API        webapi             [C#]            Web/WebAPI
Nuget Config                nugetconfig                        Config
Web Config                  webconfig                          Config
Solution File               sln                                Solution
```

FIGURE 2.4
Templates reported by the `dotnet new` command.

You can use additional arguments to the new command. For example, to force the template generator to choose a specific language, you can use the `-lang` switch (C# or F# at the time of this writing), and you have the option to specify a name for your output by using the `-n` switch.

For example, to start a new console application using F# called FirstFSharpConsole, execute the following command:

```
dotnet new console -lang f# -n FirstFSharpConsole
```

The dotnet tool creates a folder called FirstFSharpConsole and places the contents of the new project inside that folder.

dotnet restore

When executed in the same folder as a .NET Core project, the `dotnet restore` command identifies the NuGet packages to download and use with the project. If the packages are not available on the local machine's cache, they are downloaded from the NuGet repositories, configured, and placed in the local cache.

dotnet build

dotnet build is the entry point for the .NET compiler. Execute this command to request that the compiler act on a project and deliver runnable output to a bin folder with appropriate framework folders nested underneath it. You can specify the framework, a configuration, and the target output folder that you want the compiler to deliver to. Here is an example of a call to dotnet build and specifying some additional instructions for how the project should be built:

```
dotnet build c:\dev\MyProject\src\MyProject --output c:\dist\MyProject --framework
netcoreapp11 --configuration debug
```

The new project resides in the c:\dev\MyProject\src\MyProject folder and delivers the output of the compiler to the c:\dist\MyProject folder. The compiler uses the netcoreapp11 framework and applies the debug configuration to the project.

You can run the dotnet build command without any parameters, as they are all optional. If you do, the command executes against the project in the current folder and delivers output to a bin folder in the current folder as well as with the default framework and configuration specified in the project's configuration files.

dotnet publish

dotnet publish is the command to call when you want to publish an application for deployment to a remote server. It compiles your application, packages it as a NuGet package (if it is a class library), and copies all referenced packages to your destination folder in a way that makes it available for use as a NuGet package or as an application ready to distribute to a web server.

dotnet run

dotnet run is the primary command you use during development, and using it is the quickest way to get an application running with .NET Core. This command compiles (if necessary) and runs the project in the current folder if no arguments are passed to it. You can optionally pass a -p argument along with a path to a project file to run.

dotnet test

The dotnet command-line tool comes with capabilities to execute unit tests within your code and output those results as a report to disk. With the base install of the SDK, you can use dotnet test to execute unit tests for xUnit, NUnit, and MSTest.

dotnet pack

If you are working with a class library project that you want to ship as a NuGet package, you can use the `dotnet pack` command to compile and bundle your library with the necessary manifest documents for consumption by NuGet clients.

dotnet clean

`dotnet clean` removes any existing build output from your projects, using the same action available with the MSBuild tool.

dotnet sln

You can use the `dotnet sln` command to manage a solution file that contains references to one or more projects. If you do not have Visual Studio, you can start by creating a new solution file by executing `dotnet new sln`. Then you can add projects to the solution file by executing the following:

```
dotnet sln add <PATH TO PROJECT FILE>
```

You can also use the `sln remove` command to remove projects from a solution. Finally, you can review the list of projects in a solution by executing `dotnet sln list`.

dotnet add

The `dotnet add` command manipulates a project to add references to other projects or add references to NuGet packages. This command takes a project location as an optional first argument, and, if that argument is omitted, it uses the project in the current folder. The second argument is either `package` or `reference`, and finally any options about the reference that needs to be added.

You can add to the project MyProject.csproj a reference to the NuGet package Newtonsoft.Json with this command:

```
dotnet add MyProject.csproj package Newtonsoft.Json
```

dotnet remove

The `dotnet remove` command takes the same arguments and has similar structure as `dotnet add`. You can remove the reference to the Newtonsoft.Json package with this command:

```
dotnet remove MyProject.csproj package Newtonsoft.Json
```

▼ TRY IT YOURSELF

Build a Command-Line Project and Run It with dotnet

Follow these steps to write a simple command-line application and try running it with dotnet:

1. Create a new folder.

2. Execute the following at the command line inside your new folder:

   ```
   dotnet new console -n HelloHour2
   ```

3. Restore the packages in the HelloHour2 project:

   ```
   cd HelloHour2
   dotnet restore
   ```

4. Execute dotnet run to run the contents of the Program class and write the text to the console. Your results should look similar to the output shown in Figure 2.5.

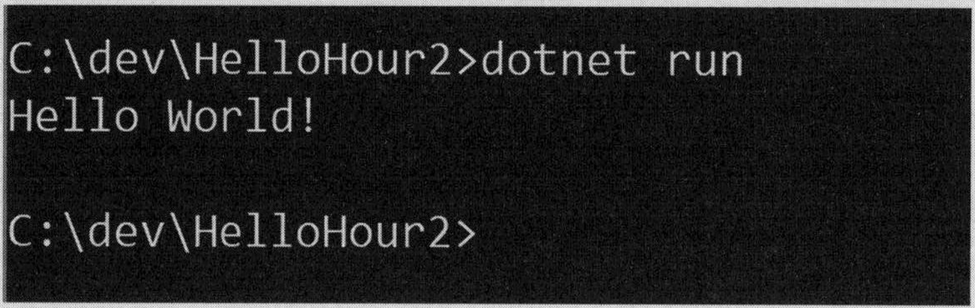

```
C:\dev\HelloHour2>dotnet run
Hello World!

C:\dev\HelloHour2>
```

FIGURE 2.5
Output of the sample console application.

Summary

This hour reviews the various ways you can configure your developer workstation to get started writing code for ASP.NET Core. There are several different options in Visual Studio products, and you can even add ASP.NET editing capabilities to your favorite text editor with the Omnisharp editor add-on. This hour you have also looked at the three key command-line applications that you will encounter while working with the ASP.NET Core tools.

Q&A

Q. Can I have more than one version of dotnet **installed on my machine?**

A. Yes, the dotnet command-line tool is very good about maintaining unique and separate versions of each install. You can find the dotnet tool in the following folders:

- ▶ On Windows: `C:\Program Files\dotnet`

- ▶ On Mac or Linux: `/usr/local/share/dotnet/bin/`

Inside that folder is the `dotnet` executable, along with an SDK folder. The SDK folder contains child folders with version numbers. These are the alternate versions of the tool that you have installed on your system. By default, the latest version of the tool will be used, but you can instruct the `dotnet` command-line tool to use an alternate version with a simple pointer file.

Say that you create a file called global.json and place the following content in it:

```
{
    "sdk": {
        "version": "1.0.4"
    }
}
```

Any execution of the `dotnet` tool in that folder or the child folders underneath it will use the version of the SDK that's referenced. This only affects the version of the `dotnet` command-line tool and not the frameworks or versions of the applications that it will run.

Q. Do I always need to run `dotnet restore` **before I run an application?**

A. Not necessarily. The `restore` command fetches and makes available new NuGet packages that you need to run your application. If you have not modified the project file where the package references are recorded, then you do not need to have subsequent executions of `dotnet restore`.

Workshop

The workshop contains quiz questions and exercises to help you solidify your understanding of the material covered. Try to answer all questions before looking at the "Answers" that follow.

Quiz

1. What are the four different Visual Studio versions that you can install?

2. What is the name of the editor add-on that you can install to enable rich .NET code-editing capabilities in a text editor like Sublime Text or `vi`?

3. What does `dotnet restore` do?

4. How can you force a compilation of a project without actually running the project's code?

Answers

1. Code, Community, Professional, Enterprise

2. Omnisharp

3. It ensures that the required packages for the current project are downloaded and available. If they are not present, it downloads them from a NuGet repository.

4. Use dotnet `build`.

Exercise

Now that you have seen how to install and get your workstation configured to begin development with ASP.NET Core, install the tools you want to use and any updates for those tools on your workstation. Starting in Hour 3, "Exploring the New Project Templates," you're going to write some code!

HOUR 3
Exploring the New Project Templates

What You'll Learn in This Hour:

▶ How to use the project templates that are included with Visual Studio 2017

▶ How to use command-line tools to get started with Visual Studio Code on Windows and other platforms

▶ Where to place C# files for compilation

▶ Where to place static content files like JavaScript, CSS, and images

▶ How to start a basic web server to begin working with a web application

Getting Started with Visual Studio 2017

New ASP.NET Core projects in Visual Studio 2017 are configured and started with a new project template. To open a template, select at: File > New > Project. The New Project dialog shown in Figure 3.1 appears.

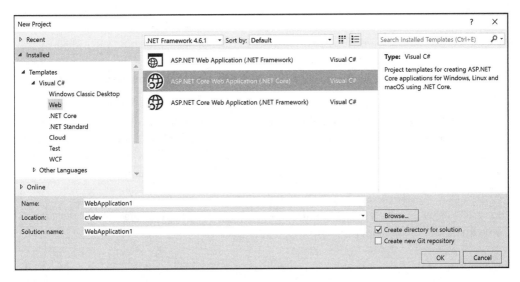

FIGURE 3.1
The Visual Studio 2017 New Project dialog.

The navigation tree in the left panel provides options for you to choose which language and project type you would like to work with. For ASP.NET Core, choose Visual C# and choose Web as the project type. In the main panel to the right, you should see the following three options: ASP.NET Web Application (.NET Framework), ASP.NET Core Web Application (.NET Core), and ASP.NET Core Web Application (.NET Framework). Table 3.1 describes these project types.

TABLE 3.1   Definitions of Web Project Types

Project Type	Description
ASP.NET Web Application (.NET Framework)	A project that will result in a runnable website that is configured to run on Windows Internet Information Server using the .NET Framework and ASP.NET 4.x or earlier
ASP.NET Core Web Application (.NET Core)	A project that builds a website using ASP.NET Core using the cross-platform-capable .NET Core framework
ASP.NET Core Web Application (.NET Framework)	A project that builds a website using ASP.NET Core using the .NET Framework on Windows and runs in Internet Information Server

In this new version of ASP.NET, the related resources that you can build and consume with your web application will be compiled directly to NuGet packages. A NuGet package is a bundle of resources that are made available for various development platforms and processor configurations. You will learn more about packaging and referencing other projects in Hour 4, "Defining ASP.NET Core Configuration."

At the top of the dialog shown in Figure 3.1 is a combo box that allows you to select the .NET Framework version. In this case, choose the largest .NET Framework version number available (for example, .NET Framework 4.6.1). Then select the third option in the box, the ASP.NET Core (.NET Framework) project type. Next, name your project on the bottom of the screen and choose the folder where you would like to save the project. (I like to work with my development projects in a c:\dev folder.)

The final item in the bottom right are the check boxes Add to Source Control and Create New Git Repository. Your project will be made available to the source control system you have configured for use with Visual Studio as a new resource to be indexed. (I prefer to use the Git source control system, and with that option activated, the project will have a .git folder created and an appropriate .gitignore file created.)

Once you click OK in the New Project dialog, you are presented with a collection of templates to choose from, as shown in Figure 3.2.

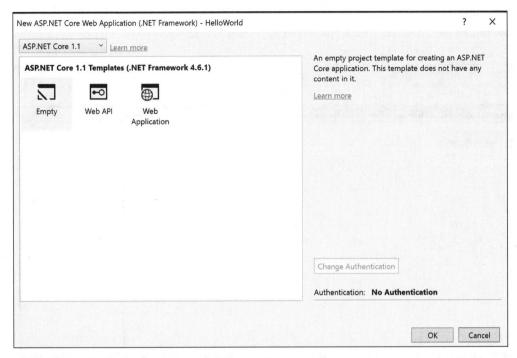

FIGURE 3.2
New web project template dialog.

This is where you finally start to see ASP.NET Core options available in Visual Studio. Table 3.2 describes the templates that are available.

TABLE 3.2   **ASP.NET Core Project Templates**

Name	Capabilities
Empty	The simplest and most basic web project, with no features enabled
Web API	A template configured for delivering machine-readable content without a server-generated user interface
Web Application	A complete template with user interface, authentication, and server-side generated content using the MVC framework

The Change Authentication button on the right side becomes available if you choose the Web Application template.

In this case, choose the Empty template and click OK. After Visual Studio does some setup work, you should see a welcome screen and layout, as shown in Figure 3.3:

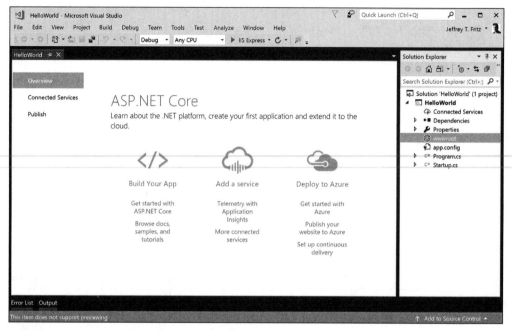

FIGURE 3.3
An empty website welcome screen and project layout.

With all the project templates, you are greeted by a very helpful Overview page that you can use to jump off to some common tasks in the management of your application. You can always return to this page in Visual Studio 2017 by choosing Project > Overview.

The Solution Explorer on the right side shows all the content of your project. With ASP.NET Core projects, this means that all the files in the folder of your project are shown.

The wwwroot Folder

The wwwroot folder is a very important folder in the structure of an application. This folder contains files that will be served without the ASP.NET process interfering with their presentation. This is where you can place HTML, CSS, images, and JavaScript files for a web server to present to your application's visitors.

You will learn more about the wwwroot folder later this hour.

Getting Started with Visual Studio Code

If you have installed Visual Studio Code on a system (regardless of operating system) with Node.js, as recommended in Hour 2, "Setting Up Your Work Environment for ASP.NET Core," then you are almost ready to begin using some startup templates. Visual Studio Code has its own ecosystem of packages, tools, and resources to facilitate more productive coding on all operating systems.

You can use the `dotnet new` command to start a new application and manage its structure, as discussed in Hour 2.

Starting a Simple Website from the Command Line

If you have everything installed properly, from either Visual Studio 2017 or Visual Studio Code, you should be able to execute the following commands from your project folder in a terminal window or at a command prompt to start your web service:

```
dotnet restore
dotnet run
```

You should see a bunch of output from the `restore` command indicating that your project's package references are installed. After executing the `run` command, you are be able to access your website at http://localhost:5000. When you navigate to this address, you should see a simple "Hello World" block of text in the top-left corner of the browser, as shown in Figure 3.4.

FIGURE 3.4
A simple Hello World result.

Congratulations! You just compiled and visited your first ASP.NET Core web application.

What actually happened here? What is the command you executed actually doing? In Hour 2, you configured the `dotnet` command-line tool for environments that don't have Visual Studio 2017, and you can use this tool in ASP.NET to compile and run web applications.

The first command, `restore`, inspects the project and identifies all the references that need to be in place to run the application. It downloads any missing references from NuGet.org and writes a lock file into the obj child folder with that package information.

In the second command you executed, `run`, the `dotnet` tool is called and instructed to begin compiling and executing the contents of the current folder. `dotnet` compiles the project contents of the current folder and starts the default web server, kestrel, hosting the results of the folder compilation.

What if there is an error in starting the `dotnet` process? Several things could be wrong. You need to determine whether there is a `dotnet` executable available in the path. Try running `dotnet --version` to report the version of `dotnet`. If nothing is returned, you might not have the command-line tool installed properly.

Moving Beyond Hello World

You've got a simple website that answers "Hello World." Let's look at what makes this little website run.

ASP.NET Core builds on the concept of a *request pipeline*. Every request from the web to the application enters the pipeline and gets evaluated for fitness of some code to execute against that request, and transmits an appropriate response. The pipeline is constructed in the `Startup` class's `Configure` method, which takes an `IApplicationBuilder` input parameter. Initially in your simple web application, this method contains only the code in Listing 3.1.

LISTING 3.1 The Initial `Configure` Method

```
public void Configure(IApplicationBuilder app, IHostingEnvironment env,
ILoggerFactory loggerFactory)
{
    loggerFactory.AddConsole();

    if (env.IsDevelopment())
    {
        app.UseDeveloperExceptionPage();
    }

    app.Run(async (context) =>
    {
        await context.Response.WriteAsync("Hello World!");
    });
}
```

Note the following about this code:

▶ The application configures the pipeline asynchronously. This is a good thing for performance of the application as the configuration will not block the running thread while the pipeline is configured.

▶ There is a logger created at the beginning, and the `AddConsole` method is called. This enables the application to write log messages to the console.

▶ The `if`-block tests whether this is the development environment. In the case that the application is running in the development environment, a `UseDeveloperExceptionPage()` method is called. (We'll look at this in a minute.)

▶ The `Run` method receives a context object—the `Microsoft.AspNet.Http.HttpContext` object, a collection of dictionaries with data about the information submitted to the server with each request. In addition, it holds a `Response` object that can be used to populate the content to be delivered to requesting clients.

▶ Content is written asynchronously to the `Response` object, allowing this operation to run in a nonblocking fashion. For the purpose of writing a simple block of text, this has little impact. If you were fetching data from another service, however, you could prevent the web server thread from blocking while awaiting the delivery of that data.

▶ The pipeline takes any context and sends the same response to all requests. This means there is no inspection of what HTTP action was received or of the path submitted with the request. All requests are served the same response text.

NOTE

Nowhere Else to Go

That last bullet is an important one: If you try to navigate your browser to a different location in your sample website, you will receive the same "Hello World" result. Go ahead, try it: Navigate to http://localhost:5000/AspNetCoreRocks or http://localhost:5000/ThisPageDoesntExist, and you will find that those results are always the same "Hello World" result.

The construction of the pipeline in this manner gives you the ability to define fallbacks when other processing of a request to the web server fails or is not handled properly. You can easily define new methods to handle when content is not found on disk, and you can also define handlers for errors that are thrown earlier in the pipeline and not handled in a polite manner before returning them to a website visitor.

We will explore the configuration pipeline and adding features to the empty website template in further detail in Hour 5, "Configuring the Service with the `Startup` Class."

Exploring the Starter Website Template

The second template we will look at is the Web Application template in Visual Studio. In the `dotnet` command-line generator, the same content can be scaffolded with the `dotnet new mvc` command.

Next, you'll start this application and check out the default template that is presented. After starting the web server by pressing F5 in Visual Studio or executing `dotnet restore` and then `dotnet run` at the command line, you should navigate to the web application at http://localhost:5000 with your browser and find the default web content on the home page, as shown in Figure 3.5.

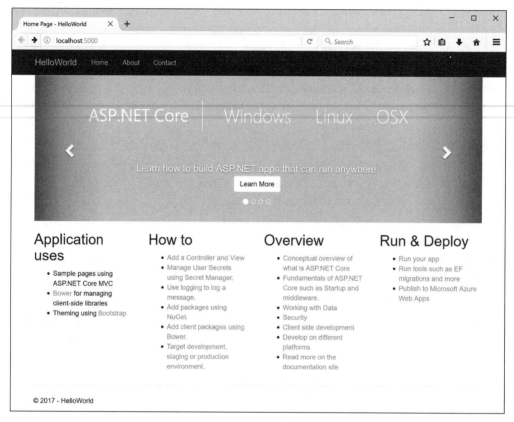

FIGURE 3.5
Home page of the Web Site template.

It's a little difficult to show in this book, but the shaded area in middle of the top of the page is called a *carousel*, and it animates, sliding through a series of elements that present various Microsoft tools and technologies that you can use with your application. This home page is designed to give you another series of jumping-off points to reference materials and to help you learn how to build various elements of the application, just like the Overview page in the Visual Studio project. Go ahead and click around the menus at the top and explore what content is already presented in this template.

Let's dive into Visual Studio and explore how this application is configured. In contrast to the Empty Web Application template, the Web Site template has a number of new folders configured, a few new files on the root folder of the project, and a number of items in a wwwroot folder, as shown in Figure 3.6.

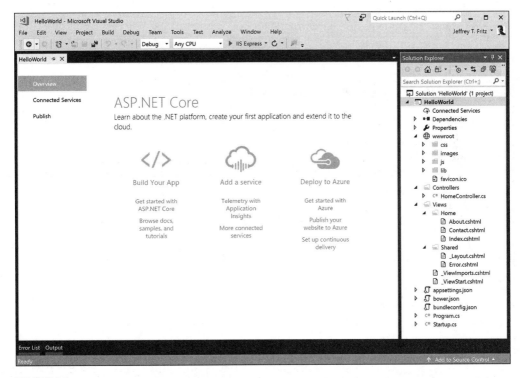

FIGURE 3.6
Visual Studio 2017 with the default Web Site template.

The new files on the root folder of the web application are the following:

▶ **bower.json**—This file contains configuration information about the packages that the project will consume from the `bower` package manager. Hour 15, "npm and `bower`: Client-Side Package Managers," provides more details on the use of `bower`.

▶ **appsettings.json**—This file contains various configuration settings that the server-side code will read and work with. Hour 6, "Configuring Your Application," provides more details on configuration settings.

▶ **bundleconfig.json**—BundleConfig is a tool from Microsoft to package and deliver minified and compressed CSS or JavaScript files. This file instructs the application to minify the site.css and site.js files in the wwwroot folder. Additional files can easily be packaged by listing them in this file.

▶ **Program.cs**—This file contains the information that .NET needs in order to start the web server from the host application.

▶ **Startup.cs**—This is the main class that dictates how the ASP.NET Core application starts and configures how it will respond to incoming requests.

Figure 3.7 shows the contents of the wwwroot folder.

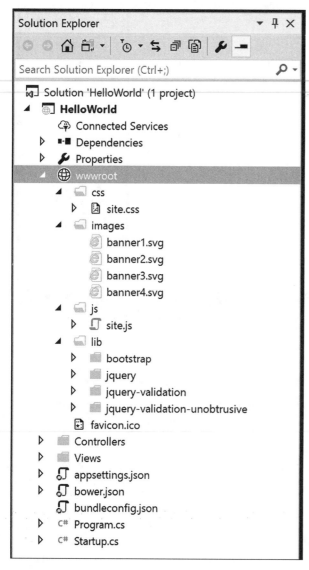

FIGURE 3.7
Contents of the wwwroot folder in Solution Explorer.

By convention, all the static files that a project needs to operate are placed in this folder. Static files are files that the ASP.NET server will not compile,parse, or otherwise transform before transmitting them to a waiting browser that has requested them from the application. In order for a web browser to request one of these files, it does not need to indicate that it is requesting it from the wwwroot folder, but it needs to instead request it from the root of the web application. For example, to request the favicon.ico file that resides on disk just inside the wwwroot folder, the browser can request http://localhost:5000/favicon.ico, and the file will be served by the web server.

TRY IT YOURSELF ▼

Create an HTML Page for ASP.NET Core to Serve

Follow these steps to create your first HTML page for ASP.NET Core to serve:

1. Add a new HTML file to the wwwroot folder by right-clicking the folder in the Visual Studio Solution Explorer and choosing the Add > New Item option from the context pop-up menu, as shown in Figure 3.8.

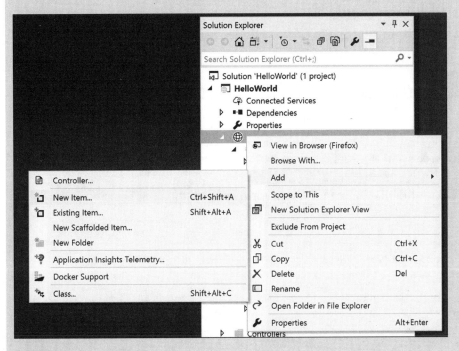

FIGURE 3.8
New Item context menu.

2. As shown in Figure 3.9, choose the HTML page template and name your page MyPage.html.

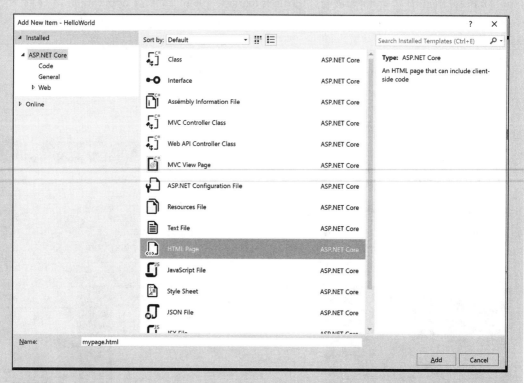

FIGURE 3.9
Adding a new HTML page.

3. Add the code shown in Listing 3.2 to your HTML page to prove that you can serve it properly.

LISTING 3.2   Initial HTML Page Content for mypage.html

```
<!DOCTYPE html>
<html>
<head>
    <meta charset="utf-8" />
    <title>My Webpage</title>
</head>
<body>
  <h2>This is my first static content</h2>
</body>
</html>
```

4. Start your web application and navigate to http://localhost:5000/mypage.html to see your page served to you. You should see a page similar to that shown in Figure 3.10.

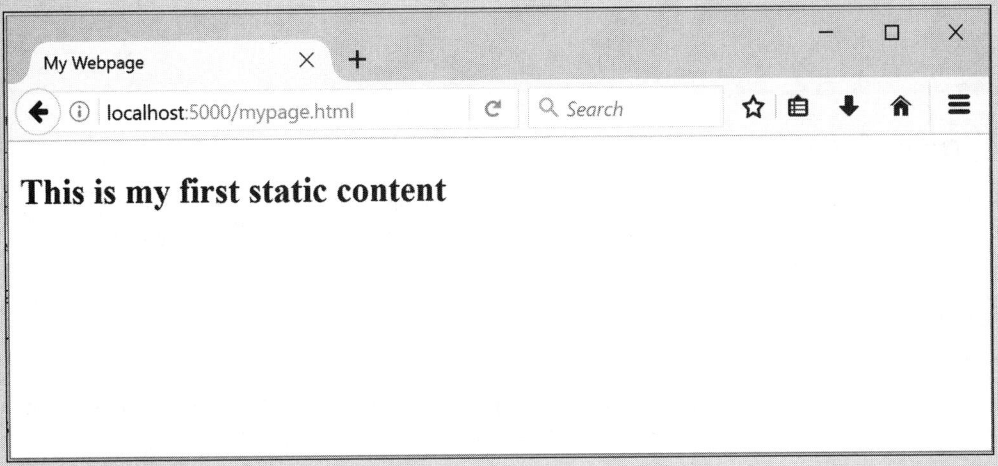

FIGURE 3.10
Your first static web page, served by ASP.NET Core.

Summary

This hour, you have learned how to start using two of the basic web application templates that are made available with ASP.NET Core from Visual Studio. You have also learned how to start using the `dotnet` tool to deliver the website templates for developers who do not have Visual Studio Professional or Enterprise. You have also explored how static files are saved and presented in an application.

Q&A

Q. What is the command to launch the `dotnet` tool and generate an ASP.NET Core web application with the default Web Application template?

A. `dotnet new mvc`

Q. What command can you use on all supported operating systems to start hosting a web application created with ASP.NET?

A. `dotnet run`

Q. What is meant by the term *static content*?

A. Static content is the content of files that are served without ASP.NET modifying them before they are transmitted to the browser.

Q. **What is the name of the folder in the default templates that stores static content files?**

A. wwwroot

Q. **In what file is the ASP.NET service pipeline configured?**

A. Startup.cs

Workshop

The workshop contains quiz questions and exercises to help you solidify your understanding of the material covered. Try to answer all questions before looking at the "Answers" that follow.

Quiz

1. ASP.NET Core projects are compiled and delivered in what distribution unit?

2. What is the default name of the topmost folder in the project hierarchy where content files like CSS, JavaScript, and images can be placed?

3. What are the names of the three project types that Visual Studio provides for ASP.NET development?

4. In startup.cs, the `Configure` method is used to configure what aspect of the ASP.NET application?

5. What Visual Studio version can you run on a Macintosh with OSX?

Answers

1. NuGet packages

2. wwwroot

3. ASP.NET Web Application, Class Library (Package), Console Application (Package)

4. The ASP.NET pipeline

5. Visual Studio Code

Exercise

Practice what you've learned to this point:

▶ Create a new ASP.NET application by using the Web Site or Web Application template and add HTML pages to show some photos from a recent trip or event.

▶ Create a new ASP.NET application by using the Empty template and modifying the standard "Hello World" response to randomly display the text of a joke from a list stored in a C# array.

Defining ASP.NET Core Configuration

What You'll Learn in This Hour:

▶ How to start a sample application from scratch
▶ What options are available with server-side project configuration
▶ What options are configured in the default project template
▶ What NuGet packages are and how to use them
▶ How to choose the .NET framework configuration for a project
▶ How to configure application commands

Introducing Our Sample Application

The sample application that you will use as the basis for all the demos from this point forward in the book is a personal travel-tracking web application called ASPTravlerz. It's named as it is because it's for a traveler who is also an ASP.NET developer, and all cool new application names these days have to have a misspelling with a Z gratuitously thrown in.

All the sample code for this application is available online in my public source code repository at http://github.org/csharpfritz/asptravlerz. To get started in this chapter, you will start with an empty project folder, then build the initial configuration files and folders to support the application. I typically use a folder called dev and store all my development projects in child folders under dev. You will see in the console window screenshots in this chapter that the project is built in dev/AspTravlerz, and you can create a similar empty folder on your workstation to begin writing this application.

Getting Started with Server-Side Configuration

With prior versions of ASP.NET, the content that was delivered to a web application visitor was mixed in with the project source code. There was no clear place to point to and see the separation between the code that would execute on the server and the code that would be delivered to the web browser for execution there. Developers would go to great lengths to create scripts folders or class modules that would contain as much server-side logic as possible. Since the release of ASP.NET Core, the line between server-executed and client-side code has been very clear.

The epicenter of a server-side project is your project file, ending with a .csproj extension. This file contains all the information necessary to direct the .NET compiler (code-named Roslyn) to build the binary executable files from C# that will run on a web server and deliver content to your web visitors. The ASP.NET team has enhanced the MSBuild tool to allow a dramatic simplification in the project file format while still supporting the entire .NET ecosystem of projects.

TIP

The Roslyn Compiler

The Roslyn compiler is Microsoft's next-generation set of compilers for the .NET platform. This compiler allows for new versions of the programming languages and ultra-fast in-memory operations against code. A number of extensions and updates have been made for and to this version of Visual Studio with this compiler. The source code of the Roslyn compiler was made open source and published to GitHub at the Microsoft Build conference in 2014; it can be found at https://github.com/dotnet/roslyn. New features that depend on Roslyn include the lightbulb analyzers that have appear on the left side of the code window since Visual Studio 2015 and the dotnet build command.

If you get started with a template, as demonstrated in Hour 3, "Exploring the New Project Templates," a sample project file is generated for you. For your sample project, you can start writing an empty project from scratch so that you have the same contents no matter which way you are starting an ASP.NET Core application, and we can discuss each element of the project as it is constructed. This book walks through setting up the sample project with Visual Studio Code, but most of the steps are automated in Visual Studio 2017 and with the dotnet command-line tool.

Fundamentals of .NET Application Structure

Before we get to configuring the application, let's take a quick look at the fundamentals of how a .NET application is structured. A .NET application's architecture is separated into four discrete layers, as shown in Figure 4.1.

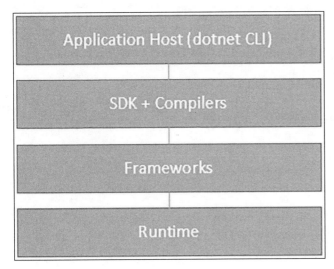

FIGURE 4.1
ASP.NET Core application architecture.

At the lowest level, a .NET application has a runtime that is specific to the operating system it runs on. In previous versions of .NET, the runtime was installed with Windows or from Windows Update, and .NET developers were able to rely on a runtime being available on a Windows machine they were targeting. Starting with .NET Core, you can deploy a version of the runtime with your application or use the runtime that is already installed on a server. The runtime includes low-level things like the just-in-time (JIT) compiler, native interop instructions for various operating systems, and the garbage collector.

Building on top of the runtime are the .NET frameworks. These frameworks enable .NET development by adding the basic implementations of .NET objects, such as collections, diagnostics, I/O management, network interactions, and thread management. In prior versions of .NET, these elements are called the Base Class Library (BCL).

Understanding the Development Options

Determining the initial set of options to configure for a web project is important to help get your filesystem configured properly, with designated folders for server-side and client-side development. In this case, you can start by initializing your project inside the empty AspTravlerz folder with the `dotnet` command-line tool, as follows:

```
dotnet new empty
```

This command generates a base web application in the current folder with some initial configuration options set to enable building an application with the new .NET Core framework that works on Mac, Linux, and Windows.

To inspect the AspTravlerz.csproj file that was generated for you, review the contents in Listing 4.1.

LISTING 4.1   AspTravlerz.csproj File Generated for an Empty Web Project

```
<Project Sdk="Microsoft.NET.Sdk.Web">

  <PropertyGroup>
    <TargetFramework>netcoreapp1.1</TargetFramework>
  </PropertyGroup>

  <ItemGroup>
    <Folder Include="wwwroot\" />
  </ItemGroup>

  <ItemGroup>
    <PackageReference Include="Microsoft.AspNetCore" Version="1.1.2" />
  </ItemGroup>

</Project>
```

This XML file is based on the long-standard MSBuild project format, but it has been greatly enhanced to make it more human readable and with sensible defaults. In addition, the nonsense that you don't need has been removed.

The first entry, the Sdk attribute on the Project element, is a pointer for MSBuild to know what type of project you are creating and instructs MSBuild to include additional tasks and properties necessary to build a web project. You can also set this value to Microsoft.NET.Sdk to build with the .NET Core SDK and not include any web-specific features.

The next entries instruct MSBuild to build this application targeting the .NET Core 1.1 runtime version, using the latest patch update available: PropertyGroup with TargetFramework referencing the netcoreapp1.1 metapackage. On Windows machines, you can find this shared framework installed at c:\Program Files\DotNet\Shared\ with a folder bearing the name Microsoft.NETCore.App (the full name of the .NET Core framework) that contains a folder with the same base version number as referenced here: 1.1.x. This metareference to the NETCore.App framework indicates that the highest version with the 1.1 base version number should be used, and that may be 1.1.0, 1.1.1, 1.1.2, or some other patch version starting with 1.1.

If you want to lock down to a specific, explicitly defined version of the framework, you can choose to add a RuntimeFrameworkVersion element with a specific version number, as shown in Listing 4.2:

LISTING 4.2   **Specifying an Explicit Runtime Framework Version**

```
<Project Sdk="Microsoft.NET.Sdk.Web">

  <PropertyGroup>
    <TargetFramework>netcoreapp1.1</TargetFramework>
    <RuntimeFrameworkVersion>1.1.0</RuntimeFrameworkVersion>
  </PropertyGroup>
```

The next section of the file is `ItemGroup`, which contains a single `Folder` element with the value `wwwroot`. This element defines the wwwroot content folder that is designed to contain static web content. You should include it here so that the `dotnet` tool knows about the folder when it comes time to compile and publish the content.

The last group in the .csproj file is the most important entry for you to understand: the collection of dependencies declared as `PackageReference` elements. ASP.NET Core parses this as a collection of NuGet packages to be used in the project, and the values of those attributes are the name and version numbers of the packages to include. ASP.NET Core delivers all parts of its framework as packages, and the packages' resolution process dynamically includes the packages that those framework packages depend on. Consequently, you can reference just the `Microsoft.AspNetCore` package, and all the features it depends on from other packages will automatically be downloaded and made available to your project without cluttering up your project file.

Extending the Project with CLI Tools

The project file and the `dotnet` command-line tool are extensible, and you can enhance them by adding another section to your project file. So add a new `ItemGroup` element at the bottom of the file, just above the closing `Project` tag. Inside `ItemGroup`, you should add a reference to the `Microsoft.DotNet.Watcher.Tools` package, using a new element called `DotNetCliReference`.

`DotNetCliReference` instructs the `dotnet` CLI to fetch and reference a NuGet package for use at the command line when in development mode *only*. The .NET command-line tool will *not* include these tools when it compiles or when you publish your application to another folder. Listing 4.3 shows the full syntax of this feature you are adding to the project.

LISTING 4.3   `DotNetCliReference` **for** `dotnet watch`

```
  <ItemGroup>
    <DotNetCliToolReference Include="Microsoft.DotNet.Watcher.Tools"
                            Version="1.0.0" />
  </ItemGroup>

</Project>
```

With this snippet inside your project file, you can run the project in watch mode, in which the Watcher tool automatically restarts the application when any of the project files change. Use the following command from the same folder as the .csproj file in order to start your application in watch mode:

```
dotnet watch run
```

Try inserting some spaces or making other changes to a file in the project, save the file, and watch the application restart for you with your changes applied.

Interesting Settings to Consider

There are a number of other settings that you may want to apply to your project file in order to tweak it to behave just right for you. Besides configuring the way that your application is going to be built, you can add a number of automation capabilities to make your development process a breeze.

Specifying a Project Version

By default, the `dotnet` compiler assigns the 1.0.0 version to your application and embeds that version number in the binary files you create. You can force a version on your project by using the `Version` element inside `PropertyGroup`, just like the one that contains the `TargetFramework` information. In this case, you can specify version 0.4.0 (a reference to Chapter 4) for your project, as shown in Listing 4.4.

LISTING 4.4   Assigning Version 0.4.0 to the Sample Project

```
<PropertyGroup>
  <TargetFramework>netcoreapp1.1</TargetFramework>
  <Version>0.4.0</Version>
</PropertyGroup>
```

NOTE

Semantic Versioning

Version numbers are an important aspect of a project, especially if you are going to share your output publicly. Semantic versioning is a good standard that defines how you should structure your version number. The version number comes in four parts separated by periods: *major.minor.patch. build*. The *build* number should be changed for any new public build of your application that has the same three other version parts. The *patch* number should be changed when your application changes to include a fix or an update that does not change the public interface at all. The *minor* number should be changed when your public interface gains new features. The *major* number should be changed when your public interface receives a breaking change such that consumers would need to learn or rewrite their applications to work with your product. For more information about semantic versioning, visit www.semver.org.

Targeting Multiple Frameworks

By default, a `TargetFramework` element instructs the compiler to build for a specific framework and version of the .NET frameworks. Perhaps you have a project or library that you want to reference that only works with a specific version of the .NET Framework. If you needed to reference a .NET 4.6.1 Framework to work with this library, you can use this feature to help enable that.

You can configure an application for multiple frameworks by using the `TargetFrameworks` element with a semicolon-separated list of frameworks that you would like your project built for, as shown in Listing 4.5.

LISTING 4.5 Configuring a Project to Build for .NET Framework 4.6.1 and .NET Core 1.1

```
<PropertyGroup>
  <!--<TargetFramework>netcoreapp1.1</TargetFramework>-->
  <Version>0.4.0</Version>
  <TargetFrameworks>net461;netcoreapp1.1</TargetFrameworks>
</PropertyGroup>
```

Notice that Listing 4.5 leaves the `TargetFramework` element in place but commented out. The `TargetFramework` element takes precedence over the `TargetFrameworks` element, so you need to remove it in order to ensure that your project will be built for the two frameworks listed in the `TargetFrameworks` element.

If you build the application with this configuration by using the `dotnet build` command, two folders are created under the bin/Debug folder, each named after the appropriate framework name. Table 4.1 lists some of the framework monikers that you can use in your ASP.NET Core application.

TABLE 4.1 Available Target Frameworks for ASP.NET Core Projects

Framework	Abbreviation
.NET Framework 4.5.1	`net451`
.NET Framework 4.5.2	`net452`
.NET Framework 4.6	`net46`
.NET Framework 4.6.1	`net461`
.NET Framework 4.6.2	`net462`
.NET Framework 4.7	`net47`
.NET Core 1.0	`netcoreapp1.0`
.NET Core 1.1	`netcoreapp1.1`

For a maintained list of all available target framework monikers, see the MSDN page https://docs.microsoft.com/en-us/nuget/schema/target-frameworks.

Optimizing for Specific Runtimes

With previous iterations of .NET Framework, you could be assured that your application would work great on any version of Windows that had the same version of .NET Framework for which your application was built. With the cross-platform features of .NET Core, you can have similar confidence that your application will run great on any platform that has a .NET Core framework installed on it. However, there may be scenarios in which you want to optimize an application to run on specific operating system runtimes. To support such a scenario, you can add the RuntimeIdentifiers element to your project file with a semicolon-separated list of the runtime identifiers your project supports. Table 4.2 lists some common runtime identifiers that you can use in your ASP.NET Core applications.

TABLE 4.2   Some of the Available Runtime Identifiers for ASP.NET Core Projects

Operating System(s) Supported	Abbreviation
Windows 7, Windows Server 2008 R2 32bit	win7-x86
Windows 7, Windows Server 2008 R2 64bit	win7-x64
Windows 10, Windows Server 2016 32bit	win10-x86
Windows 10, Windows Server 2016 64bit	win10-x64
Mac OSX Yosemite	osx.10.10-x64
Mac OSX El Capitan	osx.10.11-x64
Mac OS Sierra	osx.10.12-x64
Ubuntu Linux 16.4 (Xenial Xerus)	ubuntu.16.04-x64
Ubuntu Linux 16.10 (Yakkety Yak)	ubuntu.16.10-x64

Microsoft maintains a complete list of available runtime identifiers on MSDN, at https://docs.microsoft.com/en-us/dotnet/core/rid-catalog.

Listing 4.6 shows how you can add a simple list of runtime identifiers to your project for Windows 7, OSX 10.11 (El Capitan), and Ubuntu 16.04.

LISTING 4.6   Defining Compatible Runtimes in Your Project

```
<PropertyGroup>
  <!--<TargetFramework>netcoreapp1.1</TargetFramework>-->
  <Version>0.4.0</Version>
  <TargetFrameworks>net461;netcoreapp1.1</TargetFrameworks>
  <RuntimeIdentifiers>win7-x64;osx.10.11-x64;ubuntu.16.04-x64</RuntimeIdentifiers>
</PropertyGroup>
```

You can now build your application with the `dotnet build` command, and your output will be created in a *portable* configuration. This is a set of libraries and executables that will run wherever a specified version of the .NET Core or .NET Framework is available.

However, if you want to be able to deploy your application to an environment where the version of the .NET framework does *not* exist, you can build a *self-contained deployment* that will include all the necessary references to run the application on the target runtime with the framework of your choosing. Given your current configuration that supports Mac OSX El Capitan and .NET Core 1.1, you can create a distribution of your application appropriate to run on that environment by executing the following commands:

```
dotnet restore
dotnet publish -c Release -f netcoreapp1.1 -r osx.10.11-x64
```

The `restore` command acquires any runtime libraries needed to build for the extra runtimes listed in the project file. The `publish` command first builds the application in the `Release` configuration for the `netcoreapp1.1` framework, targeting the `osx.10.11-x64` runtime. Inside your project's bin folder, you will now find a Release folder with a netcoreapp1.1 subfolder that contains a single osx.10.11-x64 folder. Inside that folder, you'll find the binaries necessary to run the application on a Mac, and you'll also find a publish folder. The publish folder contains all the files and the wwwroot folder necessary to deploy and run your application on a Mac that does not already have the .NET Core framework installed. You can just copy the entire contents of the publish folder to a Mac and start the ASPTravlerz application to have it begin hosting the web application for you.

Executing Scripts as Part of the Build Process

The MSBuild format already provides a mechanism for you to connect and execute scripts and external tools as part of the build process for a project. You will use this feature in later chapters when you begin adding components from the npm repository to your project.

You can execute these external scripts by writing them into an `Exec` element and wrapping that element in a `Target`. In order to specify the order in which the `Target` executes, you can use `BeforeTargets` and `AfterTargets` attributes. Listing 4.7 shows a sample `Target` that runs `npm install`.

LISTING 4.7   Running `npm restore` **Before the Application Is Published**

```
<Target Name="InstallNpm" BeforeTargets="Build">
  <Exec Command="npm install" />
</Target>
```

This code block can appear anywhere as a child of the `Project` element in your .csproj file. The `Target` element takes a required name attribute, and in this case it is given the very descriptive `InstallNpm` name. The next attribute, `BeforeTargets`, indicates that the content of this target should be executed before the application is built. If you choose to use the `AfterTargets` attribute with the `Build` argument, the contents are executed after the project is built. Finally, you can also replace the `Build` target with `Publish` and trigger the actions `Before` or `After` with the `Publish` action as well. Both `Build` and `Publish` targets are triggered in Visual Studio as well as at the command line, so you can get the same automation behavior when compiling your application by hand.

The `Exec` element inside the `Target` declares the command-line executable and options that should be executed when this `Target` is triggered. In this example, the simple `npm install` command will be triggered before the `Build` operation takes place.

For a complete reference on MSBuild syntax and options, see https://docs.microsoft.com/en-us/visualstudio/msbuild/msbuild.

Managing and Referencing NuGet Packages

We quickly jumped through the topic of managing and referencing NuGet packages during the construction of the .csproj file (earlier this hour), and it needs to be covered more completely before we move on to further developing the application. Dependencies in ASP.NET Core applications are primarily delivered the same way they are in many other modern development languages and frameworks: through packages of related content. Typically, in older versions of .NET, references to other parts of the framework or third-party libraries are made through DLL (dynamic link library) files. Make no mistake, this binary delivery of software is still being used, but it has been bundled into a NuGet package.

NuGet packages allow you to deliver more than just a single library for an application to reference, as you can bundle multiple libraries that are targeted for various runtimes and framework versions. In addition, you can bundle PowerShell scripts and other content for use in your application. This package concept is very compelling for a framework that wants to deliver binary references and ensure that those references work across platforms.

The NuGet client commands are repackaged and made available through the `dotnet` command-line tool. The NuGet tool allows you to download and install packages from remote repositories or locally accessible folders. NuGet keeps a configuration file that defines some basic options about how and from where to retrieve these packages:

▶ On Windows, the NuGet.config file is kept in %AppData%\NuGet.

▶ On Mac and Linux, the NuGet.config file is kept in ~/.config/NuGet.

How do you know what packages you should install, what packages are available, and what those packages do? In Visual Studio 2017, there is a Package Manager user interface that you can access from the Tools > NuGet Package Manager menu option; you can also right-click the project in the Solution Explorer window and select Manage Packages from the context menu. This user interface allows you to search NuGet repositories, both public and private, and see the descriptions of the packages and features you have searched for. In addition, Visual Studio 2017 provides type-ahead IntelliSense for the name and version number of NuGet packages if you edit the project file by hand.

If you do not have Visual Studio, you can search the public NuGet.org repository by pointing your favorite browser at the www.nuget.org website, shown in Figure 4.2.

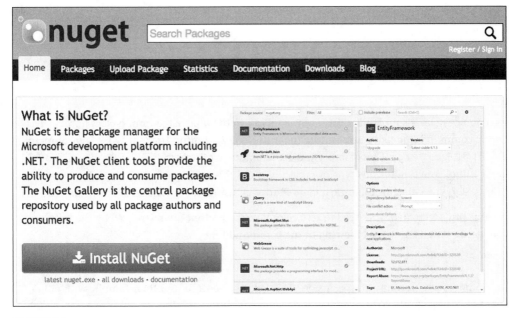

FIGURE 4.2
NuGet.org website.

You can search this public repository for packages and features that you may want to add to your project. At the time of this writing, there are more than 43,000 unique packages available to enhance your web applications.

You can also choose to write your own packages of reusable content for your web applications. In Visual Studio 2017, you can create a new project and choose Class Library (.NET Core), as shown in Figure 4.3. This project type is similar to a normal class library that you can reference in other .NET project types, but the output is a NuGet package instead of a DLL file.

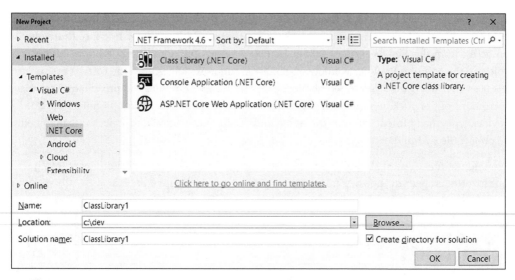

FIGURE 4.3
Creating a new class library (.NET Core) in Visual Studio 2017.

If you do not have Visual Studio 2017, how can you create a package from a class library? The dotnet command-line tool's new feature (refer to Hour 2, "Setting Up Your Work Environment for ASP.NET Core") has a Class Library project template available that will assist you in scaffolding the initial structure for this type of project. Choose this template type and, as demonstrated in Figure 4.4, you can start building a class library by using the syntax discussed in this chapter.

With this project created, you need to restore any packages that are referenced by the base template. To do this, run the following at the command line:

```
dotnet restore
```

You can now write as many classes inside the folder as you need and then compile with either the native Visual Studio 2017 compiler or another command-line tool. You can execute the following command to build your project:

```
dotnet build
```

The appropriate DLL files are then generated and written to disk for you in the bin/Debug folder off the root of this project folder. What you *really* need is the NuGet package that contains the DLL you generated. To construct the NuGet package, you can use the following command:

```
dotnet pack
```

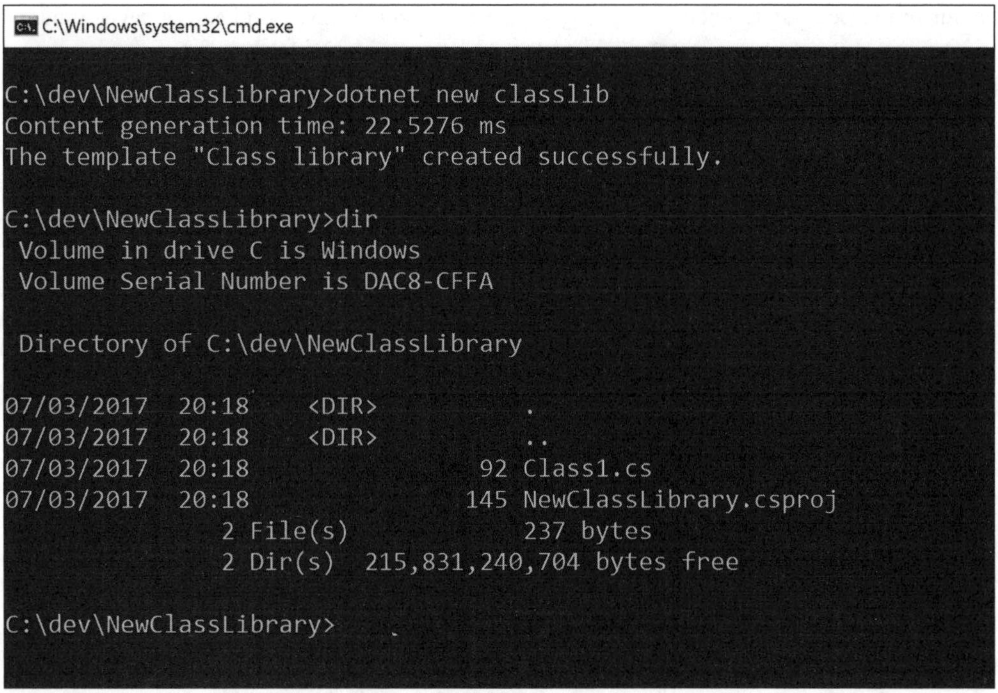

```
C:\Windows\system32\cmd.exe

C:\dev\NewClassLibrary>dotnet new classlib
Content generation time: 22.5276 ms
The template "Class library" created successfully.

C:\dev\NewClassLibrary>dir
 Volume in drive C is Windows
 Volume Serial Number is DAC8-CFFA

 Directory of C:\dev\NewClassLibrary

07/03/2017  20:18    <DIR>          .
07/03/2017  20:18    <DIR>          ..
07/03/2017  20:18                92 Class1.cs
07/03/2017  20:18               145 NewClassLibrary.csproj
               2 File(s)            237 bytes
               2 Dir(s)  215,831,240,704 bytes free

C:\dev\NewClassLibrary>
```

FIGURE 4.4
Creating a new class library from the dotnet command-line tool.

This instructs the dotnet command to build your project (if it has changed since the last build) and then package the resultant DLLs with a specification file called a "nuspec" file into a NuGet package. This package has several traits, based on how your folder structure and project are defined:

▶ The base name of the package is the name of the root folder. If you created your project in a folder called CoolProject, your package will start with the name CoolProject, followed by a period.

▶ The version specified in the .csproj file is placed next. If no version is specified in your .csproj file, the version 1.0.0 is used by default.

▶ The extension for a NuGet package is .nupkg.

Based on these examples, the CoolProject version 1.0.0 package would have the filename CoolProject.1.0.0.nupkg. The 0.4.0 version of our web project as shown earlier in the hour, called AspTravlerz, would have a filename AspTravlerz.0.4.0.nupkg.

The nupkg file (sometimes referred to as a "Nupp-Keg" by the ASP.NET and NuGet development teams) can then be shared on NuGet.org or placed in a secure folder location where other developers can reference the content to add to their projects.

▼ TRY IT YOURSELF

Find Some Free Features for Your Next Application

Follow these steps to take a look at www.NuGet.org and some cool functionality you can use to enhance your application:

1. Open a browser and navigate to www.nuget.org.

2. Enter **JSON** for JSON handling in .NET, and find the Newtonsoft.Json package. This open source library is among the most popular packages available and makes managing JSON markup a snap. There's a link to the project site on the NuGet.org package description page.

3. In your console window, add the package to your project by executing the following command:

   ```
   dotnet add package Newtonsoft.Json
   ```

4. Enter **AutoMapper** for property and object handling in .NET. This open source package helps to copy data between two objects without writing a lot of `obj.field = that.field` statements. Read more about Automapper at http://automapper.org/.

5. Check out ZXing.Net, a package that helps to scan and create barcodes and QR codes in your application. Wouldn't it be cool if you could share a link to your trips by showing your friends a QR code on the browser on your phone? You can find this package at https://www.nuget.org/packages/ZXing.Net/.

Summary

This hour covers the various options for configuring how your web application will compile and interact with the web server. You have learned how to build a .csproj file and have seen some of the most important configuration options for a project. You have learned how to get started with the NuGet package manager, where to find NuGet packages, and how to reference them in your application. Finally, you have learned how to customize the commands that interact with your project by using a `Program` class.

Q&A

Q. The SDK attribute for an ASP.NET Core project should be set to what value?

A. The SDK attribute should be set to `Microsoft.NET.Sdk.Web`.

Q. In the semantic version number 1.2.3.4, what type of version does the 2 represent?

A. The 2 is the minor version number.

Q. NuGet packages are referenced in a .csproj project definition file as part of what element?

A. The `PackageReference` element defines references to packages.

Q. What `TargetFramework` should I specify in a project file to allow the project to be executable on Mac or Linux?

A. You should specify `netcoreapp1.0` or `netcoreapp1.1`.

Q. How do I extend a project to add additional command-line tools to the `dotnet` tool?

A. You should add `DotNetCliToolReference` elements to your project file.

Workshop

The workshop contains quiz questions and exercises to help you solidify your understanding of the material covered. Try to answer all questions before looking at the "Answers" that follow.

Quiz

1. What command can you execute to compile and bundle a project as a NuGet package?

2. What project event handlers can you configure in a .csproj file?

3. How do you build an application by using the `dotnet` tool?

Answers

1. `dotnet pack`

2. `BeforeTargets Build`, `AfterTargets Build`, `BeforeTargets Publish`, and `AfterTargets Publish`

3. Use `dotnet build`

Exercise

To practice what you've learned to this point, use the `dotnet` command-line tool to generate a new console application and modify it to add two numbers together that are passed in as command-line arguments.

Configuring the Service with the Startup Class

What You'll Learn in This Hour:

- ▶ What is the Startup class?
- ▶ What is dependency injection, and how do you use it?
- ▶ Configuring an application to host ASP.NET MVC

When your web application starts for the first time, there are a number of tasks you should execute in order to apply your preferred configuration to the web service. In the ASP.NET Core framework, you can apply this server configuration through the Startup class. This hour walks through creating the Startup class for the ASPTravlerz sample application, describes the dependency injection pattern, and shows how to configure ASP.NET MVC.

Introducing the Startup Class

In Hour 4, "Defining ASP.NET Core Configuration," you used the dotnet command-line tool to construct an initial template project for your application. You also learned how to build your application, but you have not yet run it. This hour, you'll learn about the Startup and Program classes for a web application and how your web service will be configured.

The ASP.NET team has defined a standard operation in which a managed web application assembly provides a static void Main method in a Program.cs file, just like a console application project, and then launches the web server as defined in the project to apply custom configurations of the service in a Startup class. Your application begins with a static void Main method that by default contains the code shown in Listing 5.1

LISTING 5.1   Main **Method that Starts the Application**

```
public static void Main(string[] args)
{
    var host = new WebHostBuilder()
        .UseKestrel()
        .UseContentRoot(Directory.GetCurrentDirectory())
        .UseIISIntegration()
        .UseStartup<Startup>()
        .Build();

    host.Run();
}
```

This method simply creates a web host and adds the Kestrel web server to it on line 4. Then it directs the web host to use the current directory as the root of the content to deliver. On line 6, it instructs the application to use the Windows Internet Information Server (IIS) web server if it is available. On systems where IIS is not available, this method does nothing and fails silently. The next line instructs ASP.NET to configure the application with the contents of the Startup class.

The Startup class has a specific signature that the ASP.NET host processes are looking for, and if it is not found, the host throws an appropriate error and exits immediately. To demonstrate how the contents of this class operate, you can rename the template Startup.cs file to Startup.cs.bak so that the .NET compiler does not attempt to load and compile it. With that file invisible to the compiler, if you add a new, empty version of the class and try to run the application, you get an error message, as shown in Figure 5.1. Fortunately, the error thrown makes it very clear what the host process is looking for.

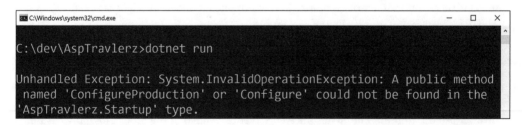

FIGURE 5.1
Error thrown when the Startup class is empty.

The message says that the ConfigureProduction or Configure method is missing from the Startup class. ASP.NET is going to choose one of these methods to configure the application. If a Configure method is available with a suffix that matches the environment name (Production), that method (ConfigureProduction) is called to initialize the application. Otherwise, the Configure method is called. You can satisfy this error message by adding a Configure method to the empty Startup class, as shown in Listing 5.2.

LISTING 5.2   Startup **Class with an Empty** Configure **Method**

```
namespace AspTravlerz {
  public class Startup {

  public void Configure() {}

  }
}
```

If you run the ASPTravlerz application now with the dotnet run command, the server responds as shown in Figure 5.2.

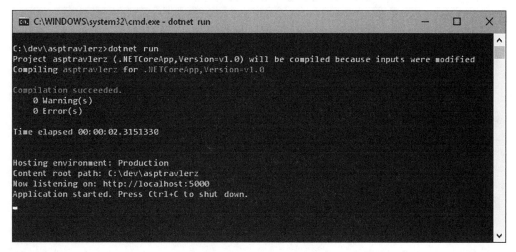

FIGURE 5.2
Successful web start with a Startup class that can be configured.

Sweet! Now you have a web server that is working, and based on the configuration specified in Hour 4, it is listening on port 5000. If you navigate to the address http://localhost:5000 now, you see nothing in your browser. Why is that?

At this point, the web service has not been configured to process any request information, nor has it been configured to serve any content. From the project.json configuration, recall that you had a dependencies configuration with two important entries: one for the Kestrel web server and one for the static files handler. The Kestrel server will host and launch this application, and now you need to configure the static files handler. The task of configuring the server-side capabilities of the web service are handled in this Configure method.

Recall from Hour 3, "Exploring the New Project Templates," the Configure method that accepted an input parameter of type IApplicationBuilder. What is that, and why not use it with the Configure method here? The answer lies in an architecture choice that is made available automatically by the ASP.NET framework: dependency injection.

Introducing Dependency Injection

Dependency injection sounds like a vaccination that you should receive before filing your taxes, but it's actually a principle that makes the development of code much simpler and less repetitive. In the source code of many sample applications, you may have seen code where objects are created with a new keyword and passed into other classes or methods. Maybe you have a central class or two named Utility to perform all kinds of simple tasks on data for you. With the dependency injection principle, you can pass in a constructor argument for a new object and objects that class may need for its work. Listing 5.3 shows what a typical workflow might look like without dependency injection.

LISTING 5.3   Sample Code Without Dependency Injection

```
public class Contact {

    public string Name {get; set;}
    public string Email {get; set;}

}

public class ContactRepository {

    public Contact GetContactByEmail(string email) {}

}

public class ContactController : Controller{

    public ContactController() {}

    public Contact ContactDetails(string email) {

        var repo = new ContactRepository();
        return repo.GetContactByEmail(email);

    }

}
```

With this model of code, ContactController creates a ContactRepository when it needs it in the ContactDetails method and gets the Contact information based on the email address passed in. This is a simple example that clearly shows that ContactController needs to know more about ContactRepository than it really should: It knows how to create ContactRepository. Should a class that will be used to build a user interface know anything about how to configure data access? No, not really; it's not that class's responsibility to know how to configure data access for the ContactRepository class. Listing 5.4 shows how dependency injection simplifies this.

LISTING 5.4 Sample Code Demonstrating the Dependency Injection Model

```
public class Contact {

    public string Name {get; set;}
    public string Email {get; set;}

}

public class ContactRepository {

    public Contact GetContactByEmail(string email) {}

}

public class ContactController {

    private ContactRepository _Repo;

    public ContactController(ContactRepository repo) {
        _Repo = repo;
    }

public Contact ContactDetails(string email) {

        return _Repo.GetContactByEmail(email);

    }

}
```

In Listing 5.4, you can see that ContactController knows nothing about how to construct or prepare the ContactRepository class, as it expects to be passed an instance of ContactRepository in the constructor's repo input parameter. The ContactDetails method then proceeds to do the only thing it should do: delegate a data-retrieval request to an already created ContactRepository. This model simplifies the code and allows you to write classes that are each focused on a single responsibility.

But how should ContactRepository be created and then passed into a new ContactController? It looks like the developer who works with the code in Listing 5.3 is going to be executing that pattern a lot in the code. The ASP.NET team thought of that, too, and has provided a dependency injection container framework.

The dependency injection container is a service class within an application that knows how to construct and provide instances of classes to objects that may be requesting access to other objects through constructor parameters or properties. In the case of ASP.NET, the container service is used with every object throughout the ASP.NET framework, and you simply need to expose a constructor parameter of the type that you desire. ASP.NET provides an appropriate matching instance as your object is being created. This brings us back to the sample code for the `Configure` method.

In the template project in Hour 3, the `Configure` method accepts an IApplicationBuilder parameter. This is an interface type that the ASP.NET Framework creates and makes available for other classes to work with through the dependency injection container. When you add this input parameter to the `Configure` method, the ASP.NET container will inject an appropriate IApplicationBuilder object, and the `Configure` method can work on building out the configuration for the application with that object.

You can start out using the StaticFiles dependencies from Hour 4. You can use the contents of this package to configure your web server to be capable of serving static content. You can do this by updating the `Configure` method to contain the code shown in Listing 5.5.

LISTING 5.5   `Configure` **Method with Method Calls to add Static File Handling**

```
public void Configure(IApplicationBuilder app) {

    app.UseDefaultFiles();
    app.UseStaticFiles();

}
```

The two new lines, `UseDefaultFiles` and `UseStaticFiles`, provide the web service with the configuration to be able to serve files saved to disk. The `UseDefaultFiles` method instructs the server to provide index.html or index.htm files if no name is specified and either of those files resides on disk. The `UseStaticFiles` directive adds the configuration that allows the server to be able to provide HTML, JavaScript, CSS, images, and other files that should not be parsed by the compiler or Razor interpreter before being transmitted to the web client.

With this simple configuration, you can write an index.html file into the wwwroot folder, and it will be served when the web application is running. Write the following content into an index.html file in your wwwroot folder:

```
<html>
  <body>
    <h1>Hello AspTravlerz</h1>
  </body>
</html>
```

You can then restart the web application at the command line with the dotnet run command, or you can build and start the application from within Visual Studio 2017. When you navigate to http://localhost:5000, you should see something like the greeting shown in Figure 5.3.

FIGURE 5.3
Your first served web page.

Congratulations! You've done it! You've served your first web page from a server that you configured by hand. You added only the features that you needed to serve this page. This is the first step of many, so you need to keep digging in and configuring more of the ASP.NET framework services on your web server.

Configuring the MVC Framework

In order to write server-side executed code in C# that ASP.NET can execute, you need to introduce the MVC framework to the server configuration. We'll dive further into what the MVC framework and architecture are and how to use them in Hour 8, "Introducing the MVC Architecture," but at this point, you just need to add some initial configuration to the application. This will happen in three steps: adding the MVC NuGet package, adding items to the dependency injection container, and configuring the MVC framework.

The NuGet package that is needed for the MVC framework is called Microsoft.AspNetCore.Mvc. This package reference should already exist in your project file's dependencies section, with a configuration like this:

```
<ItemGroup>
  <PackageReference Include="Microsoft.AspNetCore" Version="1.1.2" />
  <PackageReference Include="Microsoft.AspNetCore.Mvc" Version="1.1.2" />
</ItemGroup>
```

This makes the MVC package and its dependencies available to the ASPTravlerz project. (Don't forget to run dotnet restore from the command line if you need to make this change if you are not in Visual Studio 2017.)

To add the MVC configuration to the dependency injection container, you need to add another method to the `Startup` class that will get called by the ASP.NET framework during the initial configuration of the web server. This method, called `ConfigureServices`, ironically receives an input parameter that you can use to add your dependency configuration to. The MVC framework can be added to the dependency injection container with the following brief statement:

```
public void ConfigureServices(IServiceCollection services) {

    services.AddMvc() ;

}
```

This code makes the MVC framework and its default implementations available to the entire ASP.NET application. Now you can configure ASP.NET to use MVC if no matching static files are available. You do this by adding the following code after the `UseStaticFiles` command in `Configure`:

```
app.UseMvc(routes => {

  routes.MapRoute(
    name: "default",
    template:"{controller=Home}/{action=Index}/{id ?}");
  }

}
```

There are a number of things going on here, but we need to wait until Hour 8 to talk about them, when we explore the MVC architecture. For now, focus on the `app.UseMvc` statement on line 1. This tells the server that the MVC framework should be used in this application. Because it appears after the `UseStaticFiles` statement, the static files have a higher priority than the MVC framework. That is, if a static file and an MVC endpoint have the same name, the static file will be chosen first and served to the requesting client. This means that the order of the pipeline in the `Configure` method is very important, as requests to the server are resolved from the top to the bottom of the method. These three configuration options you have added to this method are referred as *ASP.NET middleware*.

A number of other components of middleware are available from the ASP.NET team. For example, you can add a generic handler that can run if no static file is found. You can do this by defining a handler for the generic `Run` method after the `UseStaticFiles` call:

```
app.UseStaticFiles() ;

app.Run(context => {
  throw new Exception("Not implemented yet");
}) ;)
```

With this source added, any request that does not locate a static file will throw an exception, and that's not exactly a behavior you want in a production application. For the purposes of showing how this passthrough pipeline works, if you run the web server and navigate to http://localhost:5000/missingPage, you see an empty page returned from the server. This is because there is no content called `missingPage`, and the request passed through to the thrown exception. Also, no error is reported to the console or anywhere else.

You can add some logging to your application so that you can track when exceptions occur. You can add logging by ensuring that the `Microsoft.Framework.Logging.Console` package is added to AspTravlerz.csproj with the rest of the package references.

```
<PackageReference Include="Microsoft.Extensions.Logging.Debug" Version="1.1.2" />
```

You can then activate logging in the console by adding `ILoggerFactory` to the `Configure` method's input parameters and then configuring `LoggerFactory` to use the console. We can take these steps because the Logging framework automatically registers itself with the dependency injection container. Our Configure method looks like the following:

```
public void Configure(IApplicationBuilder app, ILoggerFactory loggerFactory) {

    loggerFactory.AddConsole(LogLevel.Information);
```

You can take these steps because the Logging framework automatically registers itself with the dependency injection container. With this configuration in place, when someone navigates to a location in your application that does not have a corresponding file on disk, a log message is written to the console. This is much better; now you can start to track when and how errors occur on the server. However, it would be nice to have a more protected error page that shows error information to the visiting client. You can intercept these errors and handle them with another piece of middleware.

You can continue to add debugging and error-handling features to your project by starting to use the contents of the `Microsoft.AspNetCore.Diagnostics` package that is indirectly referenced by the `Microsoft.AspNetCore` package. This library allows you to be able to use a generic error page to help diagnose these errors. You just need to add the following statement in the `Configure` method:

```
app.UseDeveloperExceptionPage();
```

This is clean and simple, and now you can restore the packages with `dotnet restore` and restart the web server to see what it looks like when you navigate to the http://localhost:5000/missingPage location again (see Figure 5.4).

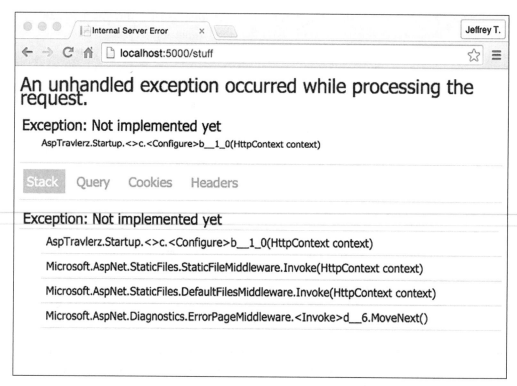

FIGURE 5.4
The standard error page.

That gives you all the diagnostic information you need to troubleshoot an error when you navigate to this page. However, what if you don't want the general public to see this error page? You can configure an ExceptionHandler instead to route people to a static error.html page if there is an error. To do this, create a new file in the wwwroot folder called error.html that contains the code shown in Listing 5.6.

LISTING 5.6   error.html File to Show to the Public When an Error Occurs

```html
<html>
  <body>
    <h2>An error has occurred</h2>
    <p>Our team has been notified and is working on the problem</p>
  </body>
</html>
```

Next, you can update the Configure method and replace the call to UseDeveloperExceptionPage with the following:

```
app.UseExceptionHandler(<< error.html >>) ;
```

With this in place, navigating to the missingPage location will result in the content of the error.html page being delivered to the client. This error scenario is logged, and the public gets a nice message indicating that the development team is working on the problem. We'll look at more configuration options and techniques in Hour 6, "Configuring Your Application," for reading and adapting to the configuration of the server based on environment variables and configuration files on disk.

Enhance Static File Interactions

The default configuration of static file handling in ASP.NET Core is very limited, but there are circumstances when you may want to open up other features for static file presentation and interaction. Follow these steps to try a few of them:

1. Add another folder called StuffOnDisk, as well as StaticFiles on your web server with static content, by using this command:

```
app.UseStaticFiles(new StaticFileOptions()
    {
        FileProvider = new PhysicalFileProvider(
            Path.Combine(Directory.GetCurrentDirectory(), @"StuffOnDisk")),
            RequestPath = new PathString("/StaticFiles")
    });
```

2. Add directory browsing to a folder under wwwroot called assets by adding UseStaticFiles to map this folder to the root of your application and then connect the DirectoryBrowsing functionality as follows:

```
app.UseStaticFiles(new StaticFileOptions()
    {
        FileProvider = new PhysicalFileProvider(
            Path.Combine(Directory.GetCurrentDirectory(),
                @"wwwroot", "assets")),
        RequestPath = new PathString("/assets")
    });

    app.UseDirectoryBrowser(new DirectoryBrowserOptions()
    {
        FileProvider = new PhysicalFileProvider(
            Path.Combine(Directory.GetCurrentDirectory(),
                @"wwwroot", "assets")),
        RequestPath = new PathString("/assets")
    });
```

You also need to connect `DirectoryBrowser` to the available services in the application with the following statement in the `ConfigureServices` method:

```
services.AddDirectoryBrowser();
```

Be careful when exposing this functionality, as you could share some application source code if you do not properly limit the folders selected by this method.

3. Extend or limit the collection of files needed (index.html, default.htm, and so on) by passing a list of the explicit filenames you would like to serve:

```
app.UseDefaultFiles(new DefaultFilesOptions
{  DefaultFileNames = new List<string> { "index.html", "defaultFile.html" }
});
```

4. Combine the two statements `UseStaticFiles` and `UseDefaultFiles` to give their default configuration by using the following statement:

```
app.UseFileServer(enableDirectoryBrowsing: true);
```

By default, directory browsing is disabled, but the statement in this form also enables that functionality.

You can easily extend or limit the files on the web server that you want to serve with these few commands. Be careful how you use them to ensure that you maintain a secure web application.

Summary

In this hour, you have learned how to configure the ASP.NET Core service to respond to requests, log information about those requests, and handle errors. You have also learned about dependency injection and how to configure the dependency injection container provided by ASP.NET.

Q&A

Q. Do I have to use the Kestrel web server when I publish my application to a production environment?

A. With the initial version of ASP.NET, you should use Kestrel combined with an enterprise-grade web server in front of it. That web server can be nginx, Apache, or Microsoft Internet Information Server. They can all be configured to proxy requests to the Kestrel server while providing hardened security and reliability for your application. You'll learn about this in Hour 22, "Deploying to Production."

Q. Do I have to use MVC in my application, or is there another server-side framework that I can use?

A. With the initial release of ASP.NET Core, the only server-side framework that is available from Microsoft is MVC. However, you did learn about middleware in this hour, and you could write your own framework to handle requests instead of using MVC.

Workshop

The workshop contains quiz questions and exercises to help you solidify your understanding of the material covered. Try to answer all questions before looking at the "Answers" that follow.

Quiz

1. What does dependency injection do for an application?

2. After you make changes to project.json to include a new dependency, to review your changes, you should stop the web server, and run `dotnet restore`. What command do you then run to relaunch the web server?

3. The ASP.NET MVC framework is available in what package?

4. What statement can you add to an application to show an error page that provides helpful information for developers when exceptions occur?

Answers

1. Dependency injection is an architecture that allows developers to write simpler classes that separate the construction and configuration of services from the objects that will use those services. It allows you to write simpler classes that each stay focused on a single responsibility.

2. `dotnet run`

3. Microsoft.AspNetCore.Mvc

4. `app.UseDeveloperExceptionPage()`

Exercise

Clean up some of the sample code that was written in this hour and make things look a little nicer in your ASPTravlerz app. Remove the exception that was thrown on every request and comment out `UseExceptionHandlerStatement`. Replace it with the `UseDeveloperExceptionPage` so that you can debug in the hours ahead.

Configuring Your Application

What You'll Learn in This Hour:

▶ Options for configuration file use
▶ The new appsettings.json file and its capabilities
▶ Changing configuration per environment
▶ Using environment variables for configuration
▶ Secret configuration options

Every application has configuration options that need to be changed and delivered in an external set of configuration files. These options have historically been delivered in text files, XML files, INI files, properties files, and even the YAML (Yet Another Markup Language) configuration format. With ASP.NET Core, applications can be configured with a number of different options to meet your application's particular needs. This hour you will explore those options and place some reasonable configuration information into your ASPTravlerz sample application.

Writing Configuration Files

In previous versions of ASP.NET and .NET applications, the preferred way to structure and manage custom application configuration was to use .config files with a prescribed XML format and read those files with a series of classes in the `System.Configuration` namespace. With ASP.NET Core, there are a number of file format options available for custom configurations, and they all deliver the same functionality from the same namespace to your configuration classes in code.

By default, the template projects provided with Visual Studio include the `Microsoft.Framework.ConfigurationModel.Json` package. This package provides the ability to write and work with JSON files and take advantage of their very flexible, hierarchical nature to parse and deliver configuration options into your application. To configure your application to read an appsettings.json file, you need to modify your `Startup` class to build out the in-memory representation of the application configuration. You didn't have a constructor before, but now you need one to ensure that you have configuration information available before the web service configuration is started in the `Configure Services` and `Configure` methods. Listing 6.1 shows the changes you need to make to the Startup.cs file.

LISTING 6.1   Modified `Startup` **Class Constructor to Read the Application Configuration**

```
public Startup(IHostingEnvironment env, IApplicationEnvironment appEnv)
{
  // Setup configuration sources.

  var builder = new ConfigurationBuilder()
      .SetBasePath(appEnv.ApplicationBasePath)
      .AddJsonFile("appsettings.json");

  Configuration = builder.Build();
}


public IConfiguration Configuration { get; set; }
```

Let's review the changes in this listing. The new constructor accepts `IHostingEnvironment` and `IApplicationEnvironment`. These two parameters will be injected by ASP.NET with the dependency injection container and represent information about the server and service that is hosting the web application. You use this information to set up a `ConfigurationBuilder` object that will assemble and make a `Configuration` object available to your application. You begin by declaring that configuration will start in the base path of the application, the same folder where the AspTravlerz.csproj file lives. Next, the appsettings.json file is read and added to the configuration builder. Finally, the configuration is "built" into a comprehensive object and stored in the `Startup` class property that is conveniently called `Configuration`.

With these changes, you can use the `Configuration` property through the rest of application startup to apply information from files and the environment to all the services and capabilities that you want to make available to the rest of the application. Let's start with a simple appsettings.json file with some information that you will want to make available to the rest of the application. Create an appsettings.json file in the base folder of the web application, next to the AspTravlerz.csproj file, that contains the code shown in Listing 6.2.

LISTING 6.2   Initial Sample appsettings.json File

```
{
  "AppSettings": {
    "SiteTitle": "Asp Travlerz",
    "ServerName": "web1",
    "AnalyticsId": "12345"
  },
  "Data": {
    "DefaultConnection": {
      "ConnectionString": "Data Source=./asptravlerz.db"
    }
  }
}
```

This configuration file has two main groups of configuration data: AppSettings and Data. These two groups don't have the same number of child objects, and it could be a little strange to navigate through these options to get the values your application needs. How should you access this information?

Accessing Configuration Data

The IConfiguration interface that the Configuration property in the Startup.cs file implements contains methods and an indexer to allow access to configuration values based on a string key. You can use this to get the entire AppSettings section of configuration with the following call:

```
Configuration.GetConfigurationSection("AppSettings");
```

This call presents the entire collection of AppSettings as another IConfiguration object that you can traverse and on which you can call an appropriate Get method to fetch a specific value from the appsettings.json file:

```
var title = Configuration.GetConfigurationSection("AppSettings").Get("SiteTitle");
```

This is very expressive code, and you could use it to traverse the file, but there is an easier way to navigate directly to the settings you need. The configuration system provides the ability to join together configuration elements with the colon (:) symbol. You can grab the SiteTitle value directly from your appsettings.json file with the following command:

```
var title = Configuration.Get("AppSettings:SiteTitle");
```

You can use the much more terse indexer syntax to call the Get method as well:

```
var title = Configuration["AppSettings:SiteTitle"];
```

This saves you a bunch of keystrokes, and you can now easily grab values from the application configuration.

If you are not sure whether the configuration contains the values that you are looking for, you can use the TryGet method on IConfiguration to verify if a value is available without an error being thrown:

```
string title = "";
bool foundTitle = Configuration.TryGet("AppSettings:Title", out title);
```

In this case, the foundTitle value can be set to false as there is no Title configuration option written in the AppSettings of your configuration file.

Configuring the Application Using Environment Variables

Besides injecting configuration information through a configuration file, the other option easily accessible to developers is to inject configuration through environment variables. This has two very nice benefits:

▶ Environment variables are available on all operating systems and are easily accessible from memory, with no disk I/O operations required.

▶ Environment variables enable easy migration to cloud-based hosting environments where systems operations teams can configure environments through a web portal. In these cases, the operations teams cannot directly access configuration files on disk, and the environment variable option is easily accessible.

A similar syntax for fetching configuration options is supported for setting configuration from an environment variable. In this case, the configuration elements are separated with underscores (_) because separation with colons is not supported on all operating systems.

Reading the environment variables into the project configuration is as simple as adding a new line to the Startup constructor, as demonstrated in Listing 6.3.

LISTING 6.3 Modified Startup **Class Constructor to Read Environment Variables**

```
public Startup(IHostingEnvironment env, IApplicationEnvironment appEnv)
{
  // Setup configuration sources.

  var builder = new ConfigurationBuilder(appEnv.ApplicationBasePath)
     .AddJsonFile("appsettings.json");

  builder.AddEnvironmentVariables();

  Configuration = builder.Build();
}

public IConfiguration Configuration { get; set; }
```

This is an easy addition to make, and the position of the Startup constructor in the order of operations is very important. With the ConfigurationBuilder object, the builder operates in a "last in wins" model, with configuration sources overwriting any previously set value. If the call to AddEnvironmentVariables() is prior to the AddJsonFile execution, then the values configured in any environment variables are overwritten by those in the configuration files on disk. By ordering configuration sources with the environment variables added last, these settings can override any development environment settings written in appsettings.json.

Defining and Configuring Application Environments

An interesting problem that all web developers face is that they typically do not work directly on the machines that are servicing the live requests to their application. Most, if not all, developers work on an environment removed from this production space that they refer to as their "development" environment. This is the developer's playground, where things can break, and the business does not have a significant customer service issue. The "production" environment is where those customers and live requests are coming into the web application, and they need to be serviced with high performance, low latency, and amazing uptime. For developers and the operators of those production environments, it's important to keep configuration of the application in each of these environments different so that customers don't end up looking at something that a developer is actively working on and a developer does not end up changing something that a customer is actively working on.

In ASP.NET Core, the environment is a "first-class citizen" in the configuration framework. There is an explicit setting that is made available in the `IApplicationEnvironment` interface that indicates the name of the environment. In Visual Studio, you can investigate the web project's properties (by selecting Project > <Project Name> Properties), and the debugging panel reports that an environment variable called `ASPNETCORE_ENVIRONMENT` is set to `Development` (see Figure 6.1). This configuration forces any interactions with the application from Visual Studio to trigger the `Development` environment settings.

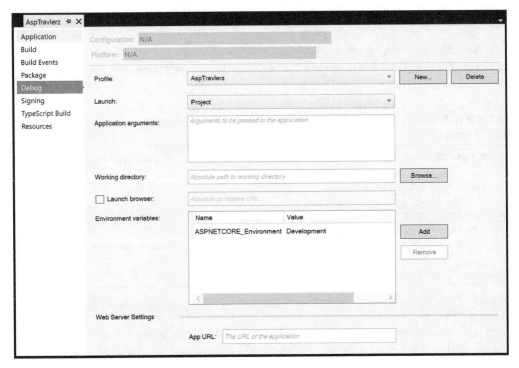

FIGURE 6.1
Environment variable configuration in Visual Studio.

How can you detect this environment name and pivot on it? The `IHostingEnvironment` parameter passed into the `Startup` constructor has several extension methods that allow you to inspect the type of environment:

▶ **IsDevelopment**—Returns `true` if the environment is named `development` and is not case sensitive.

▶ **IsStaging**—Returns `true` if the environment is named `staging` and is not case sensitive.

▶ **IsProduction**—Returns `true` if the environment is named `production` and is not case sensitive.

▶ **IsEnvironment**—Compares an environment name passed in against the current environment name and returns `true` if they match in a case-insensitive comparison.

NOTE

Extending These Options with a Static Class

You can add similar `IsProduction` or `IsDevelopment` functionality to your project by adding a static class that checks for your environment name. Perhaps you need an `IsDemo` method. Writing such a method is a snap. You can take a cue from the Microsoft source for the `IsProduction` method at https://github.com/aspnet/Hosting/blob/dev/src/Microsoft.AspNetCore.Hosting.Abstractions/HostingEnvironmentExtensions.cs.

In the default project template that is deployed with Visual Studio, the `Startup` class takes advantage of the environment name to allow a config.EnvironmentName.json file to be added to the configuration if it exists (see Listing 6.4).

LISTING 6.4 `Startup` **Class Constructor That Reads Environment-Specific Configuration Files**

```
public Startup(IHostingEnvironment env, IApplicationEnvironment appEnv)
{
  // Setup configuration sources.

  var builder = new ConfigurationBuilder(appEnv.ApplicationBasePath)
      .AddJsonFile("appsettings.json");
      .AddJsonFile($"config.{env.EnvironmentName}.json", optional: true);

  Builder.AddEnvironmentVariables();
```

The optional parameter on the call to `AddJsonFile` indicates that an error should not be thrown if the file does not exist. This gives the extra flexibility of being able to deploy a config.development.json, config.test.json, and config.demo.json set of files to all your environments, and the correct configuration will be loaded and override the settings in appsettings.json appropriately for that environment.

CAUTION

Don't Put Secure Settings in Config Files Saved to Source Control

It sounds great to be able to relax how you store and manage configuration settings by having them stored in a series of files that can be deployed to all environments. However, you shouldn't add secure information like security access keys and database passwords in these files that will be committed to source control and potentially visible to anyone in your organization. Use environment variables to set these values on the specific servers that need those secure settings.

Keeping Configuration Data Secret

In the sample appsettings.json file, you included a reference to a database connection string. This isn't a terrible practice in this case where a SQLite file is included, but when you might be connecting to a database or hosted service with a password or an access key, it could be a problem if you commit that data to source control. Even worse, it could be a real problem if you commit that data to a public source code repository like GitHub or Bitbucket. You've likely done it at some point: checked in source code with these "secret" pieces of data embedded in your code or configuration and exposed that information to other people. To prevent this type of accidental disclosure of configuration information while developing your application, the SecretManager tool was created.

SecretManager is installed by default with Visual Studio 2017, and you can easily integrate it with your project by adding this dependency in AspTravlerz.csproj:

```
<PackageReference Include="Microsoft.Extensions.Configuration.UserSecrets"
Version="1.1.1" />
```

Also, you need to add an entry for the command-line tool to manage your user secrets:

```
<DotNetCliToolReference Include="Microsoft.Extensions.SecretManager.Tools"
Version="1.0.1" />
```

When this command is executed, you should see a bunch of NuGet packages installed and configured in your workspace. The tool can then be executed with the user-secrets command. Figure 6.2 shows the help text that appears for this command.

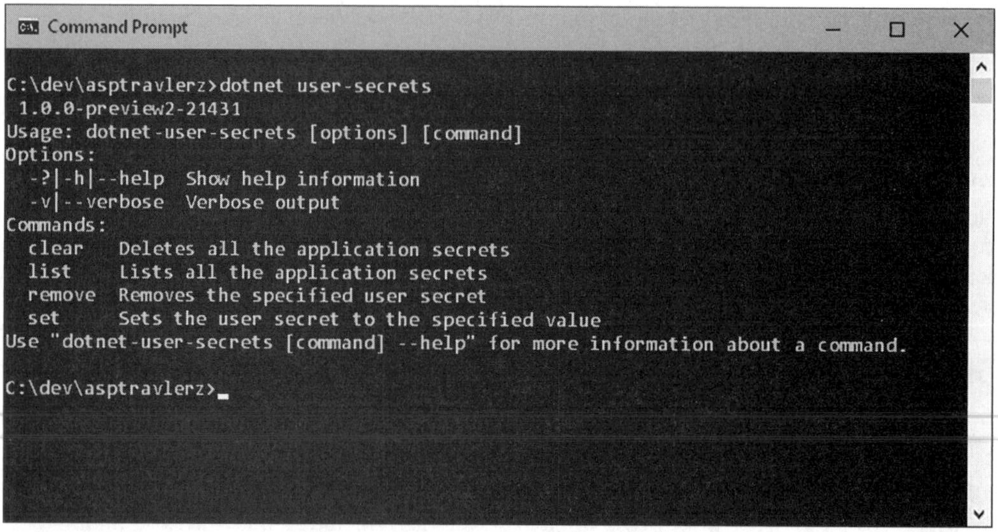

FIGURE 6.2
user-secrets command help text.

There are two parts to using SecretManager. In the first part, you create a secret store on your local disk and store your secret information in that repository. In order to tell SecretManager information about the application whose secrets are to be stored, you need to add to your AspTravlerz.csproj file a `PropertyInfo` element called `UserSecretsId` that gives a unique identifier to this project for which you want to store secrets. This should appear right next to the version information in your project:

```
<UserSecretsId>My-USER-SECRET-ID-HERE-ec0ce4f7-e6a7</UserSecretsId>
```

With this configuration added, you can then use the `user-secrets` command to set values in the secret store, like this:

```
dotnet user-secrets set AppSettings_AnalyticsId SecretId
```

This adds the value `SecretId` to the secret store for the `AppSettings_AnalyticsId` configuration key. As shown in Figure 6.3, Visual Studio 2017 allows you to right-click the project name in the Solution Explorer and choose the context menu option Manage User Secrets to view and edit the JSON file in which this was persisted.

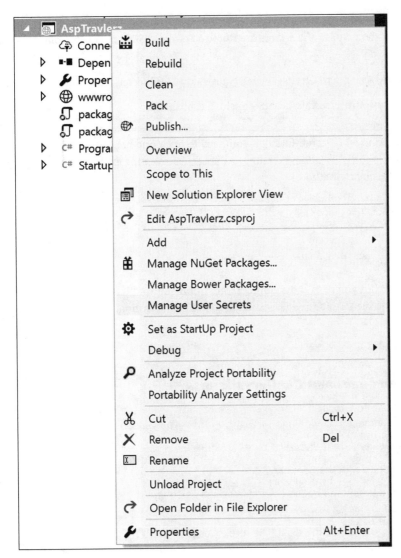

FIGURE 6.3
Managing user secrets inside Visual Studio 2017.

If this value is loaded into your application's configuration after the appsettings.json file is read, it overrides the value stored on disk. Better yet, you can remove that configuration value from the appsettings.json file entirely so that it is not shared with the public. (I recommend leaving the configuration key in the appsettings.json file but removing the value so that you know it needs to be configured in the secret store or some other location.)

This is great: You now have a way to store secrets outside the application, but where exactly are they, and how "secret" are the values? The secrets are stored in a plain JSON file in the following locations on disk:

▶ **Windows**—%APPDATA%\microsoft\UserSecrets\<userSecretsId>\secrets.json

▶ **Mac/Linux**—~/.microsoft/usersecrets/<userSecretsId>/secrets.json

For the second part of working with SecretManager, you need to fetch and get the data into your application. You can do this easily by adding a call to AddUserSecrets at the end of your configuration in the `Startup` constructor method:

```
var builder = new ConfigurationBuilder(appEnv.ApplicationBasePath)
    .AddJsonFile("appsettings.json");
        .AddJsonFile($"config.{env.EnvironmentName}.json", optional: true);

if (env.IsDevelopment()) builder.AddUserSecrets();
```

The additional line checks that you're in a development environment, and if so, it locates the secrets file on disk and adds the `UserSecrets` collection to the configuration.

▼ TRY IT YOURSELF

Try Different Environments and Configurations

Follow these steps to look at how your application changes behavior when you change the configuration through environment variables and through your appsettings.json file:

1. Set the environment variable `ASPNETCORE_ENVIRONMENT=Staging`.

2. Start the web application with the command `dotnet run`.

3. Navigate around the website and notice the log information written to the console window. Nothing has changed in the log.

4. Try navigating to a page that doesn't exist, like http://localhost:5000/ThisPageIsntHere. What is output in the console log for this page? Notice the 404 error returned in the log and the error page displayed in the browser.

5. Stop the application by pressing Ctrl+C and set the environment variable `ASPNETCORE_ENVIRONMENT=Development`.

6. Start the web application with the command `dotnet run`.

7. Navigate the browser to http://localhost:5000/ThisPageIsntHere, and notice that it returns a different error page, geared toward a developer.

8. Stop the application by pressing Ctrl+C and set the environment variable `Logging:LogLevel:Default=error`.

9. Start the web application with the command `dotnet run`.

10. Navigate the browser around the application and then to the http://localhost:5000/ ThisPageIsntHere location. What do you see in the console log?

Here you have used the environment variables to change the behavior of the application as well as to make the application log less verbose. These configuration options are available to you for extending, enhancing, and maintaining as you deploy your web application.

Summary

In this hour you have learned how to write configuration files and options into your application environment so that the web server can interpret these settings and apply them. You have discovered how to read from the appsettings.json file, environment variables, and even a secret datastore on disk. You have also learned about the different application environment names and how you can use them to manipulate the configuration of the service.

Q&A

Q. Do I always have to run in the `Development` environment while writing code?

A. No, feel free to change the name of the environment to test other environment options while you are developing an application. You can test for that environment name with the `IHostingEnvironment.IsEnvironment("MyEnvironmentName")` method. Doing so is a good practice to ensure that your application works the same in any named environment that you are planning to deploy it to.

Q. Can anyone read the secrets file from disk and get access to my other resources?

A. At the time of the release of ASP.NET Core, yes, they can. However, the "bad guys" can no longer read that information from your hosted source code repository because the user secrets file is stored outside your project's source code. Have you ever searched GitHub for the term `ConnectionString`?

Workshop

The workshop contains quiz questions and exercises to help you solidify your understanding of the material covered. Try to answer all questions before looking at the "Answers" that follow.

Quiz

1. What is the name of the JSON file that typically stores application configuration information?

2. What is the separator character for configuration hierarchy in environment variables?

3. What is the name of the default application environment?

4. What environment variable stores the name of the application environment?

Answers

1. `appsettings.json`

2. The underscore (_)

3. `Production`

4. `ASPNETCORE_ENVIRONMENT`

Exercise

Write a configuration option in appsettings.config called `HomeTimeZone` and set the value to the name of your home time zone. Next, write some code in the `Configure` method of Startup.cs to read this time zone value into a static string property called `HomeTimeZone` on the `Startup` class.

Accessing Your Data with Entity Framework Core

What You'll Learn in This Hour:

▶ What an object-relational mapping tool is and the benefits of using one

▶ How to create a new database and structures for storing, managing, and retrieving data

▶ How to use the SQLite database provider

▶ How to swap out and use other database providers

▶ Creating and populating with initial data

You have created the base configuration for your web project and defined some of the initial settings for the application, and now you need to define how and where you will store information that is created from the web. For the sample application ASPTravlerz, you will be storing information about trips, segments of trips, modes of transportation, and schedule information so that you can find them later.

NOTE

Using Any Database You Like

This hour you will see how to connect to and use the SQLite database. This is a single-file-based database that uses very few resources and is perfect for a cross-platform application that will not have very many concurrent users. However, you are free to use any database you like. We discuss other providers later this hour.

Getting Started with Data

Object-relational mapping (ORM) is a development technique that was introduced with the push for object-oriented programming. Basically, ORM allows you to work with a database as a series of objects in C# (or whatever programming language you may be using), and interactions with the database are translated for you to the database's native query language. Entity Framework Core 1.0 is the latest version of Microsoft's ORM framework for .NET developers, but there are many other ORM frameworks available, including NHibernate, Dapper, and Massive.

Entity Framework Core can be used in two modes: code first or data first. These two modes define which comes first—the .NET code or the database structures—and allows you to write applications from that point forward. In this hour, you will learn about both techniques for working with your application. The ASPTravlerz application is a brand-new application for you, and the following section demonstrates how code-first interactions are constructed. Later this hour, you will see how to work with your database in a data-first model.

Adding Entity Framework Core to Your Project

To begin working with Entity Framework Core in your project, you need to add dependencies to the project.json file to direct the `dotnet` tool to restore those packages and make their functionality available to you in the project. Add the following package references to your AspTravlerz.csproj file:

```
<PackageReference Include="Microsoft.EntityFrameworkCore.Sqlite" Version="1.1.1" />
<PackageReference Include="Microsoft.EntityFrameworkCore.Tools" Version="1.1.1"
PrivateAssets="All" />
```

These two packages add the SQLite database provider and all the Entity Framework Core references it depends on, as well as the tools you need to configure and connect to the database as a developer. The tools package is marked with the attribute of `PrivateAssets="All"` to indicate that it will not be deployed with the project and is only in use while you're writing the application. In addition, you need to add the DotNet Tools package as part of the `DotNetCliToolReference` segment of AspTravlerz.csproj:

```
<DotNetCliToolReference Include="Microsoft.EntityFrameworkCore.Tools.DotNet"
Version="1.0.1" />
```

Building Your First Model

Conceptually, you have a very simple model for tracking and managing trips in your application. There are two objects, events and segments. A *segment* is a flight, train ride, lodging information, or other information that you need for a portion of a trip. A trip is comprised of many *segments*. Figure 7.1 shows a simple entity-relationship (ER) diagram for your application.

FIGURE 7.1
Entity-relationship diagram for ASPTravlerz.

While it is very simple, this data architecture allows you to explore some of the important features of Entity Framework. By using the code-first approach to the data model, you can begin defining your database through the definition of .NET classes that will be translated and scaffolded in the database. You can start by defining some simple fields for the `Trip` object. You need to add a class in a new folder in your project called Models and name this file Trip.cs. Then add the code shown Listing 7.1 to Trip.cs.

LISTING 7.1 `Trip` **Object, as Defined in the Models/Trip.cs File**

```
namespace AspTravlerz.Web.Models
{

    /// <summary>
    /// The topmost object that defines a planned trip
    /// </summary>
    public class Trip
    {

      public int ID { get; set; }

      public string Name { get; set; }

      public string Description { get; set; }

      public DateTime StartDate { get; set; }

      public DateTime EndDate { get; set; }

    }
}
```

This seems simple enough: A trip is composed of an ID, a name, a description, and start and end dates. You can name a trip something like "Vacation to Florida" and set a description to "Visiting family and paying our respects to the mouse in Orlando." You should always have a date range and a name for a trip, so you probably want to make those three fields required. You can do this by adding `System.ComponentModel.DataAnnotations.RequiredAttribute` to these properties, and Entity Framework will help you ensure that a value is present for each of these fields. The fields now look something like this:

```
[Required]public string Name { get; set; }
```

Listing 7.1 defines a key for the `Trip` object called `ID`. The `ID` property will be a unique value that you can use to always locate a trip in the database. The ID should have a `KeyAttribute` assigned to it in order to indicate that it is a key for the `Trip` object. By convention, this is not required because Entity Framework automatically defines a field named `ID` as a primary key in a database. (I prefer to decorate the key field with a `Key` attribute to make it explicitly clear which properties are the key values in my database.)

You might prefer not to have to manually assign values to the ID property when new trips are created. You can indicate this design to Entity Framework by adding `DatabaseGeneratedAttribute` to the property as well. You can provide some direction about how the database will generate the ID with an input parameter, as follows:

```
[Key, DatabaseGenerated(DatabaseGeneratedOption.Identity)]
public int ID { get; set; }
```

The `DatabaseGeneratedOption.Identity` parameter indicates that the field should be created as a column with an auto-incremented integer value automatically assigned to the property as a new trip is saved. There are two other options for this parameter:

▶ **DatabaseGeneratedOption.Computed**—The database will compute a value when this object is inserted or updated.

▶ **DatabaseGeneratedOption.None**—The database will not generate or insert a value into this property. (This is the default setting if this attribute is not included in the `Model` class.)

With the simple `Trip` object defined, you next need to define the database context within which the trip should be managed. To do that, you need to create another class in the Models folder and call this one `TripDbContext`. You can start this class by adding the code shown in Listing 7.2.

LISTING 7.2   Initial Contents of the TripDbContext File

```
public class TripDbContext : DbContext
{

  public TripDbContext(DbContextOptions<TripDbContext> options) : base(options)
  {
  Database.EnsureCreatedAsync().Wait();
  }

  public DbSet<Trip> Trips { get; set; }

}
```

The TripDbContext file inherits from the `Microsoft.EntityFrameworkCore.DbContext` object to indicate that it is to be used to manage the connection and objects in a database. The constructor for this class accepts a `DbContextOptions` class that allows the connection information for the database and other configuration options to be passed in and managed by the base `DbContext` object. Since you will be using a file-based database, it is important that the database file be created and available for you on disk before you attempt any data processing with it. That is why the `Database.EnsureCreatedAsync` command is listed in the con-

`DbSet<Trip>` `Trips` property. Let's break down this g things to translate the .NET code to database code:

`DbSet<Trip>`. This is a collection type that Entity ıge the connection and collection of this data in

ıtes that this is a generic collection in .NET. That is, :t in the collection until one is submitted through the ct in this case.

his name is not used in the transfer to and from the

he table that it creates in the database Trips because ze the name of the class object. You can override \ttribute on the `Trip` class to set a different

interactions is to add Entity Framework and, more 'ripDbContext to the dependency injection services ınd made available to the other classes in the appli- ıp class's `ConfigureServices` method with the

:rvices Method to Configure Database

`Collection services) {`

`(options =>`
`tConnectionString("DefaultConnection")));`

is configured to use the SQLite provider with Entity ıctor parameter of type `TripDbContext` will that has been created and passed all of its configuration information. You may hear other developers refer to this as a class that is "fully hydrated," which means an instance of a class has all its dependencies provided and is ready for use.

You can now create the database file and populate it with an initial Trips table from the command line by using the Entity Framework tools defined earlier. The tools add a new command called ef to the dotnet command, and when it is executed, you are greeted by some nifty ASCII art and a list of available subcommands, as shown in Figure 7.2.

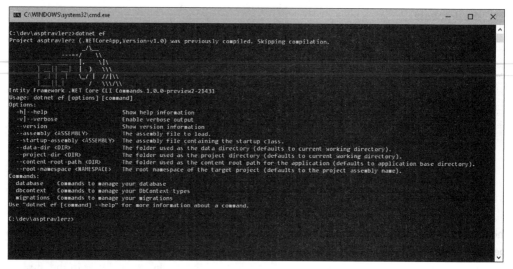

FIGURE 7.2
ef command-line help text.

Yep, that is a unicorn. The code name for a previous version of Entity Framework was "magic unicorn edition," and the moniker has stuck with the product, making an Easter egg appearance in the command-line tool.

There's a lot you can do with this ef command, so let's break it down. For one thing, you can configure which assembly (project name) and directories you want to use with the tool. In development mode, with a single web project, these configuration options are not necessary.

You can configure the namespace to use. If you are generating content from the database, you'll use this later this hour.

You have a choice of three subcommands:

▸ **database**—Allows you to manage the database the project is working with

▸ **dbcontext**—Allows you to manage the context and classes in the project

▸ **migrations**—Allows you to configure changes from the code model to the database

You can start defining the structure of the database by creating a "migration" for the initial trip design. A migration is a code-based definition of the changes needed to update the database configuration, and it also includes the code to remove the configuration changes that would be made. In this way, you can both upgrade and downgrade the state of the database with the model changes that are present in the .NET code. To generate this block of code for the `Trip` object, run the following command at the command prompt:

```
dotnet ef migrations add "Initial Trip"
```

You should see a simple `Done` statement output by this command, with some information about how to undo the command if needed. The code that was generated for you resides in the new Migrations folder in your project. You should find two files in that folder:

▶ **TripDbContextModelSnapshot.cs**—This file contains a snapshot of what the database looks like.

▶ **##_Initial Trip.cs**—This file is prefixed with numbers that constitute the date and time that you generated with the previous command. Inside this file are a series of .NET method calls that generate the appropriate database commands to construct the Trips table in the database.

You can apply this migration and build your database file by executing the following command at the command prompt:

```
dotnet ef database update
```

You should see a statement from the `dotnet` command indicating that it is recompiling your project. This is because you just added two C# files as part of the migration created earlier. Once the compilation completes, the .NET tool applies those changes, and you should see the nondescriptive `Done` message, confirming that your database is up to date. If you peek into the bin/debug/netcoreapp1.0 folder, you should see a file called WebApplication.db; this is the SQLite database that you just configured.

Adding Trip Segments to the Database with a Relationship to `Trips`

`Trips` is not the only object you want to store in your database; you also want to store information about the various segments of trips. You can therefore define a `Segment` object in a new class file inside the Models folder called Segment.cs, which contains the code shown in Listing 7.4.

LISTING 7.4 `Segment` **Object Source Code**

```
namespace AspTravlerz.Web.Models
{

    /// <summary>
    /// A reservation or some other event that has been scheduled during a trip
```

```csharp
    /// </summary>
    public class Segment
    {

        [Key, DatabaseGenerated(DatabaseGeneratedOption.Identity)]
        public int ID { get; set; }

        public int TripID { get; set; }

        [ForeignKey("TripID")]
        public Trip Trip { get; set; }

        [Required]
        public DateTime StartDate { get; set; }

        [Required]
        public DateTime EndDate { get; set; }

        [Required]
        public string Name { get; set; }

        [Required]
        public SegmentType Type { get; set; }

        [ScaffoldColumn(false)]
        public string SegmentType { get { return Enum.GetName(typeof(SegmentType),
Type); } }

        public string ReservationID { get; set; }

        /// <summary>
        /// Can be a flight seat, train class of transportation
        /// </summary>
        public string ReservationLocation { get; set; }

        public string DepartureAddress { get; set; }

        public string ArrivalAddress { get; set; }

    }

}
```

There are some familiar attributes in this class, and there are also some new ones. The first interesting attribute is the ForeignKey attribute on the Trip property. It configures a relationship
to the Trip object through the storage of the ID property (the key) in the Trip object in the

`TripID` property. This `Trip` property will serve as a navigation point back to the `Trip` object that this segment belongs to.

Another interesting attribute, the `ScaffoldColumn` attribute, indicates that the `SegmentType` property should not be created in the database. From the contents of the property, you can see that it is simply transforming the content of the `Type` property into a string that is human-readable. That `Type` property references a new type called `SegmentType` that points to a simple enumeration of the various segment types that you could schedule for a trip. The Models/SegmentType.cs file should contain the enumeration shown in Listing 7.5.

LISTING 7.5   `SegmentType` **Source Code**

```
namespace AspTravlerz.Web.Models
{

  public enum SegmentType
  {

    Lodging,
    CarRental,
    Flight,
    Train,
    Meeting,
    Other

  }

}
```

The `Segment` object references the `Type` property and will store an integer that corresponds to the appropriate value that is set on the `Segment` object. This makes the code more readable in C#, and the presence of the string `SegmentType` property makes it easy to output the name of the segment type to the browser.

You should also add a property to the `Trip` object so that it can manage the segments that belong to it. To create this one-to-many relationship, you can add a property to the `Trip` object of type `List<Segment>`, as follows:

```
public List<Segment> Segments { get; set; }
```

There is a small problem with adding this collection property: It may not be initialized with a collection when you create a new `Trip` object. To ensure that there is always a list of segments available, you can add a constructor to the `Trip` object that initializes this property, as shown in Listing 7.6.

LISTING 7.6 New Constructor for the `Trip` Object

```
public Trip()
{
  Segments = new List<Segment>();
}
```

The final step in adding the segments to your database is to add another `DbSet` property to `TripDbContext` that defines the `Segment` collection in the database:

```
public DbSet<Segment> Segments { get; set; }
```

Now you can return to the command line and add another migration to create the Segments table and relationship in your database. Execute the following at the command line:

```
dotnet ef migrations add "Adding Segments"
```

Finally, apply the migration with this command:

```
dotnet ef database update
```

You now have a database with the two tables defined and a one-to-many relationship defined between them.

Using Objects with Entity Framework

Objects in your database can now be easily created, accessed, and deleted from other classes via the `TripDbContext` object. To make your database context easy to work with, you can create a repository object that wraps the context and simplifies some of the Entity Framework interactions. Listing 7.7 shows what a sample repository class looks like.

LISTING 7.7 `TripRepository` Sample Class, Part 1

```
public class TripRepository
{

  public TripRepository(TripDbContext context)
  {
    Db = context;
  }

  public TripDbContext Db { get; }

  public IEnumerable<Trip> Get()
  {
    return Db.Trips.ToList();
  }
```

```
public Trip GetById(int id)
{

  var thisTrip = Db.Trips.Include(t => t.Segments).FirstOrDefault(t => t.ID == id);
  return thisTrip;
}

public int Add(Trip newTrip)
{

  Db.Trips.Add(newTrip);
  Db.SaveChanges();

  return newTrip.ID;

}

}
```

The repository takes a constructor parameter for `TripDbContext` that you will work with in the rest of the repository. This context is stored in the read-only property `Db` (short for database). The first method in the repository is a simple `Get` operation that fetches all trips from the database, keeps them in memory with the instance of the `TripDbContext` you are working with, and returns a reference to `Trips` to the requestor. The next method, `GetById`, finds the trip in the database that has an ID property matching the ID passed in, and it includes any `Segment` objects referenced by the trip. This `Include` statement tells Entity Framework to generate database code that will traverse the `Segments` property and return data points that are related to the trip. This trip will also be kept in memory with the `TripDbContext` instance, and a reference to it will be returned to the requesting method.

The last method shown in Listing 7.7 is the `Add` method, which simply accepts a trip and adds it to the `Trips` collection in memory followed by executing the `Save` method on the context. The `SaveChanges` method generates the appropriate database insert statement for the provider and executes that against the database, committing this new trip to the database. Remember the `DatabaseGenerated` attribute on the trip's ID property? Thanks to that attribute, you can expect the ID to be set in the `newTrip` object, and you can return that new ID to your called method after the `Save` operation has completed.

Listing 7.8 shows the last two methods for your repository, `Update` and `Delete`.

LISTING 7.8 `TripRepository` **Sample Class, Part 2**

```
public void Update(Trip savedTrip)
    {

        Db.Trips.Update(savedTrip);
        Db.SaveChanges();
```

```
}

public void Delete(int id)
{
  Db.Trips.Remove(Db.Trips.First(t => t.ID == id));
  Db.SaveChanges();
}
```

These last two methods, Update and Delete, should sound similar in simplicity to the previous two. The Update method accepts a Trip object, calls Update on it, and then saves the changes. Under the hood, the Update method on the Trips collection is matching the savedTrip object to a trip in the collection based on the ID property of savedTrip and replacing it in the in-memory collection. The SaveChanges method call on the following line generates the appropriate database update statement and sends it to the database to commit the update.

The Delete method is a little tricky because the Remove method on the Trips collection doesn't accept a key value but rather requires the concrete value of the object to remove from the collection. To ensure that you have the correct trip to remove, a quick search for the trip by ID value is submitted to the Remove method to locate the trip in the database and remove it from the in-memory collection in the ASP.NET application. The SaveChanges method persists that removal operation in the database on disk.

Using Different Database Providers

What if you want to use a different database provider, like PostgreSQL or SQL Server?

If you are interested in using a different database provider, there are several steps you need to go through in order to reconfigure your application to use that provider instead of the SQLite database:

1. Add the appropriate NuGet package dependencies for that provider instead of the Microsoft.EntityFrameworkCore.Sqlite package.

2. Update the ConfigureServices method in Startup.cs to indicate the new provider that will be used with the application.

3. Update the AppSettings.json file with the new connection string to your database.

4. Regenerate the migrations for the new provider.

5. Update the database with the new migrations.

For example, to use Microsoft SQL Server, you can reference the `Microsoft.EntityFrameworkCore.SQLServer` package and update the `Startup` or `ConfigureServices` method to contain configuration syntax similar to the following:

```
services.AddDbContext<TripDbContext>(options =>
  options.UseSqlServer(Configuration.GetConnectionString("SqlServerConnectionString"))
);
```

You can then delete the contents of the Migration folder and regenerate them for SQL Server with this single call:

```
dotnet ef migrations add "Initialize SQL Server"
```

Or you can use a similar initial migration name. All the database configuration that you previously built is then reconstructed for SQL Server, and you can apply those changes with the database `update` command:

```
dotnet ef database update
```

Now your SQL database should be configured with a similar structure for your application. Notice that none of the context or object classes in the project change; just the database configuration changes. This is one of the hallmarks of the ORM approach: You can change the database configuration without having to rewrite any of your code because Entity Framework translates your code for you when you work with the database.

Creating Some Initial Data

Now that you have a repository object and a connection to a database available, you can add a method to configure some initial data or, in this case, some sample data that you can work with as you build your application. You can do this by adding a new class in the Models folder called `SampleData` and populate it with an `InitializeData` method that will give you your initial data to work with. Listing 7.9 shows this `SampleData` class.

LISTING 7.9   `SampleData` **Class Contents with Sample Data**

```
public class SampleData
{

  public static void InitializeData(IServiceProvider provider)
  {

    using (var serviceScope = provider.GetRequiredService<IServiceScopeFactory>().
CreateScope())
    {

      var env = serviceScope.ServiceProvider.GetService<IHostingEnvironment>();
```

```
if (!env.IsDevelopment()) return;

var db = serviceScope.ServiceProvider.GetService<TripRepository>();

// Exit now if we already have trips created
if (db.Get().Any()) return;

var startDate = FirstFridayNextMonth(DateTime.Today);
var endDate = startDate.AddDays(2);

var newTrip = new Trip
{
  Name = "Weekend in NYC",
  Description = "Train to New York City for the weekend",
  StartDate = startDate,
  EndDate = startDate.AddDays(3).AddMinutes(-1)
};

var trainDepart = new Segment
{
  Name = "Amtrak Train PHL->NYP",
  StartDate = startDate.AddHours(17),
  EndDate = startDate.AddHours(19),
  DepartureAddress = "30th St. Station\n Philadelphia, PA",
  ArrivalAddress = "New York Penn Station\nNew York, NY",
  ReservationID = "123456",
  Trip = newTrip,
  Type = SegmentType.Train
};
newTrip.Segments.Add(trainDepart);

var lodging = new Segment
{
  Name = "Coolio Hotel at Times Square",
  StartDate = startDate.AddHours(19).AddMinutes(30),
  EndDate = endDate.AddHours(12),
  ArrivalAddress = "123456 Times Square, New York, NY",
  ReservationID = "ABCDE",
  Trip = newTrip,
  Type = SegmentType.Lodging
};
 newTrip.Segments.Add(lodging);

var trainReturn = new Segment
{
  Name = "Amtrak Train NYP->PHL",
  StartDate = endDate.AddHours(15),
  EndDate = endDate.AddHours(17),
```

```
        DepartureAddress = "New York Penn Station\nNew York, NY",
        ArrivalAddress = "30th St. Station\n Philadelphia, PA",
        ReservationID = "654321",
        Trip = newTrip,
        Type = SegmentType.Train
    };
    newTrip.Segments.Add(trainReturn);

    db.Add(newTrip);

  }

}

private static DateTime FirstFridayNextMonth(DateTime dateToCheck)
{

  var firstOfNextMonth = dateToCheck.AddMonths(1).AddDays(-1* (dateToCheck.Day -
1));
  var daysUntilFriday = 5 - (int)firstOfNextMonth.DayOfWeek;

  return daysUntilFriday > 0 ? firstOfNextMonth.AddDays(daysUntilFriday) :
        firstOfNextMonth.AddDays(7 + daysUntilFriday);

}

}
```

There is a single `IServiceProvider` object in the `InitializeData` method. This interface describes the dependency injection container that you configured in Hour 6, "Configuring Your Application," and you will use it to retrieve a fully hydrated `TripRepository` that you can use to populate the database. A `ServiceScope` object is created from `IServiceProvider`. This gives a limited scope to the object that you retrieve from `IServiceProvider` and ensures that it is disposed of and cleaned up properly when this method concludes operations. First, you request an instance of type `IHostingEnvironment` by calling `GetService` with the generic type `IHostingEnvironment`, as designated in the angle brackets on the `GetService` method. This hosting environment object is then asked if you are currently in the `Development` environment, and if you are not, it exits immediately. This method call allows you to ensure that you only generate sample data in your development environment and not in staging or production. In a real-world application, you may have initial database configuration code that you do want to execute in those environments to test and initialize those other tables appropriately.

The `ServiceScope` is then asked to get a service of generic type `TripRepository`, and this new `TripRepository` object is set to the variable db. db is checked to see if there are any `Trip` objects created yet. If any are found, the method exits immediately. Otherwise, a new `Trip` object called Weekend in NYC is created, with a round-trip train ride and a two-night stay at the swanky Coolio Hotel on Times Square. Once this trip and its segments are defined, they are added to the database with the Add command you wrote earlier.

Next, you need to connect this construction of sample data to your application so that it is created when you start the website. You can add a call to create this sampledata to the end of the Startup.Configure method as shown in Listing 7.10.

LISTING 7.10   Configuring Startup **to Call** SampleData.InitializeData

```
public class Startup {
///   other lines of configuration code
  public void Configure(IApplicationBuilder app, ILoggerFactory loggerFactory) {
  /// other lines of configuration code
     SampleData.InitializeData(app.ApplicationServices);


  }
```

With that SampleData.InitializeData line in place, you can feel secure that when you run your application, you will have a constructed database that contains some data for you to begin working with.

▼ TRY IT YOURSELF

Write Your Own Sample Data

Think of a recent trip or vacation that you embarked on and extend the SampleData class to include information about that trip. Your sample data will be more memorable because you will know exactly the trip that you are reviewing. Follow these steps:

1. Add a new trip to the InitializeData method, using the same new Trip() syntax that you used for the Weekend in NYC trip in Listing 7.8.

2. Write additional methods below your new Trip object with information about the various segments of the trip. Be sure to include travel and lodging.

3. Add the segments to your Trip object with a Trip.Segments.Add(myNewSegment) statement for each segment.

4. Add your trip to the database by using db.Trips.Add(myNewTrip).

5. To refresh the database on disk, delete the trips.db file in your bin/Debug/netcore1.1 folder and restart your application.

Summary

In this hour, you have learned how to configure your application to work with a database by using the Entity Framework Core tools. This introduction to Entity Framework Core shows how to do simple create, read, update, and delete operations in the database by using a DbContext object. In addition, you have generated migrations for your code structures as well as applied those migrations to a real database. You have also seen how easy it is to reconfigure the database provider to use a different database and generated some sample data to work with in your application.

Q&A

Q. Do I have to use Entity Framework Core to work with my database?

A. With the initial version of .NET Core, using Entity Framework Core is the preferred way to work with a database. Your database provider may expose other operations and endpoints that you can connect with using other APIs besides Entity Framework Core. It is for this reason that I like to create a Repository class that hides Entity Framework Core so that interactions with the data store can change between Entity Framework and the data storage's specific API.

Q. Can Entity Framework Core be configured to operate on the database asynchronously?

A. Yes! As with previous versions of Entity Framework, there are async versions of the API methods demonstrated here. You can use the async methods, use the async and await keywords, and return a task from the repository methods if you choose. For simplicity, this book does not cover async operations but focuses on synchronous interactions with the database.

Workshop

The workshop contains quiz questions and exercises to help you solidify your understanding of the material covered. Try to answer all questions before looking at the "Answers" that follow.

Quiz

1. How does SQLite store its data?

2. How is the database provider for Entity Framework configured?

3. What is ORM?

4. The sample data in your application is loaded by using the InitializeData method with a special input parameter. What does that input parameter do?

Answers

1. In a single, simple, cross-platform-capable database file

2. An entry for the provider is added to the project file, and a configuration method is executed in the `Startup` class that looks like this:

   ```
   services.AddDbContext<TripDbContext>(options => options.UseSqlite())
   ```

3. *ORM* stands for *object-relational mapping*. An ORM tool allows object-oriented code to be automatically translated and mapped to a database.

4. The `IApplicationServices` parameter contains information about the dependency injection container that was previously configured during hour 5 in the `Startup` class. You use it in the `InitializeData` method to get a Repository object and to verify the state of the application for creating sample data.

Exercise

You now have a functioning database attached to your application that can store and retrieve data about trips for you. Update the `SampleData.InitializeData` method to include some information about three of your recent trips or vacations. You will use this sample data in the hours ahead as you build web pages that work with the database.

Introducing the MVC Architecture

What You'll Learn in This Hour:

▶ Concepts of the MVC architecture

▶ Advantages and disadvantages of MVC

▶ Where do ViewModel and ModelBinding fit in?

We're going to go back to some theory in this hour and explore the MVC architecture provided in ASP.NET. It's more than just three letters; the Model-View-Controller architecture provides significant flexibility and design capabilities—but at a bit of a cost. We'll explore these topics in this hour and even cover some of the MVC-related buzzwords you may have heard, like *ViewModel* and *ModelBinding*.

NOTE

MVC Isn't Just MVC

The ASP.NET MVC framework doesn't just support the MVC architecture. It now has the capability to serve the former Web API framework as well. We'll explore more about how Web API fits into the MVC framework in Hour 13, "Writing Web API Methods."

Defining the MVC Architecture

Like many things in technology today, the MVC architecture is defined with a TLA—a three-letter acronym. MVC stands for Model-View-Controller, the three primary components of the architecture that are used to build applications. This architecture is widely used and praised for providing a clear separation of various concerns and capabilities of applications. These three parts can be further defined as follows:

▶ **Model**—This is the long-term memory of the application. Your business objects and their state are represented as models in the framework. These models reference other models only if they are anything more than primitive types.

▶ **View**—The views are the dumbest part of the application. They know nothing about your business logic, but they know how to make your models look good and how to present them to the user. They are the user interface for your models and know very little about server-side programming.

▶ **Controller**—This is the mad scientist of your application, with the knowledge to use models and views together. The controller knows how to receive user input, how to apply that input to a model, and how to deliver an appropriate view to represent the impact of that input.

Figure 8.1 puts these three components together so that you can see their interactions.

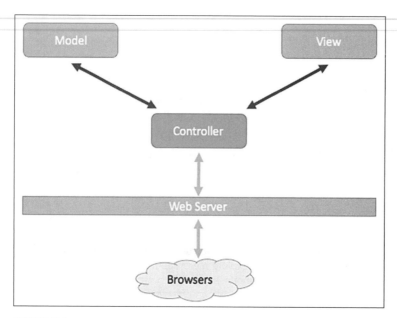

FIGURE 8.1
Interactions of the model, the view, and the controller on a web server.

The controller is activated by the web application to handle input from browsers and then translates that request into an interaction with a model and applies a view to that model. The result of the view applied to the model is then transmitted back to the web browser. In other words, models are the bytes stored in a data repository, and the view translates those bytes into (in this case) HTML representing that model for a web browser to be able to display.

With ASP.NET Core, the concepts of model, view, and controller are physically separated into folders with names appropriate for each architecture object. Figure 8.2 shows what a basic ASP.NET Core project file structure looks like.

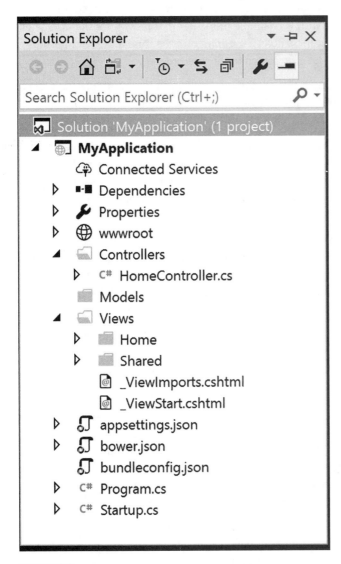

FIGURE 8.2
A basic ASP.NET Core application file layout with Models, Views, and Controllers folders.

The following sections dig a little deeper into each of these three components to help you understand their purpose.

Defining a Model

The model objects in an application typically have no business logic built into them and are sometimes referred to as POCOs, or "plain old class objects." The objects defined in Hour 7, "Accessing Your Data with Entity Framework Core," with Entity Framework—the Trip and TripSegment objects—are all models with very simple properties that provide for the storage of related data. The relationships between these objects are important because those relationships are part of how the data is stored and later presented to the web browser.

The model does not refer to a controller or a view in any way. You can have multiple controllers work with the same model objects, and you can have multiple views that present models for different user experiences.

A model stores and handles some validation capabilities for itself so that it can alert the controller and consequently the view when the model is in an invalid state. In the Entity Framework samples in Hour 7, you added attributes to the classes that dictated the sizes of the properties, the restrictions on the data that could be accepted into those properties, and error messages to display if the properties are in invalid states.

The classes in your application (in the .NET implementation of MVC) don't represent any information about how to interact with the repository that contains them. How do you retrieve information about your trips? Where do you process methods to update and add new trip information into your application? These tasks are typically handled in the controller but access a fourth component of this architecture that is very important to the model objects—the repository.

A repository is typically written to do the simple CRUD (create, read, update, and delete) work with the backing datastore. In the case of Entity Framework, the repository is the TripContext object, and you can use it from any controller to get the model objects you need and interact with their representation in the datastore.

Defining Views

The views are the Derrick Zoolander of this operation: They look amazing but know only one trick: how to make your application look good. They do not change the model in any way, nor do they provide any extra value to the browser that was not delivered to them from the controller. The view knows what the model object is but has no reference to a controller.

Business logic, data access capabilities, and decision-making code should not be written into the source of the view objects. The most processing that you want to do in a view is simple if-then or for-loop statements. If you need more logic than this, you have misplaced capabilities between your view and your controller. This is a bit counterintuitive to long-time ASP.NET developers who used the ASP.NET Web Forms framework to build user interfaces.

In the Web Forms framework, you could use blocks of logic called *web controls* that could be placed directly into the HTML that you wanted to deliver to the browser. These controls could have data access logic in them or data presentation code or pretty much any code that you wanted executed on the server. This had the side effect of making these controls very hard to test and making it very difficult to optimize processing in them.

The views in MVC should be "skinnable." That is, you should be able to apply another view with the same knowledge of the model to get a similar output for the browser. The location of user-interface components in the resultant HTML and the logic in the view should have no effect on the model being presented.

Defining Controllers

The controller is where the model and the view are put together. The controller handles user interactions and determines how to get the model the user is requesting. In addition, it decides which view the user needs and applies that view to the model that was requested.

In ASP.NET, controllers are a single class that represents a series of related actions around an area of functionality. The ASP.NET framework provides the initial handling of user input, such as the URL navigated to in your application, and routes that input to an appropriate controller to further inspect that input for processing. This routing capability could be considered a super-controller because it controls the controllers and how they interact with the browser.

You'll write your first controller in Hour 9, "Building Your First Controller," where you will start presenting a home page that shows the list of trips known to the application.

Advantages and Disadvantages of MVC

There are a significant number of advantages to using the MVC architecture that you should be aware of before you start to write code in Hour 9:

▶ The MVC pattern has been long established and practiced in other languages and environments. .NET and the web are not the first to use this pattern, and it has a proven track record of success in major projects.

▶ There is a clear separation of concerns. The user interface is clearly defined and handled in view objects that can be changed without impacting the source code that defines the model or the controller. In addition, the logic to retrieve models and handle user input can be changed without impacting the views. This also means that you could separate developers who are responsible for each of these objects: user interface designers to manage the views, database developers to manage the models, and server-side developers responsible for the controllers.

▶ Because each of the three components of MVC can be isolated, it is very easy to write unit tests to verify that a controller handles user input properly or processes business logic accurately. You can easily test a view by applying a static model to it and verifying that it does not violate any user interface concerns.

The disadvantages are heavily outnumbered by the advantages, but you should know about them as well:

▶ Knowledge of multiple frameworks and technologies is required. You need to know how to write and work with web presentation technologies as well as the database if you are on a small team.

▶ Code can be spread out across many objects to present a single screen. Some developers decry this as spaghetti code, or untidy code that is very difficult to navigate and maintain.

▶ Data access strategies are inefficient. Modern user interfaces have a very data-heavy presentation and interact with datastores frequently with strategies like AJAX to give the perception of high performance. This interaction is difficult to do, and you will see how you can accomplish this in Hour 17, "Connecting Angular to ASP.NET Core."

What Is a ViewModel?

A lot of buzzwords float around software architecture, and MVC has its share. There are variants of MVC in use, and there are implementation details in use that sound like a new form of architecture that works with MVC.

A *ViewModel* in the MVC architecture is a simplified version of a model that has been reduced to just the items that the view needs to present. Because a model has no knowledge of what a view can do, a ViewModel object is established. Some developers add validation logic to a ViewModel so that this processing can occur outside of the POCO model objects. This also means that you can grab just those related parts that you need from several models and deliver a unified data object that pulls together a single concept.

What Is ModelBinding?

ModelBinding is a feature by which the user input from the browser is directly mapped back to a model (or ViewModel) object for processing. In ASP.NET, the framework has capabilities to automatically transform input with field names similar to property names of a model. This makes handling input and validating a submitted model's information very easy to do without requiring hand-coding to load a model from every field submitted from a browser.

Examine the Individual Accounts Template

You've learned about the basic MVC architecture, and now you can take a look at a complete template application that features models, views, and controllers and peek around at how they are glued together with some knowledge of what the architecture is trying to accomplish. Follow these steps:

1. Start a new project and choose ASP.NET Core Web Application, then the Web Application template, and finally click the Change Authentication button and choose Individual User Accounts.

2. In the resultant application, start with the Controllers folder and open the `AccountController`.

3. Locate the `Login` method that has an `[HttpGet()]` attribute just above it. This statement should be within the first 50 lines of the file. Read the contents of this method. Notice that it forces the user to be signed out and ends with returning a view. This is the controller passing execution of the application to a view object.

4. Locate the Login.cshtml file in the Views/Account folder. This is the view for the `Login` method, and it contains everything needed to format the screen based on the execution of business logic in the `Login` method. This file should look fairly similar to a standard HTML page, with a few extra tags and markup. You'll learn more about views in Hour 10, "Beginning MVC: Writing Your First View."

5. The email and password fields on the view are submitted by a visitor who wants to log in. They're passed back to the second `Login` method in the `AccountController`, with an input parameter called `LoginViewModel`.

6. Locate the `LoginViewModel` in the Models/AccountViewModels folder and open this file. Notice that this class has properties for the `Email`, `Password`, and even the `RememberMe` check boxes in the view. The ASP.NET Core framework combines the posted response from the browser with this class to create a concrete .NET object that can be operated on by the controller's second `Login` method.

There you have it: A quick round-trip of data from the controller, through a view to the browser, submitted back to the server as a `LoginViewModel` to be operated on by the controller. This is a data-flow cycle that you will create and manage throughout your ASP.NET Core projects.

Summary

This hour's architectural discussion of the MVC framework has covered a number of complex topics that you will start working with firsthand in the next few hours. The views and controllers capabilities will be used extensively as you build out those objects in the following hours.

Q&A

Q. Do model, view, and controller objects need to be built in separate files?

A. Yes. In the ASP.NET framework, a templating language called Razor is used for view construction. The Razor markup and HTML are in a distinct file and a prescribed location to make organizing your project easier.

Q. How do you handle "cross-cutting" concerns like logging and security?

A. You can apply filters to controllers. The filters inspect user interactions to ensure that they are authorized and can handle output processing and tracking.

Workshop

The workshop contains quiz questions and exercises to help you solidify your understanding of the material covered. Try to answer all questions before looking at the "Answers" that follow.

Quiz

1. What does MVC stand for?

2. Of M, V, and C which one:

   A. Contains the information about the data to be persisted?

   B. Is the brains of the operation, with knowledge of the other two objects?

   C. Knows nothing about the other two objects?

   D. Can be swapped out for another object of the same type?

Answers

1. Model-View-Controller

2. **A.** Model

   B. Controller

   C. Model

   D. View

Exercise

We now understand the three components of an MVC architecture and now need to allocate space for the views and controllers source code in the project. By convention, we will store our controllers in a folder called "Controllers" and views in a folder called "Views." Add the "Controllers" and "Views" folders to the project as we will build controllers and views in the next two hours.

Building Your First Controller

This hour you'll start actually writing your first MVC code: C# code that will be compiled and run on the server. You will examine the controller object and learn how and when the controller interacts with the browser.

Reviewing the MVC Folder Structure

Figure 9.1 shows the default folder structure for a new MVC application. Pay particular attention to the new folders marked in boxes.

Separate folders are created to hold each of the model, view, and controller objects. (In addition, a folder has been allocated for ViewModels, but you are not required to use it.) You need to make sure that these first three folders are all present in your ASPTravlerz application by creating them if they do not already exist.

You're going to spend this hour in the Controllers folder, and you can get right into it and create your first controller class: TripController. Listing 9.1 shows the initial syntax for this controller.

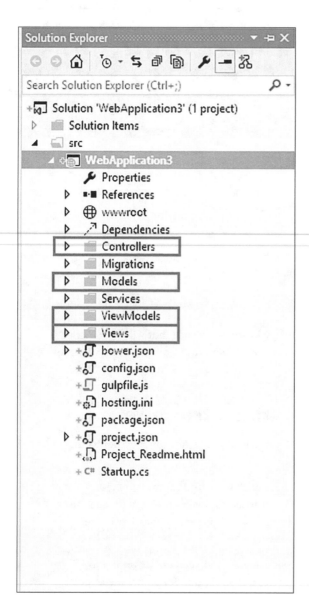

FIGURE 9.1
Standard ASP.NET MVC folder structure.

LISTING 9.1   Initial Code for the `TripController` Class

```
using Microsoft.AspNetCore.Mvc;

namespace AspTravlerz.Controllers {
```

```
public class TripController : Controller {

}

}
```

Let's examine what's happening in this code for `TripController`. The controller is named after some functionality, the *trip*, plus *controller* to help you later identify that this object is a controller. In addition, the class inherits from the `Microsoft.AspNetCore.Mvc.Controller` object. Descending from this abstract class gives us access to information about the current request context and server status when a request is handled by this controller.

Requests for content need to be handled by controllers, and the ASP.NET framework needs to know how to route those requests to the correct controller. The functionality that determines which controller handles each request is called *routing*. You already defined a brief routing configuration, called a `routing-table`, in the Startup.cs file when you initially configured the MVC framework in Hour 5, "Configuring the Service with the `Startup` Class." For reference, it's listed again in Listing 9.2.

LISTING 9.2   Initial Routing Configuration

```
app.UseMvc(routes => {

  routes.MapRoute(
    name: "default",
    template: "{controller=Home}/{action=Index}/{id?}"
  );

});
```

Now this is starting to make a *lot* more sense than when you just blindly added this code back in Hour 5. When a request comes in to the server, the template on line 5 is mapped to determine the name of the controller to handle the request. For example, if someone navigates to your application at http://localhost:5000/Trip, then a controller class named `Trip` will be located and handed this request. You just wrote that class, so this request would be handed to the new `TripController` class. If there is no controller specified in a URL like http://localhost:5000, then a default controller name is applied, and in your template, that default is specified as `Home`, and you do not yet have a `HomeController`. (We'll discuss this further later.)

The next segment of the route needs to be handled as well: `{action=Index}`. `action` is a public method in your controller class that handles a request and returns `IActionResult`. In this template, if there is no `action` segment of the URL submitted as in both of our sample URLs, then an `Index` method will be sought out in the controller.

You can configure an initial `Index` method in `TripController` with the following method syntax:

```
public IActionResult Index() {
}
```

Inside this method, you can do anything that you need to fetch data and return information to a view that will be rendered for the browser. How do you return a view to the browser? I set you up with that question. ...You return a view by returning a view. No, really; it's in Listing 9.3.

LISTING 9.3   Complete `Index` Action Method, Returning a View

```
public IActionResult Index() {

    return View();

}
```

This seems way too easy, but the framework was designed this way on purpose. No information is needed; if you don't need anything special from the server-side processing in the controller, you can just return a `View` method call from the base controller object. What if you wanted to handle some input data from the browser? The routing template in Listing 9.2 specifies an `id` element that could be submitted, but how do you work with that?

Choosing Action Method Input Parameters

Input parameters to the controller's action methods like the Index method in Listing 9.3 can come from a number of sources, including a URL folder, the text after the filename on the URL that is called a querystring, and the data posted back to the server from a web form. If you navigate to a URL like http://localhost:5000/Trip/Details/1, the ASP.NET router attempts to execute a method named `Details` on `TripController` and pass the value 1 into the method.

Other parameters can be accepted from the URL, with the parameters appearing after a ? and in `name=value` notation. Each value is passed into an input parameter with the same name that appears in the URL.

Tips for Returning a View from a Controller

A few questions arise at this point: What view object does the framework use when you return a view with that syntax? How do you choose a different view to present? How do you pass a model into the view? This section steps through some of the tips and tricks of using the `View` method in a controller.

The `View` method is built based on the idea of "convention over configuration"; it looks in the Views project folder for a folder named after the controller, seeking a file with the same name as the method that returned the view. In the case of Listing 9.3, the framework looks for a Trip folder containing an Index.cshtml file. The .cshtml extension is the standard extension for the Razor syntax, which you'll learn more about in Hour 10, "Beginning MVC: Writing Your First View."

If you don't want to name your view after the method, you can name it whatever you want or even derive a different view name and pass in the string name of the view to the View method call. If in the previous example you wanted to return a view named DefaultStuff, you could change the return statement to this:

```
return View("DefaultStuff");
```

How do you pass a model to the view? The whole point of the MVC architecture is that the view knows how to format a model, so how should that call be formatted? The model is typically an object, and not a string. You can pass the model object into the View method call in this way:

```
var model = new object();
return View(model);
```

Very nice; now you have supplied a model to your view. What if you want to specify the name of the view and return a model to the view object? In this case, you can pass two arguments—the name of the view and the model:

```
var model = new object();
return View("DefaultStuff", model);
```

Intercepting Action Methods

There are event handler methods that you can implement in the controller to enable this functionality. Let's take a look at the OnActionExecuting and OnActionExecuted virtual methods in the Controller class. The sample code in Listing 9.4 uses these methods to measure how long it takes for every method in the controller to execute and emits a header that reports the duration.

LISTING 9.4   Executing Code Before and After an Action Method

```
private Stopwatch _Timer;
public override void OnActionExecuting(ActionExecutingContext context) {

    _Timer = Stopwatch.StartNew();

    base.OnActionExecuting(context);

}
```

```
public override void OnActionExecuted(ActionExecutedContext context ) {

    context.HttpContext.Response.Headers.Add("X-ElapsedTime", new[] {_Timer.
ElapsedMilliseconds.ToString()} );

    base.OnActionExecuted(context);

}
```

This code allocates a `Stopwatch` object that keeps very accurate track of time elapsed. Before the action method is called, the timer is initialized and stored in the `_Timer` field. After the action method completes and the `OnActionExecuted` method is called, the method adds a header to the output with the value of the timer in milliseconds. Figure 9.2 shows the output that appears in the browser, including a list of headers after browsing to http://localhost:5000/Trip/Index.

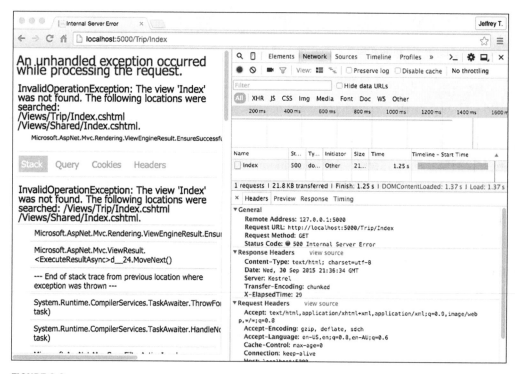

FIGURE 9.2
Output with headers from navigating to the trip index location.

You can clearly see in the Response Headers section on the right side of Figure 9.2 that X-ElapsedTime recorded that a few milliseconds elapsed while ASP.NET was attempting to locate a suitable view to present the content requested. You'll learn about the message presented on the left side in Hour 10, where you will write your first views.

You Don't Need to Return a View!

It's possible that you don't want to render HTML and return it to the browser. You may want to deliver data in some other format—even binary content—to the browser. There are a number of other methods on the controller class that you can use to help deliver ActionResult with different content. In Listing 9.5, you can see how to use the Json method to deliver data in JSON format.

LISTING 9.5   Returning JSON content

```
public IActionResult My() {

    var trips = new Models.Trip[] {
        new Models.Trip { Destination = "New York" },
        new Models.Trip { Destination = "Las Vegas"}
    };

    return Json(trips);

}
```

In this case, a Model object was assembled that was composed of a pair of Trip objects and returned as the model of the Json method in the base controller class. The Json method does all the heavy lifting work to convert the data in the trips object to JSON format and return it to the browser. Try it out by navigating to http://localhost:5000/Trip/My.

Making Controller Development Easier

In the course of developing a moderately sized web application, you will write a dozen or so controllers, and you will want them all to have some similar sense of capabilities and functionality. There is instrumentation that you may want to add, and there are common cross-cutting concerns that you will want available in all of them. How can you deliver this similar functionality to all your controllers without hand-coding all of them with the same techniques?

The way around this is to write your own abstract controller class that uses the same base controller class and then make all your controllers inherit from your new class. To see how this works, you can write a BaseController class and move your elapsed time code into that class. Listing 9.6 shows the code for the BaseController class.

LISTING 9.6 `BaseController` **Class Initial Code**

```
using Microsoft.AspNetCore.Mvc;
using System.Diagnostics;

namespace AspTravlerz.Controllers {

    public abstract class BaseController : Controller {


        private Stopwatch _Timer;
        public override void OnActionExecuting(ActionExecutingContext context) {

            _Timer = Stopwatch.StartNew();

            base.OnActionExecuting(context);

        }

        public override void OnActionExecuted(ActionExecutedContext context ) {

            context.HttpContext.Response.Headers.Add("X-ElapsedTime", new[] {_Timer.
ElapsedMilliseconds.ToString()} );

            base.OnActionExecuted(context);

        }

    }

}
```

Now, you can modify `TripController` to remove the `OnActionExecuted` and
`OnActionExecuting` methods and inherit from `BaseController` instead of `Controller`.
For every method in every controller that implements `BaseController`, the `X-ElapsedTime`
header will be added to the response.

You can also take advantage of the dependency injection container to add `LoggerFactory` to
`BaseController`. Remember that every object in ASP.NET is created through the dependency
injection container, so you can add a constructor with an `ILoggerFactory` parameter to
the `BaseController` and capture a `Logger` object for use in logging performance, as shown
in Listing 9.7.

LISTING 9.7   **Adding a Logger to** `BaseController` **Through Dependency Injection**

```
public BaseController(ILoggerFactory loggerFactory) {

    Logger = loggerFactory.CreateLogger("Controller");

}

protected ILogger Logger { get; private set;}

Logger.LogInformation($"{context.HttpContext.Request.Path} - {_Timer.
ElapsedMilliseconds}ms");
```

That was easy, and now the log reports the same information that is delivered to the browser.

CAUTION

Fat Controller Syndrome

Be careful about how much code you write into the individual controllers you are managing for an application. Many MVC projects suffer from the "fat controllers" problem, in which controller code grows to thousands of lines of code, making it unreadable and unmaintainable. Try sticking with the seven lines of code rule: If you need to write more than seven lines of code in an action method, move that code to another class, where it can be isolated, tested, and reused in another part of the application.

TRY IT YOURSELF ▼

Update `HomeController`

`HomeController` came with your application and contains some simple methods to show a home page, a contact page, and an about page. Follow these steps to update it to contain more information:

1. Open the Controllers/HomeController.cs file to begin editing.

2. Add a public method to the class called `Faq` that returns an `IActionResult` just like the `Index` method in the class.

3. Inside your new `Faq` method, create a new variable called `faq` and assign it this value:

```
var faq = new Tuple<string,string>(
    "Why did the chicken cross the road?",
    "To Get to the other side")
;
```

4. Return the `faq` object as the single argument inside the `View` statement. This is the model that you will pass into the `faq` view in Hour 10.

Summary

Controllers are a part of the MVC architecture, and you now know how to use them to handle requests from the browser. You've seen how to write action methods and how to add handlers around those action methods when you need to perform extra work on the web server. This hour you have gotten an idea of the benefits of adding a `BaseController` class to your project to provide similar functionality for multiple controllers. You have also looked at using dependency injection to deliver cross-cutting concerns, like adding a logger to your controllers.

Q&A

Q. Do I really need to place my controller objects into the Controllers folder? Can I instead organize my project by feature area and place controllers in the same folder next to their views and models?

A. You could do that, and it would require some configuration changes to support the lookup for the views from the `View()` method, but it is completely nonstandard, and most developers are very familiar with the standard project folder layout demonstrated in this hour.

Q. Can I move my controllers to another project and reference them from there?

A. In previous versions of ASP.NET, that was a possibility with a configuration option in the Startup method. Unfortunately, as of version 1.0, this feature is not yet available from Microsoft.

Q. Do I really need to inherit from the controller class? I would rather inherit from another class that gives me features I am looking for.

A. You can construct your controllers however you please, and yes, you don't need to explicitly inherit from the controller class. If your controller class's name ends with `Controller` and contains methods with the action method signature, ASP.NET will treat it as a `Controller` object, complete with dependency injection capabilities.

Workshop

The workshop contains quiz questions and exercises to help you solidify your understanding of the material covered. Try to answer all questions before looking at the "Answers" that follow.

Quiz

1. In a standard ASP.NET MVC project layout, in what folder are controllers stored?

2. What is the name of the configuration in the `Startup` class that instructs the ASP.NET framework about choosing the controller to use when a browser navigates to an application?

3. What is the name of the class that you typically inherit from when building a Controller class?

4. What object type should be returned from an action method in a controller?

5. What does the return statement in an action method look like when you want to return a view named `ContactDetails` from a method named `Details`?

Answers

1. Controllers

2. `routing-table`

3. `System.AspNetCore.Mvc.Controller`

4. `IActionResult`

5. `return View("ContactDetails")`

Exercise

Using the `TripDbContext` data access class that was created in Hour 7, "Accessing Your Data with Entity Framework Core," modify the `TripController` class as follows:

▶ Accept a `TripContext` class as an input parameter on the constructor method and store a copy of it in a property called `Repository`

▶ Add the following action methods to `TripController`:

  ▶ **Search**—Returns the full list of trips through a view

  ▶ **Details**—Returns a single trip through a view

  ▶ **Create**—Returns a blank trip through a view

  ▶ **Edit**—Gets a trip from the repository and returns it through a view

In Hour 12, "Writing Data from a Controller," you'll learn how to write this data back through the controller and to the database. For now, you need to simply set up the Search and Details methods. In Hour 10, you will write some views to present the content returned from these methods.

HOUR 10
Beginning MVC: Writing Your First View

What You'll Learn in This Hour:

▶ How to use Razor templates

▶ How to write a view

▶ How to interact with a layout template and reusable templates

▶ How to use HTML helpers

The `Trip` controller output currently looks like a collection of error messages about not being able to locate a View file. It's time to make the `Trip` controller output look like it actually belongs in a web browser. In this hour you will build your first views and start shaping the user experience of your application.

NOTE

Views Delivering HTML Content

Even though you will be using the Razor template language to craft your views this hour, the output of those templates is HTML. Everything you know about HTML is valid and should be considered appropriate output from the Razor files.

Introducing Razor Templates

The templating engine that is used by ASP.NET MVC is called Razor, and the templates that go along with it are denoted with the extension .cshtml. This extension suggests how you will write your templates: by using C# mixed with HTML. Unlike with other template frameworks, the Razor markup only denotes the start of inline C#, and the engine knows when it has reached the end of a C# statement. All C# code starts with an @ symbol and may optionally be wrapped in curly braces ({ }). It's really simple, and the Visual Studio 2017 and Visual Studio Code editors provide a lot of context in their highlighting of code to indicate what is HTML and what is C#. Let's take a look at a few examples, starting with some inline C# in Listing 10.1.

LISTING 10.1   Inline C# Mixed with HTML in a Razor Template

```
<footer>&copy; @DateTime.Now.Year - All rights reserved</footer>
```

This very simple example shows an HTML tag: the footer with a copyright notice
embedded. The copyright entity is emitted with the © code, and then the C# code starts.
DateTime.Now.Year is a C# statement to calculate the year of the current date. Notice that
there is no command to write that into the flow of the HTML, nor is there a semicolon at the end
of the value. The code just stands alone, and the value that it evaluates to is merged into the
HTML at that point. The HTML that would be delivered to the browser in the year 2018 would
look as follows:

```
<footer>&copy; 2018 - All rights reserved</footer>
```

This is easy to understand, but now look at the more complex example in Listing 10.2.

LISTING 10.2   A `for` Loop Mixing C# with HTML in a Razor Template

```
<table>
@for (var i=0; i<5; i++) {
    <tr><td>Row @i</td></tr>
}
</table>
```

This time, you have a block statement in the `for` loop, and you know you are in C# syntax
from the @ symbol on line 2. The next line starts in with HTML markup and then goes back
to C# to output the current value of i, just as in the Listing 10.1 example. The HTML ends,
and the ending curly brace is there to help identify the end of the `for` loop. Figure 10.1 is
a screenshot of this code in Visual Studio 2017. Check out how the tool helps you tell the
difference between C# and HTML.

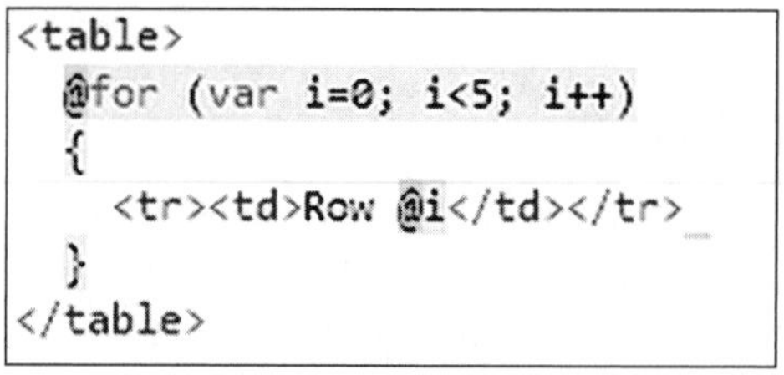

FIGURE 10.1
Razor syntax highlighting in Visual Studio 2017.

In Visual Studio, you can see that the C# code starts with a yellow background @ symbol, and
the C# code has a gray background. The HTML code is still highlighted in burgundy and blue,

with normal text in black. Even the @i inside the HTML markup is colored appropriately to indicate that code will be evaluated on the server before it is transmitted to the browser.

Listing 10.3 shows another sample of razor code that is a block of C# statements that will be executed as a group, with the variables available later in the HTML.

LISTING 10.3   A Block of C# Statements with HTML in a Razor Template

```
@{

    var daysUntil = 365 - DateTime.Now.DayOfYear;

}
<span style="font-weight:bold;">There are only @daysUntil left
in @DateTime.Now.Year</span>
```

In this case, the calculation of days remaining in the year is performed at the top of the block and then used later on, in the midst of the span element.

Writing the Search View

In this section, you can start writing the content of the search view for your ASPTravlerz web application. The focus of this page is a header and a table that shows all the trips that are currently stored in the application. The first things you need to handle in the view is receiving the Model object that was passed from the Search method in TripController. This will be a collection of Trip objects, referred to generically as an IEnumerable<Trip> (read "IEnumerable of type Trip"). You can specify the type of the Model object passed into the view with an @model statement at the top of the view. You can start writing a Search.cshtml view in a Views/Trip folder in your project with the content shown in Listing 10.4.

LISTING 10.4   A Block of C# Statements with HTML in a Razor Template

```
@model IEnumerable<AspTravlerz.Models.Trip>

<h1>Search for Trips</h1>

<table>
    <tr>
        <th>Name</th>
        <th>Destination</th>
        <th>Start Date</th>
        <th>End Date</th>
    </tr>
</table>
```

So far, it looks like normal HTML. What if you use the `for` loop syntax shown earlier to write an appropriate loop to output every `Trip` object in the model that was passed to the template? When you are working with the model that was passed in, you can use the keyword `Model` to reference that object. With the model type directive at the top of the file, you should get strong IntelliSense capabilities from Visual Studio 2017 and Visual Studio Code that help show you the properties available on the `Model` object. Listing 10.5 shows the code of the loop to add to your table.

LISTING 10.5   A Loop Statement to Output Trip Data as an HTML Table

```
<table>
    <tr>
        <th>Name</th>
        <th>Destination</th>
        <th>Start Date</th>
        <th>End Date</th>
    </tr>
@foreach (var trip in Model) {
    <tr>
        <td>@trip.Name</td>
        <td>@trip.Destination</td>
        <td>@trip.StartDate.ToString("d")</td>
        <td>@trip.EndDate.ToString("d")</td>
    </tr>
}
</table>
```

The `foreach` statement instructs the Razor template engine to repeat the enclosed code once for each trip in the collection. Each trip in the collection is represented by the local variable `trip`, and you can use the `Trip` object properties in each of the columns of the table as shown. With some sample data loaded, the search page now looks as shown in Figure 10.2.

This is a nice start, but say that you would really like to wrap the contents of this search page with a nice header bar and a footer. To do that and to ensure that this layout is available to all pages in the application, you can use a Layout template, as described in the following section.

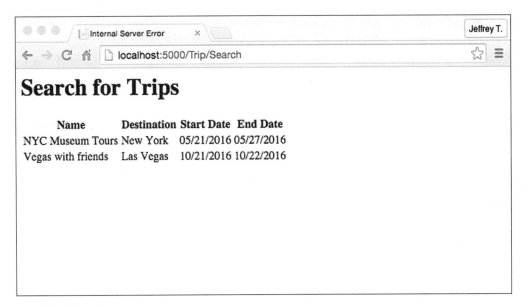

FIGURE 10.2
Output of the initial search template.

Creating Razor Layout Templates

To create and enforce a shared layout template on all pages in the application, you only need to create two templates with some code in them that directs the Razor engine how to appropriately include child templates. The first of the two templates is called _ViewStart.cshtml, and it resides at the root of the Views folder.

The _ViewStart.cshtml template is typically a single line of code, a directive telling the engine where to find the layout to apply to any Razor template that is requested. _ViewStart.cshtml is a "magic filename" for the Razor template engine that it will discover and execute first. Listing 10.6 shows the contents of the _ViewStart.cshtml file for the ASPTravlerz site.

LISTING 10.6 _ViewStart.cshtml Content That Specifies a Common Layout File

```
@{
   Layout = "_Layout";
}
```

In Listing 10.6, the definition of Layout as a file called _Layout takes advantage of the file locator built into the Razor engine, and it looks in several places for this file. You have already seen reports of where the Razor engine looks, way back in Hour 5, "Configuring the Service with the Startup Class," when you first started running a method in a controller without having a view file present. You probably saw error output that looked similar to the contents of Figure 10.3.

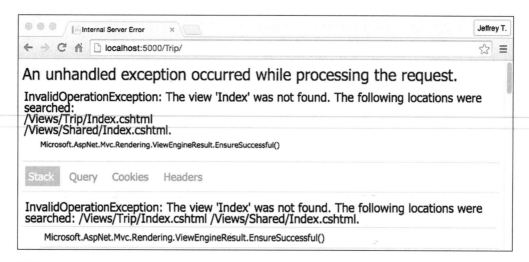

FIGURE 10.3
Error message indicating where the Razor engine is looking for view files.

In Figure 10.3, the Razor engine is very helpfully reporting an error with all the locations that it searched for the Index.cshtml file. It first looked in the folder with the same name as the controller that is requested, and then it looked in a folder called Shared. That is where you will place the common _Layout.cshtml file—in a folder called Shared under the Views top-level folder.

Now you're ready to write a layout with appropriate HTML 5 formatting, header, and footer. Add the contents of Listing 10.7 to your Views/Shared/Layout.cshtml file.

LISTING 10.7 Initial Content of _Layout.cshtml to Format Pages as HTML 5

```
<!DOCTYPE html>
<html>
  <head>
    <title>ASP Travlerz - Trip Tracking for you!</title>
  </head>
  <body>

    <footer>&copy; @DateTime.Now.Year - ASP Travlerz</footer>
  </body>
</html>
```

This is a fairly standard collection of markup for an HTML 5 page. Make sure to include the DOCTYPE directive at the top so that browsers know that you are delivering HTML 5 markup. You can see in the footer that this code reuses the copyright demonstration from the Razor templates introduction earlier this hour. The next part to add to this page is the "landing zone"—the area where the contents of the child template should be placed. You can add an entry just above the footer element in the page with this syntax to include the child template:

```
@RenderBody()
```

The body of the child template will be included at this point of the HTML page. If you run your application now, your search results page will look as shown in Figure 10.4.

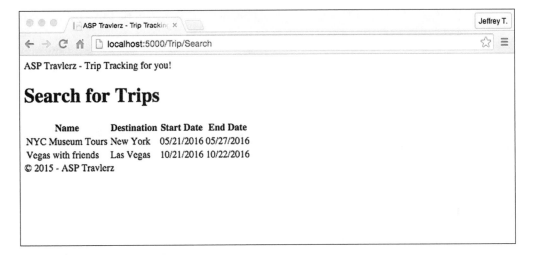

FIGURE 10.4
Search page with layout applied.

You have a header, a footer, and some clear content in the middle of the search results page. It's not beautiful, but then you haven't applied any images or styles to it yet.

At some point, you're going to want to click on your trips and navigate to a page that shows their detailed information. In the next section, you'll see how to modify your table markup with an HTML helper to help build that link.

Introducing HTML Helpers

In the Search.cshtml page, you can modify the name of the trip to no longer output plain text but to be a hyperlink to the appropriate details page for that trip. For this, you can use an ActionLink HTML helper that will use some C# code to format the text as a hyperlink. An *HTML helper* is a method in a C# library that can be called directly from the Razor markup to perform some formatting of HTML code for you.

Listing 10.8 shows how to modify the Name column of the table to use the `ActionLink` helper.

LISTING 10.8   Using an `ActionLink` HTML Helper to Format a Hyperlink

```
@foreach (var trip in Model) {
    <tr>
        <td>@Html.ActionLink(trip.Name, "Details", new {id=trip.TripId})</td>
```

The `ActionLink` method uses these three arguments:

- ▶ The text to display in the hyperlink

- ▶ The name of the action on the same controller as the requested controller

- ▶ A collection of information to help in building the route to the action (in this case, the `TripId` to be found)

You now have a table with names that are hyperlinks to pages with more information about the trip listed in the table.

CAUTION

Keeping Razor Dumb

Do not add any "smarts" to your Razor views beyond what they need to deliver a good-looking presentation onscreen. Never interact with your data repository, modify the contents of your model, or do any network communications from within the C# used in the Razor markup. Such tasks significantly slow the rendering of your pages and increase the utilization of your web server's processor unnecessarily. The application of a Razor template should be very fast, with very little processing required from your web server.

▼ TRY IT YOURSELF

Add a View for the `Faq` Method

At the end of Hour 9, "Building Your First Controller," you created an `Faq` method in `HomeController` and had it return a simple question-and-answer object to a view. Follow these steps to create that view now:

1. Add a new file to the Views/Home folder called Faq.cshtml and open it for editing.

2. Inside this view, start with the statement @model Tuple<string,string>, which indicates that you expect a model to be passed in of type Tuple<string,string>.

3. Add an HTML H2 tag with the content "Frequently Asked Questions".

4. Below the header, write the following code:

```
<p><b>Q:</b>@Model.Item1</p>
<p><b>A:</b>@Model.Item2</p>
```

5. Save your view, start the application, navigate to http://localhost:5000/home/faq, and observe how your view formats and presents the simple `faq` model that was passed to it.

This is a simple demonstration of formatting view data—in this case a question with an answer. You can extend this sample further with additional questions in an array as your model and loop over that content to write the questions into your HTML.

Summary

This hour you built your first Razor view for your web application's search page, and you learned how to use the Razor template syntax. In addition, you started a simple layout for use in your web application. You hand-authored these segments of your application, and it took some time to write them. In Hour 11, "Scaffolding User Interfaces," you will learn how Visual Studio and the `dotnet` tools can help you generate an initial snapshot of the view code you need in your application.

Q&A

Q. Can I have multiple layouts in my application and choose an appropriate one at the top of my Razor template?

A. You certainly can do this, but you will end up with a bit of code duplication.

Q. Do I have to use Razor markup with ASP.NET Core? Is there another type of markup that I can use?

A. Razor is the only templating engine delivered with the initial release of ASP.NET Core. The community is welcome to make Spark, Web Forms, or any other templating toolkit available.

Workshop

The workshop contains quiz questions and exercises to help you solidify your understanding of the material covered. Try to answer all questions before looking at the "Answers" that follow.

Quiz

1. What is the file extension for Razor syntax?

2. What is the special name of the Razor template that is loaded first if it is present on disk?

3. What is the command for a layout page to call to indicate where contents of a child template should be placed within the page?

4. What is the character that indicates the start of C# code in a Razor template?

Answers

1. .cshtml

2. _ViewStart.cshtml

3. `RenderBody()`

4. `@`

Exercise

Write a Details.cshtml view for the details of the trip that is returned from `TripController`'s `Details` action. This view should show all the information about the trip in an easy-to-read page.

Customize the layout.cshtml file to add styles and formatting that bring some color to your application.

HOUR 11
Scaffolding User Interfaces

What You'll Learn in This Hour:

▶ How to use the new scaffolding tools in Visual Studio 2017 to create user interface components

▶ What the output of the various templates looks like and how to start developing with the templates to meet your needs

In this hour you're going to look at some of the scaffolding options that ship with Visual Studio 2017. You will explore these automation tools and use them to automate the construction of some controllers and razor views to help speed up the construction of your application.

NOTE

Scaffolding Is Not Limited to Visual Studio

There are lots of templates and scaffolding options available to help make you more productive with ASP.NET Core and web development outside Visual Studio. Remember that you can use the `dotnet new` command to start building a new application, and there are several templates available there.

Introducing Scaffolding in Visual Studio 2017

Scaffolding is a term used to refer to the automated construction of code from a template based on some inputs from the user of the scaffolding tool. Scaffolding takes a number of forms in developer tools—command-line executables, editor commands, and graphical step-by-step wizards to name a few.

Visual Studio was built to be a very productive integrated development environment, and there are productivity-enhancing tools buried throughout the application. The scaffolding tools for ASP.NET Core are embedded in the Solution Explorer window and can be found when you right-click on a folder and choose Add. You can start looking at the templates by right-clicking the Controllers folder, as shown in Figure 11.1.

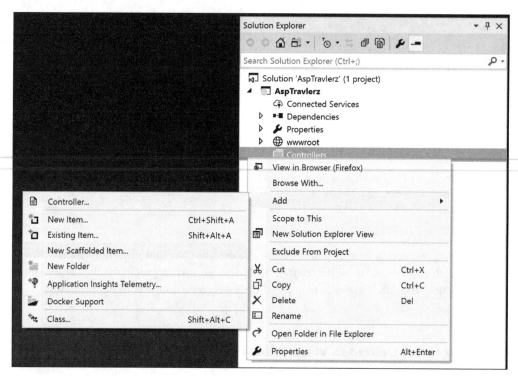

FIGURE 11.1
Adding a new scaffolded item in Visual Studio 2017.

Click the New Scaffolded Item menu option to open the Add Scaffold dialog, as shown in Figure 11.2.

The default templates available in the Add Scaffold dialog help you construct controllers and views based on the contents of the code you have already written and the data access capabilities already made available in your project with Entity Framework. The Entity Framework information you learned about in Hour 7, "Accessing Your Data with Entity Framework Core," seems like a *really* good idea now because you can just create cookie-cutter user interface elements for all your objects and be done with your sample project 13 hours early. Or you can dig in a bit further and make your sample project something *really* cool.

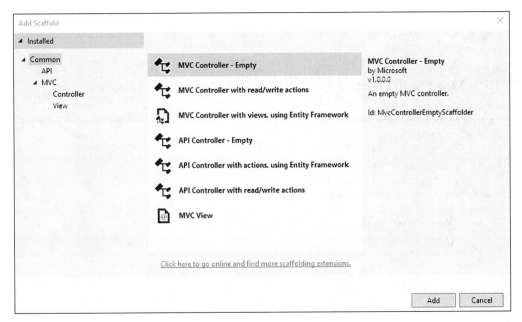

FIGURE 11.2
The Add Scaffold dialog with the default collection of templates to choose from.

Investigating the Templates

Let's take a look at each of the templates shown in Figure 11.2 and the code they can generate for your application. Each of these templates adds functionality and generates more code
than the previous, in an effort to reduce the amount of identical code that you would need to
rewrite for each scenario.

Trying the MVC Controller - Empty Template

MVC Controller - Empty is one of two very simple templates. When you choose this template,
a simple prompt box opens and allows you to specify the name of the controller class that
you want to create, as shown in Figure 11.3.

FIGURE 11.3
The prompt window for the MVC Controller - Empty template.

With the template name MVC Controller - Empty, you know you're not going to get a lot in the way the generated code. Take a look at Listing 11.1 to see the sparse code this template generates for your application.

LISTING 11.1   Code Generated by the MVC Controller - Empty Template

```
using System;
using System.Collections.Generic;
using System.Linq;
using System.Threading.Tasks;
using Microsoft.AspNetCore.Mvc;

namespace asptravlerz.Controllers
{
    public class TripController : Controller
    {
        public IActionResult Index()
        {
            return View();
        }
    }
}
```

If you like to build things by hand and want to just get started with the minimum, this is a nice place to start. After using the template a few times, you may find it quicker to type the class name and constructs by hand.

Trying the MVC Controller with Read/Write Actions Template

With the MVC Controller with Read/Write Actions template for MVC controllers, methods are created with different signatures for `Details`, `Create`, `Edit`, and `Delete`. When you select this template from the Add Scaffold dialog, you get a prompt box that allows you to specify the name of the controller class that you want to create, just like the one shown in Figure 11.3. Listing 11.2 shows this template's code.

LISTING 11.2   Code Generated by the MVC Controller with Read/Write Access Template

```
using System;
using System.Collections.Generic;
using System.Linq;
using System.Threading.Tasks;
using Microsoft.AspNetCore.Http;
using Microsoft.AspNetCore.Mvc;
```

```
namespace asptravlerz.Controllers
{
    public class EventsController : Controller
    {
        // GET: Events
        public ActionResult Index()
        {
            return View();
        }

        // GET: Events/Details/5
        public ActionResult Details(int id)
        {
            return View();
        }

        // GET: Events/Create
        public ActionResult Create()
        {
            return View();
        }

        // POST: Events/Create
        [HttpPost]
        [ValidateAntiForgeryToken]
        public ActionResult Create(IFormCollection collection)
        {
            try
            {
                // TODO: Add insert logic here

                return RedirectToAction("Index");
            }
            catch
            {
                return View();
            }
        }

        // GET: Events/Edit/5
        public ActionResult Edit(int id)
        {
            return View();
        }

        // POST: Events/Edit/5
        [HttpPost]
        [ValidateAntiForgeryToken]
```

```
public ActionResult Edit(int id, IFormCollection collection)
{
    try
    {
        // TODO: Add update logic here

        return RedirectToAction("Index");
    }
    catch
    {
        return View();
    }
}

// GET: Events/Delete/5
public ActionResult Delete(int id)
{
    return View();
}

// POST: Events/Delete/5
[HttpPost]
[ValidateAntiForgeryToken]
public ActionResult Delete(int id, IFormCollection collection)
{
    try
    {
        // TODO: Add delete logic here

        return RedirectToAction("Index");
    }
    catch
    {
        return View();
    }
}
    }
}
```

You get the same class definition and empty index method from the previous template, as well as some very deliberate methods with a lot of TODO comments embedded.

The Details method is intended to show the content of one item that the controller manages—in this case a single Event object. It is up to you to write the logic and code necessary to load the Event model and pass it to the view.

The first `Create` method does not receive any arguments and is the action that handles that screen you navigate to with the empty form awaiting information about the event you would like to create.

The second `Create` method has a pair of attributes decorating it and receives an `IFormCollection` argument. This is the method that will handle the HTTP Post action when a visitor submits the form on the create page. The `HttpPost` attribute marks this method to be used only when the web server is handling an HTTP Post action. The `ValidateAntiForgeryToken` attribute is part of a security strategy to prevent cross-site scripting. The collection that is submitted through the input parameter is a string-keyed collection of string values that were submitted. This means you can access the value of the `FirstName` field that was submitted with some code like the following:

```
var firstName = collection["FirstName"]
```

NOTE

Using `IFormCollection` Is Not the Only Way to Access Your Data

Form collection from fields submitted is not the only way to access the submitted data. You could add individual field names as parameters to your methods and capture each field as a separate parameter. That would also be a lot of maintenance work each time you wanted to change your application's fields. With the next template, you'll see how you can do this a bit more easily with ModelBinding.

The two generated `Edit` methods are identical to the `Create` methods in that one is configured to be the `Edit` method executed to edit a specific object identified by the integer ID value submitted, and the second method is the method that will be executed when the first posts to the web server for a specific ID value.

The two `Delete` methods function the same way as the `Edit` and `Create` methods. The first `Delete` method should give a user an opportunity to review the object he or she is deleting and click a Confirm button to approve removal of the object. The second method should handle that confirmation and remove the object from your datastore.

Trying the MVC Controller with Views, Using Entity Framework Template

The MVC Controller with Views, Using Entity Framework template promises to do even more with your base objects. When you choose this template, you're prompted for more than a simple name for your controller, as shown in Figure 11.4.

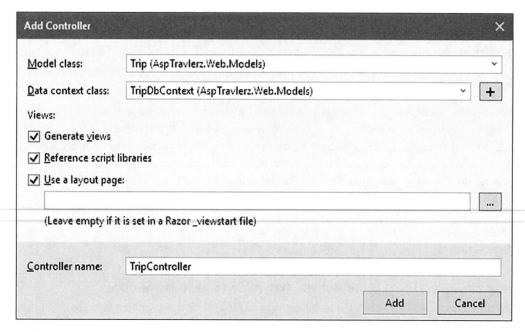

FIGURE 11.4
The prompt window for the MVC Controller with Views, Using Entity Framework template.

With this dialog, you can configure a number of options for the code to be generated. This template generates a controller and prepopulates all the database interaction methods based on the Entity Framework objects you specify in the first two combo boxes in this dialog. It is important that the model chosen can be managed with the class specified in the Data Context Class combo box. The button with the plus symbol on it allows you to specify the name of a new data context class if you have not yet written one for your model class.

The Generate Views check box is intuitive: Do you want views generated for the controller actions? The Reference Script Libraries check box allows you to specify whether the template should use a view residing in /Views/Shared/_ValidationScriptsPartial.cshtml to load JavaScript to help validate the contents of your forms on the browser. The Use a Layout Page check box allows you to specify the location of an alternate layout page if you are not using the standard /Shared/_Layout.cshtml page that comes with the default templates. Finally, the Controller Name text box allows you to name your new controller class and file.

The contents of the controller class have the same method names and similar signatures as the first two template, with a few notable exceptions:

▶ There is now a public constructor method that accepts an instance of the data context chosen in the dialog. This context is assigned to a read-only controller-scoped field.

▶ All methods now run asynchronously and return `Task` objects. This is accomplished by adding the `async` keyword to the method signature and returning a `Task` object of type `IActionResult`. `IActionResult` is the typical action result object you would return from a controller when you return a view or JSON result.

▶ The methods that previously accepted `IFormCollection` now accept a `Trip` object, as demonstrated in the `Create` method signature in Listing 11.3.

LISTING 11.3   New `Create` Method Signature

```
// POST: Trip/Create
  [HttpPost]
  [ValidateAntiForgeryToken]
public async Task<IActionResult>
Create([Bind("ID,Description,EndDate,Name,StartDate")] Trip trip)
{
     if (ModelState.IsValid)
     {
         _context.Add(trip);
         await _context.SaveChangesAsync();
         return RedirectToAction("Index");
     }
     return View(trip);
}
```

What makes this code interesting is that it now uses a `Bind` hint on the input parameter to specify to ASP.NET which field names from the posted form should be populated on the object of type `Trip`. The next few lines are typical code to validate the state of the `Trip` object and commit to the database. You'll learn more about how this database update code works in Hour 12, "Writing Data from a Controller."

NOTE

`Bind` **Is Great, in Some Situations**

The `Bind` hint does a great job of limiting the insertion of values to the trip model. This creates another maintenance issue when you want to add new fields to the model. A third option would be to create a ViewModel class that contains *only* the fields you would like to capture. You can then write a method on your ViewModel to copy its contents into a new instance of your model that will be saved. In this way, all the logic for maintaining your model and what data is inserted into your model is moved out of a controller and into a class that knows how to manage the model.

In addition to the controller class that is created, a collection of Razor templates are created and added to the /Views/Trip folder that match the names of the methods that were generated. We'll take a look at their content in the next section, about the MVC View template.

Let's skip the three API controller templates for now; we will return to them in Hour 13, "Writing Web API Methods," where we discuss API controllers. For now, you need to know about the MVC View template.

Trying the MVC View Template

There are actually five different child templates for the five different actions in the generated controller: Create, Delete, Details, Edit, and List. When you choose the MVC View template, you are prompted with a dialog similar to those you get for the other templates, as shown in Figure 11.5.

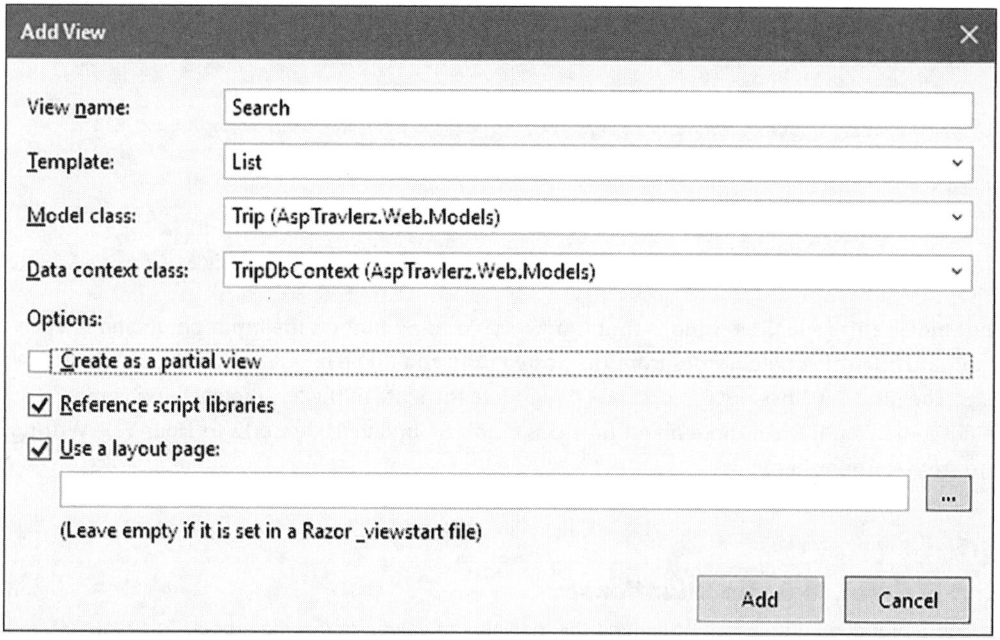

FIGURE 11.5
The prompt window for the MVC View template.

Figure 11.5 shows how you can create a view for a Search action, based on the List template for `Trip` objects. Notice that you don't have to specify a controller for this view. Views by their nature are "dumb objects" that don't know anything about their controller and just accept content that is passed to them to work with. It is up to you to place the resultant .cshtml file into a folder for the controllers to use appropriately. (See Hour 10, "Beginning MVC: Writing Your First View," for more information about locating views in an application.)

This template quickly generates a simple page with a grid that has columns allocated for each of the fields in the `Trip` object. Listing 11.4 provides the template-generated source code for the search view.

LISTING 11.4 Template-Generated Content for a Search View

```
@model IEnumerable<AspTravlerz.Web.Models.Trip>

@{
    ViewData["Title"] = "Search";
}

<h2>Search</h2>

<p>
    <a asp-action="Create">Create New</a>
</p>
<table class="table">
    <thead>
        <tr>
            <th>
                @Html.DisplayNameFor(model => model.Description)
            </th>
            <th>
                @Html.DisplayNameFor(model => model.EndDate)
            </th>
            <th>
                @Html.DisplayNameFor(model => model.Name)
            </th>
            <th>
                @Html.DisplayNameFor(model => model.StartDate)
            </th>
            <th></th>
        </tr>
    </thead>
    <tbody>
@foreach (var item in Model) {
        <tr>
            <td>
                @Html.DisplayFor(modelItem => item.Description)
            </td>
            <td>
                @Html.DisplayFor(modelItem => item.EndDate)
            </td>
            <td>
                @Html.DisplayFor(modelItem => item.Name)
            </td>
```

```
            <td>
                @Html.DisplayFor(modelItem => item.StartDate)
            </td>
            <td>
                <a asp-action="Edit" asp-route-id="@item.ID">Edit</a> |
                <a asp-action="Details" asp-route-id="@item.ID">Details</a> |
                <a asp-action="Delete" asp-route-id="@item.ID">Delete</a>
            </td>
        </tr>
}
    </tbody>
</table>
```

As you learned in Hour 10, this view is automatically wrapped by the layout view, and this content will appear in the "middle" of that layout. The anchor tags that contain asp- attributes are tag helpers that help generate appropriate links to other actions in the application. These anchor tag helpers specify information about the action method in the current controller that you should route to, and in other uses of these tag helpers, you will see that you can also specify the id value for the route to use in formatting a URL. You will learn more about tag helpers in Hour 14, "Introducing Reusable User Interface Components."

The rest of this page is a table with a for loop around the creation of each row in the table. The header row uses the DisplayNameFor method to output an appropriate label for each property. The body rows use the DisplayFor method to inspect each of the properties of the Trip object and write the value of the property into the table row.

The Create template uses similar logic to generate property labels and makes use of tag helpers to generate text boxes and validation comments. Listing 11.5 shows the Create.cshtml code that the template generates.

LISTING 11.5   Template-Generated Content for a Create View

```
@model AspTravlerz.Web.Models.Trip

@{
    ViewData["Title"] = "Create";
}


<h2>Create</h2>

<form asp-action="Create">
    <div class="form-horizontal">
        <h4>Trip</h4>
        <hr />
        <div asp-validation-summary="ModelOnly" class="text-danger"></div>
        <div class="form-group">
```

```
        <label asp-for="Description" class="col-md-2 control-label"></label>
        <div class="col-md-10">
            <input asp-for="Description" class="form-control" />
            <span asp-validation-for="Description" class="text-danger" />
        </div>
    </div>
    <div class="form-group">
        <label asp-for="EndDate" class="col-md-2 control-label"></label>
        <div class="col-md-10">
            <input asp-for="EndDate" class="form-control" />
            <span asp-validation-for="EndDate" class="text-danger" />
        </div>
    </div>
    <div class="form-group">
        <label asp-for="Name" class="col-md-2 control-label"></label>
        <div class="col-md-10">
            <input asp-for="Name" class="form-control" />
            <span asp-validation-for="Name" class="text-danger" />
        </div>
    </div>
    <div class="form-group">
        <label asp-for="StartDate" class="col-md-2 control-label"></label>
        <div class="col-md-10">
            <input asp-for="StartDate" class="form-control" />
            <span asp-validation-for="StartDate" class="text-danger" />
        </div>
    </div>
    <div class="form-group">
        <div class="col-md-offset-2 col-md-10">
            <input type="submit" value="Create" class="btn btn-default" />
        </div>
    </div>
    </div>
</form>

<div>
    <a asp-action="Index">Back to List</a>
</div>

@section Scripts {
    @{await Html.RenderPartialAsync("_ValidationScriptsPartial");}
}
```

The asp-for attributes on the input and label elements are tag helpers that instruct
the Razor syntax compiler to generate a label containing the name of a property or to place
the value of a property into the label or input element, as appropriate. Similarly, the

`asp-validation-for` attribute is a tag helper that outputs any error messages from the validation process that occur in the `Create` HTTP post method. Finally, the `asp-validation-summary` attribute is a tag helper which indicates that errors about the model submitted should be reported within the `div` element.

The Edit template is identical to the Create template, with some slight text changes to indicate that it is handling the Edit action and not the Create action. In addition, there is a hidden field on the Edit template for the ID property of the trip.

The Delete and Details templates are almost identical as well. Listing 11.6 shows the code for the Delete template.

LISTING 11.6   Template-Generated Content for a Delete View

```
@model AspTravlerz.Web.Models.Trip

@{
    ViewData["Title"] = "Delete";
}

<h2>Delete</h2>

<h3>Are you sure you want to delete this?</h3>
<div>
    <h4>Trip</h4>
    <hr />
    <dl class="dl-horizontal">
        <dt>
            @Html.DisplayNameFor(model => model.Description)
        </dt>
        <dd>
            @Html.DisplayFor(model => model.Description)
        </dd>
        <dt>
            @Html.DisplayNameFor(model => model.EndDate)
        </dt>
        <dd>
            @Html.DisplayFor(model => model.EndDate)
        </dd>
        <dt>
            @Html.DisplayNameFor(model => model.Name)
        </dt>
        <dd>
            @Html.DisplayFor(model => model.Name)
        </dd>
```

```
        <dt>
            @Html.DisplayNameFor(model => model.StartDate)
        </dt>
        <dd>
            @Html.DisplayFor(model => model.StartDate)
        </dd>
    </dl>

    <form asp-action="Delete">
        <div class="form-actions no-color">
            <input type="submit" value="Delete" class="btn btn-default" /> |
            <a asp-action="Index">Back to List</a>
        </div>
    </form>
</div>
```

The Delete template provides a simple list of property names and property values, but the main difference between the Delete and Details views are the actions at the bottom. On the Delete template, you see a form with a Submit button to delete the item currently displayed. The Details template does not have a form and contains a link that allows you to edit the item.

Generate an FAQ with Multiple Questions

Follow these steps to enhance the FAQ that you created in Hours 9, "Building Your First Controller," and 10, "Beginning MVC: Writing Your First View," by allowing multiple questions to be created and listed on the page:

1. Create a new class in the Models folder called `Faq` with two string properties: `Question` and `Answer`.

2. Right-click the Views/Home folder and choose Add > View.

3. Name your view `FaqList` and choose the Details template. Be sure that the Create as a Partial View check box is unchecked and click Add.

4. In the resultant .cshtml file, change the top line to define the model as follows:

   ```
   @model IEnumerable<AspTravlerz.Models.Faq>
   ```

5. Wrap the four dd and dt tags in the view with a `@foreach (item in Model)` statement.

6. Update the dt content to contain the words `Question` and `Answer`, as appropriate. Update the dd content to output the item's `Question` or `Answer` property, as appropriate.

7. Return to `HomeController` and update the Faq action to build an `Faq` object instead of a `Tuple`, and assign the question to the `Question` property and the answer to the `Answer` property.

8. Update the `return View` statement to return a new array of `Faq` objects and targeting the new `FaqList` view by using this statement:

```
return View("FaqList", new[] {faq});
```

Run the application and navigate to your FAQ page. You should be greeted with the content of the question in a nicely formatted page. You can now add additional questions and answers to your Faq action, and they will be automatically formatted on this page for you.

Summary

Templates for ASP.NET Core can save you significant time in generating simple and standard looks for an application. The templates that can be used to generate controllers and views help you create basic create, details, delete, edit, and index operations with just a few clicks that you can then customize easily to meet your needs.

Hour 12 shows how you can write data from the controller back to your database.

Q&A

Q. Can I use my own templates with scaffolding in Visual Studio?

A. You can't do this with the current release of ASP.NET Core, but this is something that has been accommodated in previous versions of ASP.NET and should happen in the future.

Q. What other template-generation tools are available?

A. There are templates created for the Yeoman tool that have several mechanisms and child templates that you can use in your application. If you would like to use these templates to help automate your development process, you can find instructions for constructing new templates on the Yeoman website (http://yeoman.io/authoring/).

Workshop

The workshop contains quiz questions and exercises to help you solidify your understanding of the material covered. Try to answer all questions before looking at the "Answers" that follow.

Quiz

1. What types of files can be scaffolded by using Visual Studio?

2. What extra code might you need to add to the controller templates that do not include Entity Framework but provide Insert and Update actions?

Answers

1. You can generate C# classes for controllers and Razor views.

2. Code for the controllers in the templates does not contain any logic for validating, adding, or updating your models.

Exercise

Generate controllers and user interfaces for the `Trip` and `Segment` objects. Write some extra code to display the segments for a trip to the Trip/Details view and allow users to add, edit, and delete views for that segment of the trip.

Writing Data from a Controller

What You'll Learn in This Hour:

▶ Enhancing code generated by the scaffolder

▶ Validation techniques for your methods

▶ API strategies for allowing data to be submitted to a controller

▶ Asynchronous data-writing techniques

Fetching data and presenting user interfaces are simple tasks that don't really involve working with and waiting on other systems that you integrate your applications with. This hour you'll look at how to structure your controller methods and your service APIs as well as how to validate your data as it is processed on an ASP.NET Core application.

NOTE

Code Generation Gets You Halfway There

In Hour 11, "Scaffolding User Interfaces," you generated code for some data-writing or modification routines. There are other ways to write data if those signatures don't work for you, and this hour you'll look at some of the code that you need to write to complete those methods.

Enhancing Scaffolded Code

The code initially generated by the scaffolder in Visual Studio is very generic code for creating, updating, and deleting data in your database. In most applications, you want to perform some level of validation before committing any data, and this is especially true for Internet-facing applications. For such public-facing applications, you should *never* trust the data that is sent to you from your application users; you should inspect such data prior to taking any action on it.

Listing 12.1 reviews the initial and overly simple Create method that was generated in Hour 11 when you created a TripController class for your project with the MVC Controller with Views, Using Entity Framework template.

LISTING 12.1   Default `Create` Method Generated by the Scaffold Template

```
[HttpPost]
 [ValidateAntiForgeryToken]
 public async Task<IActionResult>
Create([Bind("ID,Description,EndDate,Name,StartDate")] Trip trip)
 {
     if (ModelState.IsValid)
     {
         _context.Add(trip);
         await _context.SaveChangesAsync();
         return RedirectToAction("Index");
     }
     return View(trip);
 }
```

Notice the interesting bit that reads if `ModelState.IsValid`. What is that actually doing, and how can you can have the `IsValid` property perform the validation checks that you need on your `Trip` model object?

Validating Data in Controller Methods

You generated a lot of code in Hour 11. Listing 11.3 shows code generated with Entity Framework action methods connected to your controllers, that contains some simple code generated around the `ModelState` object. These methods simply check whether `ModelState` is valid and proceed from there. But what does this `ModelState` do, and how can you control it?

`ModelState` is loaded and managed by a feature of ASP.NET Core called ModelBinding. With ModelBinding, you can receive fully defined classes in your input parameters of controller methods and have those classes automatically populated by the framework from the contents of the submitted form, querystring, or cookies.

Listing 12.2 shows an HTML form generated for the `Create` action with fields that represent the `Trip` object.

LISTING 12.2   HTML Input Fields for Creating a `Trip` Object

```
<input class="form-control" type="text"
    id="Description" name="Description" value="" />
<input class="form-control" type="datetime"
    data-val="true" data-val-required="The EndDate field is required."
    id="EndDate" name="EndDate" value="" />
<input class="form-control" type="text"
    data-val="true" data-val-required="The Name field is required."
    id="Name" name="Name" value="" />
<input class="form-control" type="datetime"
    data-val="true" data-val-required="The StartDate field is required."
    id="StartDate" name="StartDate" value="" />
```

That's a lot of stuff in those input boxes, but there are a few things that you need to take from this:

▶ The names of the fields in the HTML match the names of the properties in the C# Trip object.

▶ Coincidentally, the types of these HTML fields are also similar to the types of the fields in the C# object. The new datetime type in HTML 5 gives mobile device users and modern browser users a nice date picker widget to choose a date to submit into the field.

▶ The other data-val attributes are generated by the Visual Studio scaffolder and used for the client-side validation of the Trip object.

Because the names of the fields match the names of the properties of the Trip object, ASP.NET can map those fields directly into a Trip object that it creates and passes into your Create method. The Create method has a Bind attribute that defines exactly which fields you need to map from the HTML form into our Trip object:

```
public async Task<IActionResult>
Create([Bind("ID,Description,EndDate,Name,StartDate")] Trip trip)
```

The Bind hint is not required, but it provides a level of control that you may want to assert over the creation and submission of objects to your controller.

By default, the scaffolded HTML attempts to validate data on the browser before it ever reaches your server. This is a nice attempt, but you should *never* trust data submitted from the browser.

CAUTION

Always Verify and Validate Data Submitted By Users!

I cannot reinforce this enough: You should always verify and validate data submitted by users. Untrusted data submissions are the top attack vector for applications. The validation provided by the default server-side configuration requires that you add some annotations to the Trip object in order to define which fields are validated and how they are checked by the framework.

You have already decorated the Trip object with Required attributes to help the database understand which fields need to be present when writing a record. This attribute works for the ModelState check as well, with non-null and non-empty string values being rejected as invalid. A number of other data annotations work similarly, including the following:

▶ **CreditCard**—Verifies that the value submitted is formatted as a credit card number

▶ **DataType**—Verifies that the value submitted matches the data type specified

▶ **EmailAddress**—Verifies that the value submitted matches an email address format

▶ **MaxLength**—Verifies that the value does not exceed the length specified

▶ **Phone**—Verifies that the value is a well-formed phone number

▶ **Range**—Verifies that the number submitted falls within a range of values

▶ **RegularExpression**—Verifies that the value submitted passes a test of the specified regular expression

▶ **StringLength**—Verifies that the string submitted satisfies a minimum and maximum length requirement

▶ **Url**—Verifies that the value submitted is formatted as a URL (that is, a web address)

These attributes can be applied to any field. They assist Entity Framework in providing a specific-sized field in your database, and they also provide simple validation for your object.

In addition, each of these attributes provides the ability to configure an error message to report to the calling method when the validation fails.

CAUTION

Regular Expression Validation Can Be a Security Risk

Security analysts have reported that the use of regular expressions as validation expressions can be a security risk as text can be submitted that causes a regular expression to loop infinitely. Be careful with the syntax of your expressions and how you use them to validate data. For current discussion and description of this security scenario, visit http://www.regular-expressions.info/catastrophic.html.

What if you need more complex validation? In this case, you previously marked the StartDate and EndDate as required, but that does not guarantee that the StartDate occurs before the EndDate. It would be very strange to have a trip end before it even started!

You can add an additional level of validation by having the Trip class implement the IValidateableObject interface, which provides a single method Validate, that allows you to check the state of the object and report back any problems. You can implement the IValidateableObject interface and add the Validate method to verify the relationship of the StartDate and EndDate fields with the code shown in Listing 12.3.

LISTING 12.3   `Validate` **Method for the** `Trip` **Object**

```
public class Trip : IValidatableObject
{
public IEnumerable<ValidationResult> Validate(ValidationContext validationContext)
{

  var myTrip = (Trip)validationContext.ObjectInstance;
  var results = new List<ValidationResult>();
  if (myTrip.StartDate > myTrip.EndDate)
  {
```

```
    var msg = "Start Date cannot occur before End Date";
    var fields = new[] { "StartDate", "EndDate" };
    results.Add(new ValidationResult(msg, fields));

}

return results;

}
}
```

The `Validate` method is then called whenever the `ModelState` is checked, and then there is a simple `StartDate` before `EndDate` check, as shown on line 9. To indicate that a problem was found, a `ValidationResult` is created with the error message and the list of fields affected. That `ValidationResult` is added to the returned collection to be interpreted by ASP.NET as an error in the validation of the `Trip` object.

Investigating Controller Interaction Strategies

Your controller methods will be submitted from the browser, and if the controller method takes too long to respond, your visitors may become frustrated and start refreshing the browser in an effort to get your application to respond. A common approach to reduce your application's exposure to this type of interaction is a strategy called *redirect after submit*. Figure 12.1 shows a simple demonstration of this interaction.

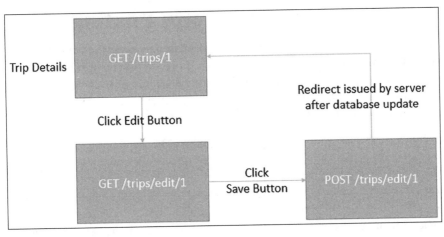

FIGURE 12.1
Page flow in redirect after submit.

In your generated code, you can see this convention used in the `Create`, `Edit`, and `DeleteConfirmed` methods that are decorated with an `HttpPost` attribute. In these methods, after the database interaction is complete, the `RedirectToAction` method is called, which sends an HTTP 302 response to the browser. This response instructs the browser to navigate to another location, and the `RedirectToAction` method takes the name of the action (and an optional controller name) to formulate the location to redirect to. Listing 12.4 shows this strategy with the `Create` method.

LISTING 12.4   **Redirect After Post Strategy in the** `Create` **Method**

```
[HttpPost]
[ValidateAntiForgeryToken]
public async Task<IActionResult>
Create([Bind("ID,Description,EndDate,Name,StartDate")] Trip trip)
{
    if (ModelState.IsValid)
    {
        _context.Add(trip);
        await _context.SaveChangesAsync();
        return RedirectToAction("Index");
    }
    return View(trip);
}
```

The save operation takes place on line 9, with the `SaveChangesAsync` method, and the application immediately redirects to the Index action, which shows a list of trips in the sample application.

Preventing Unwanted Cross-site Posting

Another recommended configuration is to use the anti-forgery token in forms that will be submitted to the application server. The anti-forgery token is a randomly generated hash that is transmitted to your application users in a hidden form field or an HTTP cookie. This token value is validated when a method is executed on the server that is decorated with a `ValidateAntiForgeryToken` attribute, as shown in Listing 12.4.

You can ensure that a token is added to your form by using the HTML helper `@Html.AntiForgeryToken()` inside the `Form` element in your views. This call is not always needed if you decorate your form element with the `asp-action` attribute to direct the form to submit to a specific MVC action. The `asp-action` attribute turns the form element into a tag helper, which you'll learn more about in Hour 14, "Introducing Reusable User Interface Components." This tag helper automatically adds an anti-forgery token to the bottom of the form, using the same technique as with the HTML helper mentioned earlier.

With both the tag helper and HTML helper, a simple hidden element is generated with the name __RequestVerificationToken and a value assigned to a very long hash of characters that the server can parse. If an incorrect value is submitted in this field to a method decorated with the ValidateAntiForgeryToken attribute, you are greeted by an error message similar to the one shown in Figure 12.2.

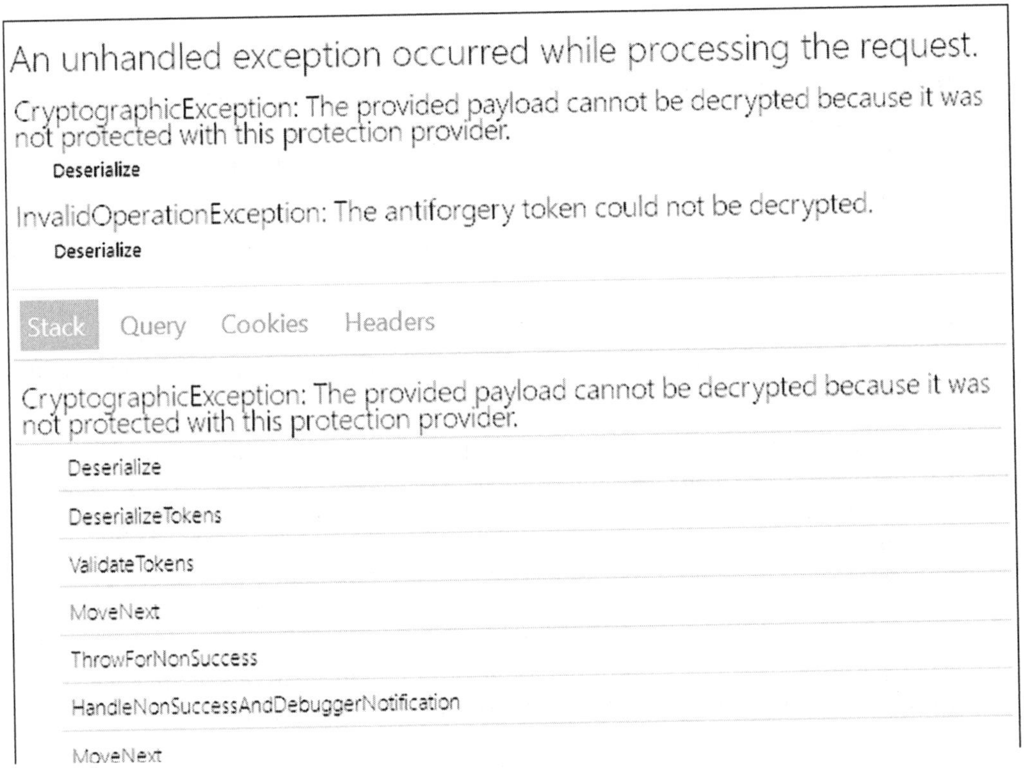

An unhandled exception occurred while processing the request.

CryptographicException: The provided payload cannot be decrypted because it was not protected with this protection provider.

  Deserialize

InvalidOperationException: The antiforgery token could not be decrypted.

  Deserialize

Stack   Query   Cookies   Headers

CryptographicException: The provided payload cannot be decrypted because it was not protected with this protection provider.

  Deserialize

  DeserializeTokens

  ValidateTokens

  MoveNext

  ThrowForNonSuccess

  HandleNonSuccessAndDebuggerNotification

  MoveNext

FIGURE 12.2
Error condition when an invalid anti-forgery token is submitted.

I used some JavaScript to change the token value in the browser in order to force this error condition, but you can provide your own error handlers to hide this page and present a nicer message to your visitors.

Speeding Up Data Access with Asynchronous Techniques

C# 5 introduced the ability to mark methods as asynchronous and gave developers the ability to avoid managing threads, parallel executions, and other multithreaded concerns by hand. With the `async` and `await` keywords that were introduced in C# 5, these concerns were shifted to the just-in-time code compiler, which now emits the proper handling to manage the multithreaded concerns in an application.

If you look back at the code generated for the `Create` method, as shown in Listing 12.4, you will notice the method signature:

```
public async Task<IActionResult> Create(Bind[...] Trip trip)
```

The use of the async keyword here indicates that this method can run asynchronously, and parts of it may later operate outside the thread that executes it. The `Task` object is a generic object that manages the state of the asynchronous operation. The `IActionResult` generic parameter (inside the angle brackets) defines the output type that will be returned when the operation has completed.

However, the introduction of the `Task` return type and `async` keyword also raises a few concerns for the content of the method:

▶ You should return an object of the type generically referred to in the task—in this case, `IActionResult`. The `Task` return type will automatically be created for you and wrap the object that you are returning.

▶ Other methods marked with `async` may be called with an `await` keyword. The use of this keyword forces the method to release the current thread while the method used with the `await` method is executing. This *could* occur on a different thread, but it will never block the current thread.

▶ You cannot use `await` with a method call inside another method that is not marked `async`. An async method called from a non-async method must be given instructions about how to handle the `Task` object that is returned. For methods that return a value inside a task, you can easily request the result of the task with a method call like this:

```
context.GetTrip().Result
```

In the `Create` method, you can see that the `SaveChangesAsync` method is marked with an `await` modifier (refer to Listing 12.4). While the database is updating records in the Trips table, this method releases the current thread, and it resumes processing once the database has completed its operation.

The `async` and `await` operations allow your application to potentially make better use of resources on a server. The release and reuse of threads while operations are taking place on another server enables your web server to handle more concurrent operations as those application services complete processes for you.

Write FAQ Questions to Your Datastore

Follow these steps to configure `HomeController` to allow you to create and edit FAQ questions:

1. Add a property to the `TripsDbContext` class for the `Faq` model like this:

   ```
   public DbSet<Faq> FAQ {get;set;}
   ```

2. Add the `TripsDbContext` class as an input parameter to the `HomeController` constructor and store a copy of it as a field in the class.

3. Update the `FaqList` method in `HomeController` to return the list of `Faq` objects from the datastore.

4. Add `CreateFaq` and `EditFaq` methods to `HomeController` to facilitate the creation and management of questions and answers for the FAQ.

With these extra methods for the management of FAQ questions, you can now present and manage this content in the `HomeController`.

Summary

This hour, you have reviewed some of the code that was generated to assist your application in writing data from the MVC controllers. You have learned some techniques to help protect your application from bad actors and how to make the most of your computing resources by making data-writing methods asynchronous.

Q&A

Q. Can I use async techniques similar to those demonstrated this hour with a database when writing to file storage?

A. Yes. Any I/O operation or call to a service outside the web process should be triggered and managed asynchronously.

Q. Do I really need anti-forgery tokens on my web methods?

A. The anti-forgery tokens protect against cross-site scripting attacks and guarantee that a request originated from your server. That's a pretty good reason to use them.

Q. Does redirect after submit processing prevent "double-postback" to a page in my application? Can someone double-click a Submit button and cause the same action to occur twice?

A. No. Redirect after submit does not prevent double-postback interaction, but it does help prevent users from bookmarking a page that they shouldn't be directly navigating to that contains the result of a save operation.

Q. Do I need to use data annotations on my models?

A. No. You don't need to use data annotations. You can write simple if-then checks in your methods to validate the contents of your models that are posted to your server. You could use just the IValidatableObject interface and implement all of your business logic checks there.

Q. Does the CreditCard attribute really check for a valid credit card number?

A. There is an algorithm for a credit card number, and this attribute simply tests against that algorithm to ensure that it could be a valid number. You need to do further checks to verify whether a number is valid or available for charging.

Workshop

The workshop contains quiz questions and exercises to help you solidify your understanding of the material covered. Try to answer all questions before looking at the "Answers" that follow.

Quiz

1. What do data annotations on model classes help with?

2. How does ASP.NET automatically validate models?

3. The `await` keyword can be used only with methods that are decorated with what keyword?

4. What method call can you use in your controllers to enable redirect after post processing?

Answers

1. Data annotations help with defining data storage requirements and the validations that need to be performed on the various properties of the class.

2. The `ModelState` object is populated with metadata about the model object that is received as an input parameter to a controller class. You can check the `IsValid` property of `ModelState` to verify that all validations passed.

3. The keyword `async` is required because asynchronous methods are the only methods that are allowed to contain an `await` keyword.

4. You can use the `RedirectToAction` method to emit an HTTP 302 response code to direct the browser to navigate to another MVC action and, optionally, on another controller.

Exercise

For further practice, enhance `SegmentsController` to validate start and end times as required fields and add code to the Segment object to ensure that the start time is before the end time. Also verify that anti-forgery tokens are present for all `SegmentsController` methods. Then review the `SegmentsController Create, Edit,` and `DeleteConfirmed` methods to ensure that they are taking full advantage of asynchronous processing.

HOUR 13
Writing Web API Methods

What You'll Learn in This Hour:

▶ Web API concepts and history
▶ Integrated MVC and Web API controllers
▶ HTTP verbs
▶ Routing attributes
▶ XML formatting
▶ Options to make your project an API-only application

Sometimes you want to interact with a user using a web server and you don't want to serve a user interface. Maybe you want to reuse your logic to serve data to another machine for processing. In such cases where you don't want to be bothered with HTML and you just want to push some data around, you can use the Web API features of the MVC framework to work directly with the HTTP protocol and web server endpoint.

In the Old Days of ASP.NET[...]

In versions of ASP.NET prior to ASP.NET Core, Web API was a separate framework that could be chosen and integrated into the web application to provide interface-less interaction. Such interaction is particularly useful when you're integrating systems or providing services for browser-side JavaScript to query to make the user experience significantly better.

The goal with Web API was to make a framework that adhered tightly to the HTTP protocol, that felt like coding an already familiar MVC controller, that could handle various media types in a no-nonsense pluggable architecture, and that provided flexibility to extend and handle route information just like the rest of ASP.NET All these features continue to be available in the new incarnation of Web API in ASP.NET Core.

With the merger of Web API into the MVC framework, the same old Web API features are available as extensions and special syntax on top of the same controller object that you use to deliver HTML content to the browser. This hour you'll see how you can provide your search operation from `TripController` as a collection of `Trip` objects that can be retrieved from the service.

You define Web API methods in a controller with the four HTTP verbs that they support: You can create `GET`, `POST`, `PUT`, and `DELETE` methods that Web API will work with when those HTTP verbs are executed against the URL your controller is listening to. Listing 13.1 shows how to add a `GetTrips` method to `TripController`.

LISTING 13.1   A Simple `GetTrips` API Method

```
[HttpGet("api/Trips")]
public IEnumerable<Models.Trip> GetTrips()
{
    return _context.Trips.ToList();
}
```

Let's analyze what this code is doing. First, it resides in a controller class and does not return `IActionResult` but instead returns a collection of `Models.Trip` objects from the repository you configured at the end of Hour 10, "Beginning MVC: Writing Your First View." The magic happening in this code is the attribute `HttpGet` above the method. This attribute instructs the ASP.NET router to listen for the HTTP `GET` verb and respond with the contents of this method if the URL requested matches the `api/Trips` template. This code does not specify what to do with the data, but Web API has you covered for that. By default, Web API formats any requested data as JSON and returns it as such. Figure 13.1 shows the content of the browser when you navigate to http://localhost:5000/api/Trips; the browser performs an HTTP `GET` to retrieve this content, and a JSON formatter formats the content to make it readable.

It looks like two trips have been written to the database, and they are the same as the sample data that was presented for constructing the Search view in Hour 10.

If you name your methods so that they start with the HTTP verb that they will be handling, ASP.NET Core will automatically handle the verb with the method that starts with the same name. For example, a "Post" method will automatically be configured to handle HTTP POST actions, and a "PutContent" method would be configured to handle HTTP PUT actions. However, to make things more explicit for other developers who will need to read your code after you are done writing it, it is much clearer to use the verb attributes to indicate the purpose of the controller method.

Similarly, you can provide a feature that fetches a single trip by accepting an input parameter that specifies the ID of the trip to fetch. Listing 13.2 shows the code you can add for the `GetById` method.

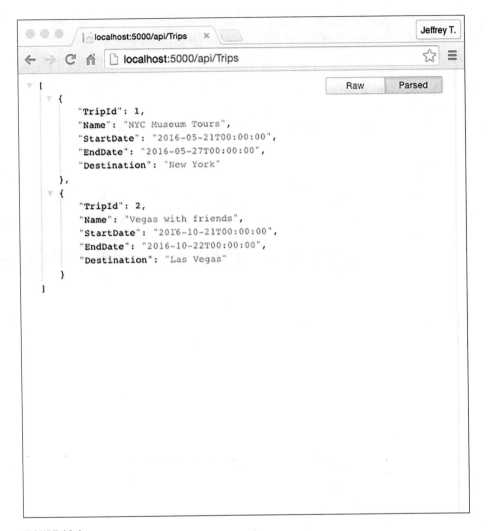

FIGURE 13.1
Web API GET content result in the browser.

LISTING 13.2   Getting Data for a Single `Trip` Object

```
[HttpGet("api/Trips/{id}", Name="GetTrip")]
public Models.Trip GetById(int id) {
    return Repository.Trips.FirstOrDefault(trip => trip.TripId == id);
}
```

Once again, you have a method that is not returning an `IActionResult` object. This time, you're performing a query against the repository to find the specific trip that is identified by the id value submitted to this method. In addition, the `HttpGet` attribute has a very similar URL template as before, but now it has an `{id}` placeholder at the end. This value, if present, will be passed as the input parameter to this method. Also, the `HttpGet` attribute is added to a Name parameter for the route that hosts this method. You can navigate to http://localhost:5000/api/Trips/1 and see the New York trip returned as JSON to the browser, as demonstrated in Figure 13.2.

FIGURE 13.2
Web API `GET` for a specific ID in the browser.

Creating a New Trip with Web API

Let's take a look at writing a new trip to the datastore. The HTTP verb that you will use for this operation is `POST`. In this scenario, you can add a method signature and content similar to what was in your `Create` method, but with some slight changes, as shown in Listing 13.3.

LISTING 13.3 Post **Method to Add a Single** Trip **Object**

```
[HttpPost("/api/Trips")]
 public async Task<IActionResult> Post([Bind("ID,Description,EndDate,Name,
                                    StartDate")] Trip trip)
{
  if (ModelState.IsValid)
  {
    _context.Add(trip);
    await _context.SaveChangesAsync();
    return CreatedAtRoute("GetTrip", new { id=trip.ID }, trip);
  }

  return BadRequest(ModelState);

}
```

This looks and feels very similar to the code in your generated Create method, but let's look more closely. Yes, you have the same Trip input parameter and the same ModelState.IsValid check to verify that the content passes validation. The two return methods are just slightly different.

Remember that when you are working with API endpoint methods, you are returning data that should be readable to machines first and humans second. In order to inform a machine that the data that was posted to this method was properly saved and an object created, you should issue an HTTP 201 Created status code to the calling method. The HTTP 201 status code is a standard that all API consumers should recognize; it returns information about the location where you can find the object you just created. You can properly utilize this communication standard by using the CreatedAtRoute method. This method takes the name of the route to return, GetTrip, and you need to specify the ID of the Trip object to help finish formatting that URL route. The final parameter of the CreatedAtRoute method is the object that was created. You can test this method by using the PostMan extension to Google Chrome to post data to your API endpoint. You can find this extension in the Google Chrome Extension store. Figure 13.3 shows the result of posting a simple Trip object with PostMan.

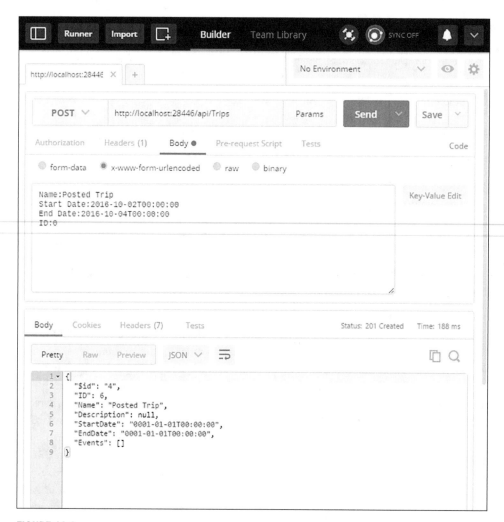

FIGURE 13.3
Web API POST using PostMan.

In cases where there is an error, you need to signal to the caller that the error occurred and give some information so that the caller can correct the attempt and try again. The last line of the method returns the BadRequest method to trigger an HTTP 400 status code, which indicates that there was a problem with the content submitted. The BadRequest method takes ModelState as an input parameter and properly formats that validation failure as content to present to the caller, as shown in Figure 13.4.

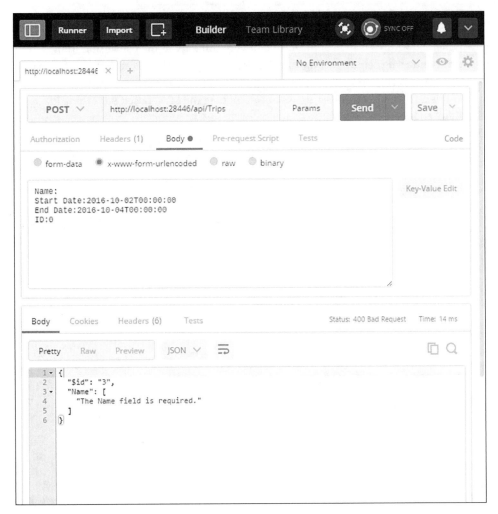

FIGURE 13.4
Web API POST using PostMan with errors reported.

In Figure 13.4, you can see that a 400 Bad Request status is returned when the required Name field is omitted. The content of the response message contains an array with the text of the error message: "The Name field is required." This is ASP.NET's way of helping you help the users of your application by making it very easy to format those error messages.

Updating a Trip with Web API

The Update method with Web API can be looked at very similarly to the conversion from Create which handled a user interacting with a form in the browser, to Post that handled an API interaction. The HTTP verb for this operation is PUT, and you can decorate your Update method with this attribute. Listing 13.4 shows how to update the MVC-based Edit code to support an API PUT endpoint.

LISTING 13.4　PUT Method to Update a Single Trip Object

```
[HttpPut("/api/Trips/{id}")]
public async Task<IActionResult> Update(int id, [Bind("ID,Description,EndDate,Name,
                                        StartDate")] Trip trip)
{
  if (id != trip.ID)
  {
    return NotFound();
  }

  if (ModelState.IsValid)
  {
    try
    {
      _context.Update(trip);
      await _context.SaveChangesAsync();
    }
    catch (DbUpdateConcurrencyException)
    {
      if (!TripExists(trip.ID))
      {
        return NotFound();
      }
      else
      {
        return StatusCode(500, "Unable to update the data store.  Please try again");
      }
    }
    return Ok(trip);
  }
  return BadRequest(ModelState);
}
```

Once again, this looks very similar to the code in your generated Edit method, with those same changes around the returning of status codes that you saw in the POST API. This time, you return an HTTP 404 NotFound status code if the trip with the ID submitted does not exist in the datastore. Of course, you could make this a legitimate operation by updating this code to save the trip as a new object if there is no object with a matching ID currently available.

If the save operation hits a concurrency exception, you force an HTTP 500 status code to indicate that there was an internal problem not caused by the data submitted by the user. HTTP status codes in the 500s typically mean "something happened inside the application that was not the fault of the user." You use the StatusCode method to specify the 500 status code and provide some helpful text to the calling system.

Finally, if the object was updated properly, you return an HTTP 200 OK status to the system to indicate that the update was successful.

Figure 13.5 shows the result of posting a simple Trip object with PostMan:

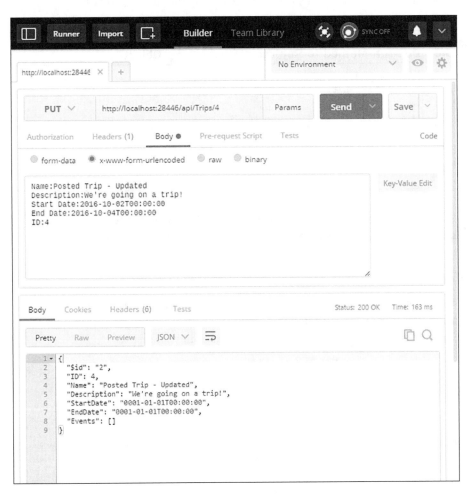

FIGURE 13.5
Web API PUT using PostMan.

You can clearly see that the API returned a 200 OK status code as well as the updated content of the trip that was submitted. This acknowledgment of changes being applied to the `Trip` object is a polite response for calling systems to process.

Deleting a Trip with Web API

The information in this section should look familiar because the `Delete` method with Web API is almost identical to the `DeleteConfirmed` method. The HTTP verb for this operation is `DELETE`, and you can decorate your `DeleteApi` method with this attribute. Listing 13.5 shows how the MVC-based `DeleteConfirmed` code is updated to support an API `DELETE` endpoint.

LISTING 13.5   `Delete` **Method to Remove a Single** `Trip` **Object**

```
[HttpDelete("/api/Trips/{id}")]
public async Task<IActionResult> DeleteApi(int id)
{
  var trip = await _context.Trips.SingleOrDefaultAsync(m => m.ID == id);
  _context.Trips.Remove(trip);
  await _context.SaveChangesAsync();
  return Ok();
}
```

This method received the single `id` parameter to identify the `Trip` object to remove, and it attempts to remove that immediately. There is no error check, and the method returns the HTTP 200 OK status once it has completed the work in the datastore.

Figure 13.6 shows the result of posting a simple `Trip` object with PostMan.

This time, you can see that no content is returned, and you get the HTTP 200 OK status code. Once again, this is the polite and standard way to indicate to calling systems that the operation completed successfully, and the content is no longer in your system.

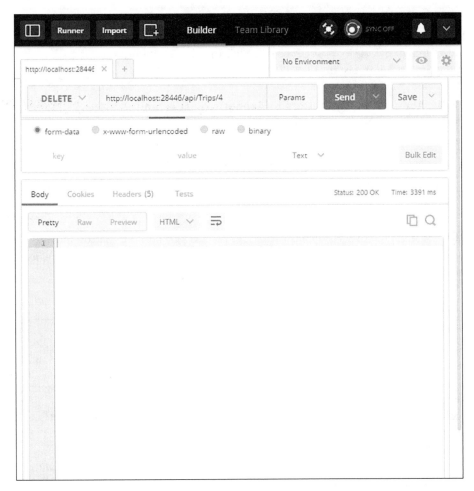

FIGURE 13.6
Web API delete using PostMan.

Negotiating and Formatting Content

By default, ASP.NET Core includes JSON formatting capabilities when you add the MVC feature to your project file. What if your application needs to interact with another system that expects XML or some other data format? This adjustment of data format, called *content negotiation*, is the process by which ASP.NET Core inspects the HTTP Accept header to determine what data format to respond with.

You can add those format capabilities to an application easily with just a few configuration updates. In order to add XML formatting, you need to add the `Microsoft.AspNetCore.Mvc.Formatters.Xml` NuGet package to your application, as shown in the project file in Listing 13.6.

LISTING 13.6   Adding XML Formatters to AspnetTravlerz.csproj

```
<ItemGroup>
  <PackageReference Include="Microsoft.AspNetCore" Version="1.1.2" />
  <PackageReference Include="Microsoft.AspNetCore.Mvc" Version="1.1.3" />
  <PackageReference Include="Microsoft.AspNetCore.Mvc.Formatters.Xml"
                   Version="1.1.3" />
</ItemGroup>
```

Next, you need to configure the MVC application to use the XML formatting. You can modify the call to `UseMvc` in the `Startup` class's `ConfigureServices` method to add this feature, as shown in Listing 13.7.

LISTING 13.7   Configuring XML Formatters in Startup.cs

```
public void ConfigureServices(IServiceCollection services)
{

    services.AddMvc().AddXmlSerializerFormatters();
```

As you can see, this is a simple change: You just add the `AddXmlSerializerFormatters()` method call, which configures the API endpoint to understand the `Accept: text/xml` header and transform your output content to be in XML format. It also handles the `Accept: application/xml` header and behaves identically. Using PostMan to get data with this header configured yields the result shown in Figure 13.7.

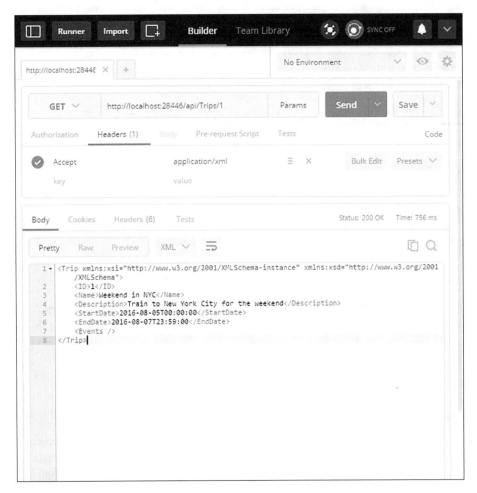

FIGURE 13.7
Web API getting data in XML format.

Trimming the Fat: An API-Only Application

If you're building an application that does not require a user interface—perhaps you're building a microservice or some other HTTP endpoint that will handle machine-to-machine communications—you can remove the extra MVC capabilities for managing views and formatting requests with a content type that you do not want to support. To reduce your project to just the minimum needed to support this HTTP endpoint model, you can replace the `Microsoft.AspNetCore.Mvc` package in your project with the `Microsoft.AspNetCore.Mvc.Core` package. In addition, you need to add an explicit reference to the JsonFormatter or `XmlFormatter` package, as needed, for your application. The project file should contain at least the entries shown in Listing 13.8.

LISTING 13.8   Minimum Set of Dependencies for API Endpoints

```
<ItemGroup>
  <PackageReference Include="Microsoft.AspNetCore.Mvc.Core" Version="1.1.3" />
  <PackageReference Include="Microsoft.AspNetCore.Diagnostics" Version="1.1.2" />
  <PackageReference Include="Microsoft.AspNetCore.Mvc.Formatters.Json"
                   Version="1.1.3" />
  <PackageReference Include="Microsoft.AspNetCore.Server.Kestrel" Version="1.1.2"
/>
  <PackageReference Include="Microsoft.Extensions.Logging.Console" Version="1.1.2"
/>
</ItemGroup>
```

Your `ConfigureServices` method inside `Startup.cs` now needs to reference adding `MvcCore` instead of `Mvc`, and it also needs to include some configuration for the formatters available in your project, so you can add this:

```
public void ConfigureServices(IServiceCollection services)
{
  services.AddMvcCore().AddJsonFormatters();
}
```

The `Configure` method inside Startup.cs still needs to include an `app.UseMvc()` call in order to enable the controller functionality for the HTTP endpoints you will be constructing. The last change that you need to be aware of is that the abstract controller class is not available, and you need to instead create your controllers so that they inherit from the `ControllerBase` class:

```
[Route("api/[controller]")]
public class ValuesController : ControllerBase
{
```

You can then build your application by adding controllers and their business logic. This application will then only accept and deliver content with the content format you specified—JSON in this small example.

TRY IT YOURSELF ▼

Convert the FAQ to an API

You added methods to allow the creation and modification of FAQ questions at the end of Hour 12, "Writing Data from a Controller." Now, to update those methods and add a method to allow the reading of FAQ questions as an API, follow these steps:

1. Update the `HttpPost` and `HttpPut` attributes on the `CreateFaq` and `EditFaq` methods in `HomeController` so that they are listening on the URL `api/faq`.

2. Create an additional method on `HomeController` called `FaqApi` that returns the current FAQ questions and answers that are in the datastore.

3. Add a `Route("api/Faq")` attribute to this new `FaqApi` method.

You should now be able to browse to http://localhost:5000/api/faq and see your questions returned as a JSON collection.

Summary

In this hour, you have learned how to build HTTP endpoints that were formerly called Web API. In previous versions of ASP.NET, they were built with a different program model, and in ASP.NET Core you can simply add new features to your existing Controller objects. You have also learned what components you need, at a minimum, to build these interactions for your consumers. This minimum set of components may be very desirable in a project if you want to squeeze the most performance out of your application while still making use of the controller metaphor to build your application. Of course, if you don't want to use controllers, you can interact directly with the request by using middleware, as you saw in Hour 5, "Configuring the Service with the `Startup` Class."

This hour you have learned how to add formatters to your application to allow controllers to interact with clients using XML format. There are other formatters available from open source contributors on NuGet.org that allow you to make use of other data formats your application can interact with. You can find formatters for protocol buffers, comma-separated lists, and even Excel format.

Q&A

Q. Are there other HTTP verbs supported besides `GET`, `POST`, `PUT`, and `DELETE`?

A. Yes. You can also use `HEAD`, `OPTIONS`, and `PATCH`.

Q. Can I provide multiple methods for the same verb?

A. Yes. Each method needs to accept different parameters, but providing multiple methods for the same verb is supported. Examine the differences between the two Get methods demonstrated this hour.

Q. Can I use other data formatters besides JSON and XML?

A. Yes. There are other formatters available on NuGet, including one for protocol buffers called protobuf-net. You can also build your own formatter to support your individual needs by implementing the classes `InputFormatter` and `OutputFormatter`. To enable a custom formatter, you add a new instance to the MVC InputFormatters and OutputFormatters collection. Finally, in the MVC options, you can use the `FormatterMappings.SetMediaTypeMappingForFormat` method to define which HTTP content type should be identified with your formatters.

Workshop

The workshop contains quiz questions and exercises to help you solidify your understanding of the material covered. Try to answer all questions before looking at the "Answers" that follow.

Quiz

1. What HTTP verb corresponds to an `Update` operation?

2. What is the attribute that should be used to decorate a controller method that is intended to return a collection of data?

3. What HTTP status code is returned to indicate a successful operation, with no further data?

4. What is the polite HTTP response to a `Create` operation?

5. What content formatter comes with the default MVC configuration?

6. What is the package to reference instead of `Microsoft.AspNetCore.Mvc` if you want a minimum set of options available to build your API application?

Answers

1. HTTP `PUT`

2. `HttpGet`

3. HTTP 200 OK

4. HTTP 201 Created with a response body that contains the object that was created

5. JSON

6. `Microsoft.AspNetCore.Mvc.Core`

Exercise

To prepare for making your data available for a client-side JavaScript framework, update `TripsController` to contain only an `Index` method that returns a view and convert the remaining methods to be API endpoints. In this way, all interaction with the data for your trips will be through a fast interaction with JavaScript. Convert `EventsController` to include only API methods, so it does not use any views to return data.

HOUR 14
Introducing Reusable User Interface Components

What You'll Learn in This Hour:

▶ What tag helpers and view components are
▶ Tag helpers that ship with ASP.NET Core
▶ Other reusable components
▶ How to write your own tag helpers
▶ How to write your own view components

This hour gets you back to building a user interface for your application. In this hour, you're going to learn how to build reusable components that you can use throughout your application. With ASP.NET Core, there are several ways to build HTML user interface components that can be used again and again throughout your application. The most interesting and exciting of these is to use tag helpers.

Introducing Tag Helpers

When you look around the landscape of modern user interface construction in other web frameworks, a myriad of technologies—such as directives, controls, and widgets—are available. With ASP.NET Core, Microsoft wanted to correct the troubles of its previous control capabilities by introducing a very focused and tag-like mechanism. A tag helper is involved in server-side rendering technique, using .NET code to interact with only the content that appears between the start and end tags of the tag helper. Listing 14.1 shows a common tag helper that is used in the standard template's layout page: the environment tag.

LISTING 14.1 The environment Tag Helper in Use in _Layout.cshtml

```
<environment names="Development">
  <link rel="stylesheet" href="~/lib/bootstrap/dist/css/bootstrap.css" />
  <link rel="stylesheet" href="~/css/site.css" />
</environment>
```

This markup is not standard HTML, and `environment` is an HTML tag that was invented by the ASP.NET team. When you look at this code in Visual Studio with the default light theme (see Figure 14.1), the `environment` text is highlighted in bold purple.

```
File   Edit   View   Project   Build   Debug   Team   Data Lake   Tools   Test   Analyze   Window   Help
```
```
_Layout.cshtml + X
       7
       8         <environment names="Development">
       9             <link rel="stylesheet" href="~/lib/bootstrap/dist/css/bootstrap.css" />
      10             <link rel="stylesheet" href="~/css/site.css" />
      11         </environment>
```

FIGURE 14.1
Visual Studio showing the Listing 14.1 code is a tag helper.

The `environment` tag helper does a check on the name of the current development environment (`Development`, `Staging`, or `Production`), and if the current environment matches one of the values in the `names` attribute, then the content inside the tags is written into the resultant page; the `environment` tag never appears in the HTML transmitted to the browser. The `names` attribute can contain one environment or several attributes, separated by commas.

Listing 14.2 shows another tag helper: the `anchor` tag helper.

LISTING 14.2   The `anchor` Tag Helper in Use in _Layout.cshtml

```
<li><a asp-area="" asp-controller="Home" asp-action="Index">Home</a></li>
<li><a asp-area="" asp-controller="Home" asp-action="About">About</a></li>
<li><a asp-area="" asp-controller="Home" asp-action="Contact">Contact</a></li>
```

Wait a second! This looks different from the previous tag helper example. Isn't a a legitimate HTML tag? Yes, it is, but in this case, the attributes next to it are what turn this into more than just normal HTML: Now you have .NET-enabled code. These `asp-` attributes enable extra functionality—in this case, it's building an HREF attribute for the tag based on routing information. This second flavor of tag helper is enabled with the presence of these attributes; otherwise, the a tag would be rendered as normal text and transmitted to the browser, with no .NET involvement.

With both of these types of tag helpers, Visual Studio offers IntelliSense capabilities and information based on the attributes, help markup, and configuration offered by the tag helper, as shown in Figure 14.2.

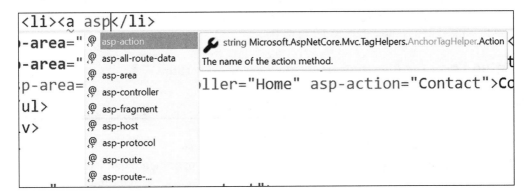

FIGURE 14.2
Visual Studio helping out with tag helper syntax and usage.

Visual Studio shows that this attribute is managed on the server side with the @ icon. In addition, the type and description text that mark the attribute definition in the `TagHelper` class are displayed here to help the developer. (Later this hour, you'll see where and how attributes are configured when building a tag helper.)

In addition, tag helpers that enhance the capabilities of an existing HTML tag (such as the `anchor` tag helper) allow you to continue to use standard HTML attributes. Feel free to decorate your a tag with a `CLASS` or `STYLE` attribute, and those attribute(s) will be preserved in the output transmitted to the browser.

You can trigger interaction from .NET code on your HTML inside the view with either a unique tag name or the presence of special attributes on a normal HTML tag. How do you configure the Razor engine so that it knows that there are tag helpers that it can trigger and use? This configuration is defined through the use of a page directive that looks as follows:

```
@addTagHelper <NAME>, <ASSEMBLY>
```

CAUTION

Don't Forget to add `@addTagHelper`

Forgetting to place an `@addTagHelper` directive on a Razor page results in the tag helper syntax being copied directly into the output of the view without being interpreted by the `TagHelper` class.

Optionally, you can surround the name and assembly with quotes. You can also use an asterisk wildcard character with the `name` parameter to instruct the interpreter to include all tag helpers in an assembly with a matching `name` segment. This directive line can appear at the top of any page to activate tag helpers on that page, or you can add it to the /Views/_ViewImports.cshtml page to include the tag helpers on all pages. If you look in that _ViewImports.cshtml file, you should see the contents shown in Listing 14.3.

LISTING 14.3   The Default Contents of _ViewImports.cshtml

```
@using <MY APPLICATION'S NAMESPACE>
@addTagHelper *, Microsoft.AspNetCore.Mvc.TagHelpers
```

Including the tag helpers on the /Views/_ViewImports.cshtml page causes all the default tag helpers that Microsoft ships to be available inside of your application. What if there are some that you don't want to use? How do you deactivate tag helpers? You can use the removeTagHelper directive at the top of a page or in _ViewImports with the same syntax used with addTagHelper. If you wanted to disable the environment tag helper on every page, you could add the following to the contents of _ViewImports.cshtml:

```
@removeTagHelper Microsoft.AspNetCore.Mvc.TagHelpers.EnvironmentTagHelper,
Microsoft.AspNetCore.Mvc.TagHelpers
```

You can also disable the use of a tag helper in a specific instance by prefixing the opening tag name with an exclamation point:

```
<!a asp-action="Contact">Contact</!a>
```

A final configuration for tag helpers is to specify a prefix that all elements in your views need in order to be considered tag helpers. Simply add the following directive to _ViewImports.cshtml or to any other page to force a prefix before any tag name:

```
@tagHelperPrefix "tag:"
```

For any tag that you would like to have behave as a tag helper, you need to use this prefix. Note that it does not force any character to separate your prefix from the tag name. With this tag: prefix configured, the earlier environment and anchor examples need to be called with this configuration in order to trigger the server-side behavior:

```
<tag:environment names="Development"></tag:environment>
<tag:a asp-area="" asp-controller="Home" asp-action="Index">Home</tag:a>
```

This explicit marking of the tag helper is completely optional. Some developers find that it helps to reduce confusion between server-side interpreted tags and directives that may be interpreted client side as web components or by a framework such as Angular.

Tag Helpers That Ship with ASP.NET Core

The ASP.NET team put together a group of tag helpers to showcase the capabilities of this feature in the framework and to enable some interesting scenarios that developers may run into. The collection that is available when you first install ASP.NET Core includes the following:

▶ **AnchorTagHelper**—The a tag can be configured with information about a server-side route, and this tag helper formats the link appropriately.

▶ **CacheTagHelper**—This custom cache tag stores items in memory in the local web server and is not reexecuted until the cache expires.

▶ **DistributedCacheTagHelper**—This custom distributed cache tag performs similarly to `CacheTagHelper` but instead stores its cache entries in a service defined by the `IDistributedCacheTagHelperService` interface and registered with the dependency injection container. This makes the content of the cache available in a multi-web server scenario.

▶ **EnvironmentTagHelper**—The `environment` tag allows you to define which system environment names (`Development`, `Staging`, `Production`) the tag's content should be delivered on.

▶ **FormTagHelper**—This tag enhances the standard `form` tag with attributes to enable the form's `action` attribute to be defined by a route.

▶ **ImageTagHelper**—This tag enhances the `img` tag to allow you to better manage dynamically generated images. It includes features like appending the version number of the application as a cache-buster token on the URL of the image source.

▶ **InputTagHelper**—This tag enhances the `input` tag with capabilities to help verify content and connect to model properties. It supports HTML 5 input text box types.

▶ **LabelTagHelper**—This tag enhances the `label` tag with the ability to set label content based on the name of an attribute on a model.

▶ **LinkTagHelper**—This tag enhances the `link` tag to allow version number cache-buster tokens to be added, as well as the ability to specify a CDN (Content Delivery Network) location with fallback capabilities.

▶ **ScriptTagHelper**—This tag enhances the `script` tag in the same ways as `LinkTagHelper`.

▶ **SelectTagHelper**—This tag enhances the `select` tag to map to model properties and handle a .NET-based collection of options.

▶ **TextAreaTagHelper**—This tag enhances the `textarea` tag to map to a model property.

▶ **ValidationMessageTagHelper**—This tag enhances a span tag with an `asp-validation-for` attribute that inserts into the span an error message for a given model property that has a failed validation in `ModelState`.

▶ **ValidationSummaryTagHelper**—This tag enhances a `div` tag with an `asp-validation-summary` attribute to indicate that the contents of the `div` should be any errors found in `ModelState`.

You can find the source code for all these tag helpers, as well as new "in the box" tag helpers, on GitHub, at https://github.com/aspnet/Mvc/tree/dev/src/Microsoft.AspNetCore.Mvc.TagHelpers.

Building Other Reusable Components

Besides tag helpers, you can also use two other mechanisms to build reusable components: view components and partial views. View components are more closely related to the user control model of older ASP.NET, where a markup component and a server-side component work together to execute and deliver a block of user interface code to the browser. Both view components and partial views are referenced from a view and can be called asynchronously.

Listing 14.4 shows the code for a simple view component to get the upcoming trips and render them as a list.

LISTING 14.4 A View Component for the Next Three Trips

```
[ViewComponent(Name ="Upcoming")]
public class UpcomingTripsViewComponent : ViewComponent
{

  public UpcomingTripsViewComponent(TripRepository repo)
  {
    Repository = repo;
  }
  public TripRepository Repository { get; private set; }

  public async Task<ViewViewComponentResult> InvokeAsync(int count)
  {

    var nextTrips = Repository.Get()
      .Where(t => t.EndDate > DateTime.Now)
      .OrderBy(t => t.StartDate).Take(count);

    await Task.FromResult(0);

    return View(nextTrips);
  }

}
```

By convention, view components are created in a class that inherits from the `ViewComponent` class and are named with the suffix `ViewComponent`. The name of the component as it will be called from a view is the name of the class preceding the `ViewComponent` suffix. In Listing 14.4, this component would be referenced as `UpcomingTrips`. You can override this naming convention by decorating the class with `ViewComponentAttribute`, as shown in Listing 14.4 on line 1, and specifying the name of the component that should be used to reference it from the view.

We can execute this view component from a view with the following:

```
@await Component.InvokeAsync("UpcomingTrips", new{count=3})
```

This code executes a view component that responds to the `UpcomingTrips` name and passes in an anonymous object to satisfy an input parameter called `count`.

In this class, you take advantage of dependency injection by requesting a `TripRepository` object in the constructor and keeping a reference to it on the `Repository` property. `InvokeAsync` is the method that will actually be called to render the view component for the browser. You don't have to receive parameters on this method, but to make this more interesting, here you accept a `count` parameter. You then fetch the collection of trips that end soon and order them by when they started, limiting the result to the counted items submitted on the `count` parameter. After a token `await` statement to indicate to the calling view that this method is done immediately, the code returns a view with the trips selected. It returns a view? Where does that live?

The view components can return views and/or straight content that will be rendered as a string inside the calling view. The views will live in one of the following locations, and ASP.NET searches for the views in this order:

▶ Views/<controller_name>/Components/<view_component_name>/<view_name>

▶ Views/Shared/Components/<view_component_name>/<view_name>

If you do not specify a view name when returning from the `Invoke` method, the Default.cshtml filename will be sought out by convention. The contents of Default.cshtml for this view component can be as simple as the markup in Listing 14.5.

LISTING 14.5 A Simple `UpcomingTrips` View Component's Markup

```
@model IEnumerable<AspTravlerz.Web.Models.Trip>
<ul>
  @foreach (var trip in Model)
  {
    <li><a asp-controller="Trips" asp-action="Details" asp-route-id="@trip.ID">
@trip.Name</a></li>
  }
</ul>
```

This markup should look very similar to the markup for other views, with the only difference being that it is called from a `ViewComponent` class instead of a controller.

Conversely, a partial view is called from a view and is just another block of Razor markup that is included and executed at the spot where it is referenced. You can pass objects into the partial view, and they will be treated as the model. Finally, all `ViewBag` content from the parent view is visible to the partial view. By default, ASP.NET searches in the following folder locations for a partial view:

▶ /Views/<controller_name>/<partial_view_name>

▶ /Views/Shared/<partial_view_name>

You can write a partial view to standardize the format of a link to a trip by creating a file at /Views/Shared/Trip.cshtml with the contents shown in Listing 14.6.

LISTING 14.6 A Partial View to Standardize the Format of a Trip Link

```
@model AspTravlerz.Web.Models.Trip

<a asp-controller="Trips"
    asp-action="Details"
    asp-route-id="@Model.ID">@Model.Name</a>
```

You can then include this partial view in a view with the following command:

```
@Html.Partial("Trip", myTrip)
```

You can also call the `PartialAsync` method, like so:

```
@await Html.PartialAsync("Trip", myTrip)
```

For practice, you can try updating the view component code to reuse the trip partial view that you just created.

Writing Your Own Tag Helper

Say that you want to reimplement the list of upcoming trips as a tag helper. To get started, you can create a C# class called `UpcomingTripsTagHelper` in a new /TagHelpers folder. You are not required to use a folder named TagHelpers, but you should use a folder with this name for ease of communication with your other project contributors who need to locate the tag helpers available in this project. There is a Razor Tag Helper template available in the Visual Studio 2015 New File dialog that will help you start your new class (see Figure 14.3).

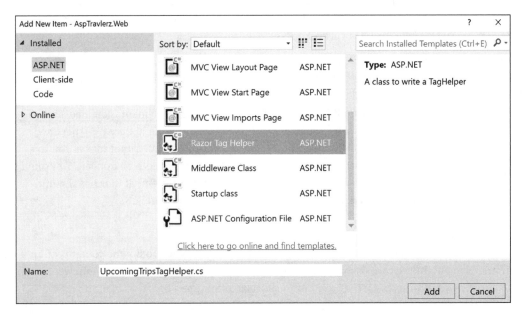

FIGURE 14.3
Razor Tag Helper template in the Visual Studio New File dialog.

Listing 14.7 shows the code Visual Studio gives you to start with in the Razor Tag Helper template.

LISTING 14.7   Razor Tag Helper Code Generated by Visual Studio

```
namespace AspTravlerz.Web.TagHelpers
{
  // You may need to install the Microsoft.AspNetCore.Razor.Runtime
  // package into your project
    [HtmlTargetElement("tag-name")]
    public class UpcomingTripsTagHelper : TagHelper
    {
        public override void Process(TagHelperContext context,
                                     TagHelperOutput output)
        {

        }
    }
}
```

Let's take a closer look at this template code. The name of the tag helper class is UpcomingTripsTagHelper, and that's important. By convention, if you name a tag helper class so that it ends with TagHelper, then you can use the tag helper in your Razor file as a tag with the name that proceeds `TagHelper`. For example, for a class named `FooTagHelper`, you could use that tag helper with an HTML element `foo`.

That's the convention, but there also is an override to this convention, and that override is presented in the Razor template code. The class is decorated with the `HtmlTargetElement` attribute, and this attribute explicitly defines the element name in Razor syntax that should be used to refer to this class. By default in this template, the `tag-name` element is defined. You can change that so that you can use this tag helper with the element name `upcoming`. There are other options on this attribute, including a parameter called `Attributes` that allows you to define HTML attributes that must be present in order for this tag helper to be applied. You could therefore configure the tag helper so that it is applied to any HTML element that has the attribute `upcoming` with an `HtmlTargetElement` attribute that looks as follows:

```
[HtmlTargetElement(Attributes="upcoming")]
```

With this definition and no element attached, your tag helper could modify the contents of an existing element. In the case of this upcoming trips tag helper, you can replace all the content in the `upcoming` tag with a `div` that contains a short list of planned trips.

Writing a Constructor

The upcoming trips tag helper fetches some data from your database about the upcoming trips, and it needs to do a simple database lookup to acquire that data. In order to ensure that you can connect to the database and get that data, you can write a constructor that requires a `TripRepository` object as an input parameter. Tag helpers, like other classes in ASP.NET Core, are instantiated with the help of the dependency injection container, and this input parameter will be satisfied by the class registered in the `Startup` class that you referenced in Hour 7, "Accessing Your Data with Entity Framework Core." You also need an `IHtmlGenerator` object to help with hyperlink generation later. You can store these parameters in class properties for use later. The contents of this tag helper class should look like the following:

```
public UpcomingTripsTagHelper(IHtmlGenerator generator, TripRepository repo)
{
    this.Generator = generator;
    this.Repository = repo;
}

    [HtmlAttributeNotBound()]
    public IHtmlGenerator Generator { get; }

    [HtmlAttributeNotBound()]
    public TripRepository Repository { get; }
```

The `Repository` and `Generator` properties are read-only because of the C# 6 `auto-read-only` property feature. When the `set` parameter of this property is omitted, a value can only be assigned to the property in a constructor. You should also use the `HtmlAttributeNotBound` attribute on these properties to ensure that the Razor engine that will call this tag helper does not assign any values to this property. Without this attribute on the property, an HTML attribute on the upcoming tag named `repository` or `generator` would be assigned to this. Because these properties are not .NET primitive types and are also read-only, ASP.NET would throw an error.

You also need to capture the view context of the tag helper for use in HTML generation later. You do this by adding a property of type `ViewContext` and decorating it with `ViewContextAttribute`:

```
[ViewContext(), HtmlAttributeNotBound()]
public ViewContext ViewContext { get; set; }
```

You can use this view context for passing information about the current page request context, and you can use it to help generate hyperlinks in the tag helper's content.

Counting the Number of Trips

You can make an option available for consumers of the tag helper to specify a count of trips by including a `Count` property on the tag helper that can be submitted to limit the size of the database query and the number of records presented onscreen. You can add this feature as a simple auto-property:

```
public int Count { get; set; } = 3
```

This simple property with a primitive type will be assigned if the HTML attribute `count` is present on the `upcoming` tag. The presence of the `= 3` notation sets a default value for the property if no value is assigned in HTML.

You can change the HTML attribute that is mapped to this property by decorating it with the `HtmlAttributeName` attribute and the name of the attribute to use, as follows:

```
[HtmlAttributeName("trip-count")]
  public int Count { get; set; } = 3
```

Now the attribute `trip-count` is mapped to the `Count` property.

Formatting Your Trips

You can start processing your data and formatting the HTML to present for your trips in the `Process` method that was generated for you. There are two input parameters to this method: `context` and `output`. `context` gives information about the current context of the page at the location where the tag helper is referenced. `output` is a handle that you can use to write content to be inserted into the page where the helper resides. Unlike with previous versions of ASP.NET, you cannot make changes to the rest of the page but can only affect the content between the begin and end tags of the tag helper.

You can set the element name that you want the tag to output by setting the `TagName` property of the `output` parameter. By setting this to `div`, you force the `<upcoming>` element to be converted to a `<div>` HTML element.

Next, you can write a little code to take any CSS class that is applied to the element and add a specific `upcoming-mini` class to it in the resultant HTML. You should first check whether the class attribute has already been set by a developer in the Razor template and add your class as appropriate. By default, all attributes of the tag helper are copied to the output. You need to check the output and add your CSS class to this list as needed, as seen in the following code

```
var newClass = "upcoming-mini";
if (output.Attributes.ContainsName("class"))
{
  newClass += " " + output.Attributes["class"].Value;
}
output.Attributes.SetAttribute("class", newClass);
```

Next, you can add a small header to indicate that this is a list of upcoming trips. You can use the `output.PreContent` property to define an H4 element with this text:

```
output.PreContent.AppendHtml($"<h4>Next {Count} Trips</h4>");
```

`PreContent` is defined as content that is displayed before anything that was defined between the tags in the Razor template.

Once you start modifying the content of the `output` parameter, anything that was written into the content area between the `<upcoming>` tags will be erased and replaced with the content that you instruct the tag helper to emit. You can start writing a standard HTML unordered list to the output content with the `AppendHtml` command:

```
output.Content.AppendHtml("<ul> ");
```

To build the list of trips, you can use a simple LINQ query to return only the next trips that you want to display:

```
var trips = Repository.Get()
  .Where(t => t.EndDate > DateTime.Today)
  .OrderBy(t => t.EndDate)
  .Take(Count);
```

The predicate methods on the `Get()` call add a filter to return only trips that end later than today and order them by most recently ending trip first. Finally, the `Take` method ensures that you retrieve at most the number of trips defined in the `Count` property. With this collection of

Trip objects from the database, you can now write a `for` loop to generate list items with hyperlinks to the trip details page for more information. Listing 14.8 shows this `for` loop.

LISTING 14.8   For Loop to Generate a List of Trips

```
foreach (var trip in trips)
{
  var anchor = Generator.GenerateActionLink(ViewContext, trip.Name,
    "Details", "Trips", "", "", "", new { id = trip.ID }, null);
  output.Content.AppendHtml("<li>");
  output.Content.AppendHtml(anchor);
  output.Content.AppendHtml(
    $" ({trip.StartDate.ToString("d")}-{trip.EndDate.ToString("d")})</li>");
}

output.Content.AppendHtml("</ul>");
```

The interesting part of this loop is the definition of the `anchor` variable. You use the `IHtmlGenerator` object that was injected into the tag helper to generate an `action` link using the routing information for the controller and action that you want the resultant hyperlink to target. The second-to-last argument for this method defines the route attributes to use in formatting the link; in this case, you specify the value of the trip's ID. Recall from Hour 9, "Building Your First Controller," that this is an input parameter to the Details action in `TripsController`'s `Details` method.

Finally, you add the dates of the trip in a nicely formatted "short-date" string, by using the d formatting specifier. For U.S. English locales, this forces the date to be formatted in month/day/year format.

Using Your New Tag Helper

You need to create an entry in the _ViewImports.cshtml page to indicate that you now want to use tag helpers that exist in this project. To do that, you can add an @addTagHelper entry at the end:

```
@addTagHelper *, AspTravlerz.Web
```

You can now place a list of upcoming trips on the home page by using the `<upcoming>` tag.

NOTE

Tag Helpers Were Inspired by Angular

When the ASP.NET team was testing AngularJS 1.0 directives with ASP.NET MVC 5, it was inspired to create a similar construct that could be built on the server side. This server-side directive became the foundation for tag helpers.

▼ TRY IT YOURSELF

Create an FAQ Tag Helper

You currently have a standard presentation of a question and answer on your FAQ. Follow these steps to add a new tag helper for an FAQ so that you get a consistent format:

1. Create a new `FaqTagHelper` class in your TagHelpers folder.

2. Ensure that the class inherits from `TagHelper` and add a single property called `Item` of type `AspTravlerz.Models.Faq`.

3. Copy the formatting from your FaqList.cshtml page and use it to format the content in the `Process` method of the `FaqTagHelper` class. You should create code that looks something like this:

```
output.Content.AppendHtml($"<dt>Question:</dt><dd>{Item.Question}</dd>");
output.Content.AppendHtml($"<dt>Answer:</dt><dd>{Item.Answer}</dd>");
```

4. Return to your FaqList.cshtml page and replace all the HTML inside the `for` loop with a single call to the new `FaqTagHelper`:

```
<faq item="@item"></faq>
```

Start your application and navigate to http://localhost:5000/home/faq, and you should see the contents of your FAQ.

Summary

There are many ways to simplify and reuse HTML content throughout an ASP.NET Core application. In this hour, you have learned what tag helpers are available, how to use tag helpers and view components, and how to write your own tag helpers and view components.

In Hour 15, "npm and bower: Client-Side Package Managers," you will start to add JavaScript and stylesheet components to your application by using package managers such as npm and bower.

Q&A

Q. Can I use tag helpers in earlier versions of ASP.NET MVC?

A. No, tag helpers only work with ASP.NET Core.

Q. Can tag helpers be compiled and distributed for use in other projects?

A. Yes. A number of tag helpers packages are available on NuGet.org that you can add to your project. Some community members have built tag helpers for Bootstrap CSS framework components to make development with them easier. Some vendors are writing high-end tag helpers that deliver significant JavaScript and CSS capabilities for you to use in your web applications.

Q. Can view components be compiled and distributed for use in other projects?

A. No. Because there is a Razor component to the view component, it cannot be bundled and deployed. Use a tag helper if you want to distribute a web feature.

Q. Can HTML helpers from ASP.NET MVC 5 and earlier be used in ASP.NET Core?

A. Yes, with some work. They need to be recompiled for compatibility with .NET Core if they are to be distributed and run on other platforms, such as Mac and Linux.

Workshop

The workshop contains quiz questions and exercises to help you solidify your understanding of the material covered. Try to answer all questions before looking at the "Answers" that follow.

Quiz

1. Besides view components and tag helpers, what other reusable components can be used in MVC views to encapsulate HTML content?

2. What features do `ScriptTagHelper` and `LinkTagHelper` provide?

3. How do you inject features into the `TagHelper` classes?

4. In what folders does ASP.NET Core look for view component Razor views (.cshtml files)?

5. What attribute can you place on a `TagHelper` class to change the HTML element name that it will act on?

Answers

1. Partial views and HTML helpers were both available in older versions of ASP.NET MVC and are not recommended solutions but are provided for compatibility.

2. `ScriptTagHelper` and `LinkTagHelper` allow you to specify a CDN location for a script or stylesheet and also allow you to specify whether a cache-buster token should be used when new versions of your project are deployed.

3. To inject features into the `TagHelper` classes, add an input parameter to the tag helper constructor method of the type of object that you need in your class.

4. It looks in:

   Views/<controller_name>/Components/<view_component_name>/

   Views/Shared/Components/<view_component_name>/

5. `HtmlTargetElement`

Exercise

You wrote a very simple tag helper and view component to format the list of upcoming trips. Expand on those samples to make them reusable on the home page and on your Trips/Index action so that you have a single view component to format and show your list of trips.

npm **and** bower: **Client-Side Package Managers**

What You'll Learn in This Hour:

▶ What npm and bower are

▶ How to use package managers to fetch CSS and JavaScript frameworks

▶ How to extend npm and bower to assist in ASP.NET Core development

You have written a lot of server-side code in this book so far; all of the code you've written to this point will be executed by a web server and returned to a client that is typically a web browser. This hour, you will start taking a look at using and reusing code for formatting your web pages for visitors to your application. There are thousands of CSS and JavaScript libraries available that you can use to beautify your application at no charge to you.

What Are npm **and** bower?

Up to this point, you've made use of a number of packages from the NuGet package manager system. NuGet delivers features and frameworks for .NET applications, and it previously used to provide web frameworks and widgets for use in ASP.NET applications. The problem with this approach is that web framework maintainers do not want to distribute their product for just the .NET ecosystem, so instead they use different package managers that are built specifically for delivering projects for formatting and building web pages.

npm (which stands for Node Package Manager) is a command-line tool that is available across platforms for use in fetching and managing packages of content to be consumed—typically by Node.js projects. The packages delivered by npm can deliver user interface frameworks, other command-line tools, or modules needed for building a Node.js application. When using npm with ASP.NET Core, you will make use of the first two areas of functionality.

bower is a package manager that was originally written by some folks at Twitter as a way to deliver user interface components easily from their GitHub repositories. It has since expanded and taken on a life of its own as a way to deliver and manage user interface frameworks from

Git repositories. Unlike with npm, with bower there is no utility model and there are no scripting capabilities that allow you to enhance the behavior of the bower command-line tool.

Doesn't Microsoft Provide a Client-Side Framework and Tools?

Alas, unlike in previous versions of ASP.NET, where Microsoft managed a library of controls to give some initial and limited enhanced features for web development, Microsoft has opted out of creating and maintaining client-side tools for this edition of ASP.NET. In addition, Microsoft is no longer promoting the use of the NuGet tool for delivering these packages for use with ASP.NET Core projects. There are three primary reasons for this design decision:

▶ JavaScript and CSS libraries in NuGet were never maintained by the open source projects that owned them. Instead, packages like jQuery in NuGet were maintained by Microsoft employees and were guaranteed to never receive updates at exactly the same time that the owners of the project would publish updates.

▶ There are already thousands of libraries and packages available that the web development ecosystem outside .NET already uses and loves. If you really like using jQuery UI with your project, Microsoft thought it would be best to enable you to use that library with the tools that the library maintainers want you to use with their product.

▶ By integrating with npm and bower, Microsoft brings ASP.NET Core into parity with other server-side frameworks, like Ruby on Rails, Node.js, and PHP, that already integrate nicely with these tools to allow web developers to work easily with their output.

Do I Really Need to Use npm and bower with My Project?

No, you don't need to use these tools with your ASP.NET Core project. Microsoft has only included some sample configuration files in the project templates in an effort to help get you started more easily. If your project team does not want to use these tools and would rather manage the JavaScript and CSS libraries by hand or with a different tool, you are more than welcome to delete the files and folders that were created for you and instead integrate with your favorite tools and libraries.

Getting Started with npm

The Node Package Manager uses the same package.json file to define the packages referenced by an application and the contents of a package to be registered and available for other applications to install. This package.json configuration file is provided in a simple JSON format that can be read and managed either by hand or with a series of commands issued with the npm command-line tool.

By default in Visual Studio 2015, ASP.NET Core creates the package.json file with very limited content, as shown in Figure 15.1.

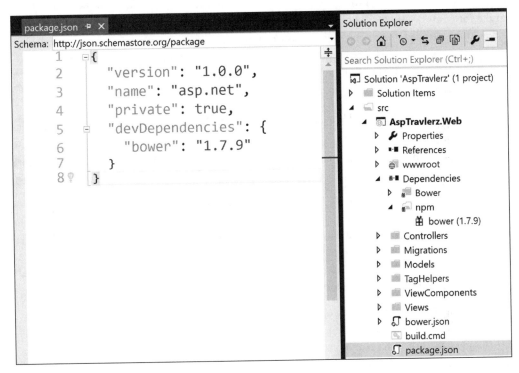

FIGURE 15.1
Visual Studio default package.json content.

It's not very exciting content. At this point, it's only being used to add the bower functionality and define some baseline version information. The devDependencies element declares that the bower reference should only be included as a developer tool and should not be included in any deployment capacity. You can also define packages in a Dependencies section which indicates that the contents of those packages should be made available for production compilation and deployment of your application.

Visual Studio provides some insight about what is referenced by npm in the new Dependencies child element in the Solution Explorer and lists npm packages under the npm parent element. That's a nice way to easily see what packages are included without having to read through the package.json file directly.

When Visual Studio 2015 sees a change saved to the package.json file, it automatically runs the npm command-line tool to ensure that the packages installed within your project accurately reflect what is defined in this file. You do not need to execute any extra commands or gestures in Visual Studio to get it to trigger npm for you.

npm packages are defined on the https://npmjs.org registry. You can browse to and search this website for packages that will help you build your next web application. Visual Studio 2015 and Visual Studio Code provide type-ahead assistance, so if you know what packages you're looking for, they will help you in keying in the names of the packages and in choosing the appropriate notation to get the version of the package you need. When referencing a package version from package.json, there are several distinct version markings that deliver different behaviors:

▶ A version number with no additional markup attempts to fetch exactly the package version defined.

▶ A version number preceded with a tilde (~) matches the major and minor versions requested and installs the latest patch version available. For example, ~1.2.3 installs version 1.2.3 and automatically updates to 1.2.4 when it becomes available and you instruct npm to install updates.

▶ A version number preceded with a caret (^) matches the major version number and installs the latest minor and patch versions as they become available. For example, ^1.2.3 installs version 1.2.4 and 1.3.0 as they become available, with a preference for 1.3.0 since it is the highest available version.

▶ You can alternatively provide an asterisk (*) for the version to indicate that you want absolutely the highest version available to be installed in your project. This is an aggressive approach, as major version number changes on a package indicate significant changes in API that could have adverse effects on your project.

In addition to editing and maintaining the package.json file by hand, you can use the npm command-line tool to manage the contents of this file by using following commands:

▶ **npm init**—Initializes a new package.json file to begin using with a project in the current directory

▶ **npm install**—Installs any missing packages

▶ **npm update**—Updates any packages to their latest published versions that match version specs in the package.json file

▶ **npm install *"package name"* --save**—Installs the latest version of *"package name"* and saves a reference to it in package.json's Dependencies section

▶ **npm install *"package name"* --save-dev**—Installs the latest version of *"package name"* and saves a reference to it in package.json's devDependencies section

▶ **npm uninstall**—Removes a package from this project

With each of the `install` commands, `npm` places the contents of the package in the local node_ modules folder. Any new command-line tools that are added will have their scripts placed into a root .bin folder that can be used to execute those commands.

If you want to add a command-line tool with `npm` so that it can be executed anywhere on your workstation or server, you can execute the `npm install` command with a global flag, as follows:

```
npm install -g bower
```

This command places the libraries and executable files for `bower` in the executable path of your machine. On Windows, the executable is placed in %APPDATA%\npm and on a Unix-based system it is placed in /usr/bin.

Getting Started with `bower`

`bower` is a simpler package manager than `npm` that acts as a management layer on top of the `git` protocol. `git` is a source control system that is very popular in the open source community and has gained a lot of traction in the enterprise development market as well. `bower` maintains a registry of packages at https://bower.io, where you can search for packages to use in your application.

Packages managed by `bower` in an application are configured in a bower.json file with a `bower` command-line tool that can assist in maintaining entries in this file. These packages also use the bower.json file to add, update, or remove packages from your project. Much like npm, `bower` is part of the default configuration with the default ASP.NET Core templates, as shown in Figure 15.2.

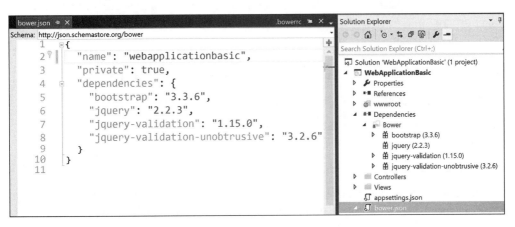

FIGURE 15.2
Visual Studio default `bower` configuration.

In Figure 15.2, you can see that the JavaScript and CSS libraries for Bootstrap, jQuery, and jQuery validation are referenced by `bower` and listed in the `Dependencies-Bower` segment in the Solution Explorer of Visual Studio, much like the `npm` packages.

Unlike with the `npm` packages, with `bower` you have a little more control over where the `bower` packages are placed on disk. There is a .bowerrc file hidden under bower.json in the Solution Explorer that contains an override directive for the location to place the `bower` packages. Listing 15.1 shows this file.

LISTING 15.1 The Default .bowerrc File

```
{
  "directory": "wwwroot/lib"
}
```

This file simply directs that all `bower` packages will be placed in the wwwroot/lib folder instead of the default bower_components folder in the same folder as the bower.json configuration file. This is a simple configuration that places all the files from the `bower` package in the publicly accessible webroot space of your application. If someone browsing your web application knows that the jQuery folder from `bower` is available, he or she can potentially browse to and download any of the files from that folder. This may be acceptable for your application, but perhaps you only want to ship the distributable parts of jQuery that you want running on your application's web server. (You'll learn more about manipulating the contents of these folders in Hour 16, "Introducing Angular.")

If you have installed Visual Studio 2015, there is a copy of `bower` available when you use the developer command prompt. If you would like to make a copy of `bower` available to all command lines, you can install a global copy of `bower` by using the following `npm` command:

```
npm install -g bower
```

You can also use the following commands with `bower` from the command line:

- **bower init**—Initializes a new `bower` project in the current directory

- **bower install**—Installs any missing packages

- **bower install "*package name*" --save**—Installs a package and saves the package as a dependency

- **bower install "*package name*" --save-dev**—Installs a package and saves the package as a developer dependency that should not be deployed to production instances

- **bower uninstall**—Uninstalls a package from the current project

So you can run `bower` from the command line or key in those package names directly in your bower.json file. In addition, Visual Studio has a package manager for `bower` that you can access from the Solution Explorer window. To open it, right-click the project name and choose Manage Bower Packages, as shown in Figure 15.3

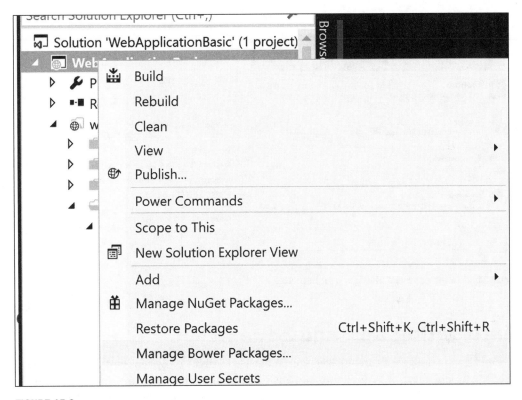

FIGURE 15.3
The Visual Studio Manage Bower Packages command.

This command launches the Bower Package Manager tool and shows you the Manage Bower Packages window (see Figure 15.4).

In this view, you can search for packages by using the text box, and you can see the results of your search in the left panel and the details of a selected package in the right panel. You can also easily see which packages are currently installed and which packages have updates available. There are easy-to-use Install and Uninstall buttons located next to each package that allow you to add these libraries to your project easily.

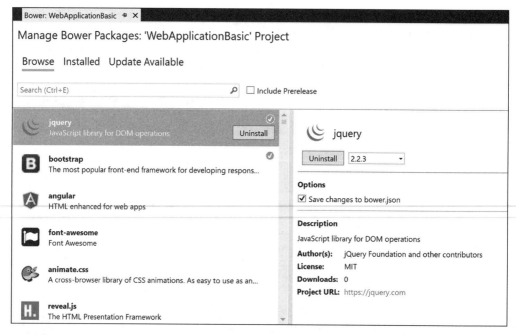

FIGURE 15.4
Visual Studio Bower Package Manager user interface.

Automating npm and bower

npm and bower are very clearly tools that exist outside the .NET ecosystem that do not interact directly with any of the .NET tools that you have seen to this point. There are, however, extension points on the .NET project system and tools that you can use to integrate and automate the use of npm and bower in your projects.

Extending Your Project with Scripts

There are several extension points in the project file that you can use to automate the execution of command-line applications. You learned a bit about these points in Hour 4, "Defining ASP.NET Core Configuration," and this hour recaps those techniques.

You can add scripts to execute in your project file by adding a new Target element off the top level of the project and defining Exec elements with the script names to execute. You can execute your target at different steps of the build process by adding BeforeTargets and AfterTargets attributes with one of the following values:

- ▶ **build**—Executes your script just before or after the project is compiled
- ▶ **publish**—Executes your script just before or after the publish action takes place

The scripts assigned to these actions are triggered regardless of the development tool that is issuing the `compile` or `publish` commands. Visual Studio and the `dotnet` command-line tool both execute these commands when the appropriate event is triggered.

Task Runner Explorer

Integrated within Visual Studio is a tool that allows you to execute tasks for your project. The Task Runner Explorer window is built to allow you to execute these command-line tools as part of your normal interactions with your .NET project. By default, the Task Runner Explorer comes with bindings for the JavaScript Grunt and Gulp tools, which many developers have discontinued using due to a preference in using scripts in npm directly. In this hour, you'll add the npm Task Runner extension to Visual Studio. Select Tools > Extensions and Updates and search for and add the npm Task Runner extension. This extension enables package.json interactions for the Task Runner Explorer window.

Next, launch the Task Runner Explorer by selecting View > Other Windows > Task Runner Explorer. You should see a docked window at the bottom of Visual Studio that looks like the one in Figure 15.5.

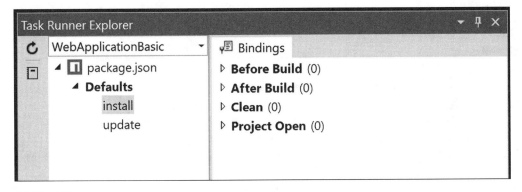

FIGURE 15.5
Visual Studio Task Runner Explorer configured for npm.

From this dialog, you can right-click the Install or Update option on the left side and choose to run it immediately. The more interesting part is on the right side of the window. These are bindings to events in your .NET project. You can configure the `install` or `update` commands to execute whenever these events occur during the life cycle of your project. Consider the following:

▶ When you execute a standard Visual Studio Build > Clean Solution command, you can install all npm packages automatically.

▶ When you open your project in Visual Studio, you can have npm check for updates and apply those updates so that your project has the latest package versions available to it.

To bind these events to your npm commands, right-click the npm command on the left and choose the event you want to trigger the command. Figure 15.6 shows how to connect the update command to the Project Open event as an example.

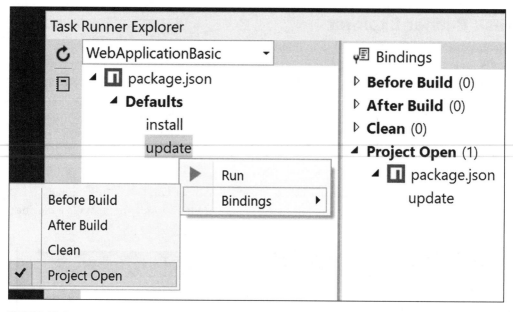

FIGURE 15.6
Binding the update command to the Project Open event.

That's a pretty neat effect, but where is Visual Studio storing this event binding? Is it adding markup to your project file that is going to break your project for teammates who are not using Visual Studio? Not at all. The npm Task Runner extension adds an entry to the end of your package.json file that looks like this:

```
"-vs-binding": { "ProjectOpened": [ "update" ] }
```

Other tools that are using npm ignore this configuration element in your package.json file.

Installing Newer Versions of npm and bower

Visual Studio installs set versions of bower and npm as of the date that you install Visual Studio, and it does not readily expose these tools to you. What happens when newer versions of these tools are released and you want to update your toolkit?

Let's look at Visual Studio and see where it installs these tools. By default, Visual Studio installs Node.js, npm, bower, git, and several other tools in the C:\Program Files (x86)\Microsoft Visual Studio 14.0\Web\External folder. You will find CMD files in this folder that route to the appropriate locations on disk to launch each of these tools. They are a nice default and are on the path when you launch the Visual Studio command prompt on your Windows-based workstation.

If you want to install and manage your own versions of these tools, you can download and install the latest Node.js from http://nodejs.org. With Node.js installed, when you install global copies of these tools by using the -g switch as shown here, npm places a copy of the executable at %appdata%\npm on your Windows workstation:

```
npm install bower -g
```

This is nice, but it's not in the path where Visual Studio will be looking to run your tools. Where is Visual Studio looking for these tools, and how can you control it? You can expose this configuration by selecting Tools > Options > Projects and Solutions > External Web Tools, as shown in Figure 15.7.

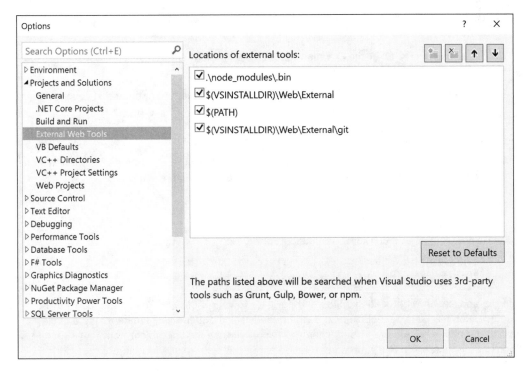

FIGURE 15.7
Visual Studio external tool configuration locations.

Visual Studio searches in these locations from top to bottom, and it stop at the first folder that contains the executable it is looking for. When you want to restore your bower packages, it first looks in the node_modules folder of the current project and then the default Visual Studio installation directory's web/external folder. Next it searches on your system's path, and finally it looks in the git folder for Visual Studio.

When you install Node.js, the global installation folder for `npm` (%appdata%\npm) is added to your path. You can force that location to take a higher priority in Visual Studio by either adding that folder to the top of this list or simply moving the $(PATH) option to the top of the list.

With this little bit of configuration in place, you can execute the `npm update -g` command occasionally to ensure that Visual Studio is using the latest versions of all your globally installed Node.js command-line tools.

▼ TRY IT YOURSELF

Add the font-awesome Package to Your FAQ Page

Follow these steps to add the font-awesome package to your application by using `bower` and then add some icons to your questions and answers:

1. Add an entry to your bower.json file for font-awesome version 4.7.0, right below the entry for Bootstrap.

2. Run `bower install` at the command prompt to download the font-awesome package and add it to your wwwroot/lib folder.

3. Update Views/Shared/_Layout.cshtml with a CSS link to the font-awesome stylesheet after the Bootstrap stylesheet in the HTML header:

   ```
   <link href="~/assets/font-awesome/css/font-awesome.min.css" rel="stylesheet"/>
   ```

4. In the code for `FaqTagHelper`, prefix the text inside the `dt` and `dd` elements with an icon from font-awesome. For the question, add this code just inside the `dt` tag:

   ```
   <i class=\"fa fa-question-circle\" style=\"color: blue;\
   " aria-hidden=\"true\"></i>
   ```

5. For the answer, add this code just inside the `dd` tag:

   ```
   <i class=\"fa fa-check-circle-o\" style=\"color: green;\
   " aria-hidden=\"true\"></i>
   ```

Run the application with these changes and navigate to your FAQ page. You should now have a blue question mark inside a circle next to the question and a green checkmark inside a circle next to the answer. There are lots of icons you can easily use in your project from font-awesome. Check out fontawesome.io for more information about this easy-to-use font library.

Summary

In this hour you have learned how to integrate several client-side tools with your ASP.NET Core project. ASP.NET Core doesn't have an opinion with regard to these tools and enables you to use the tools that you feel best meet the needs of your project.

Q&A

Q. Do I have to use `npm` and `bower` with my project?

A. No. You are not required to use these tools. Visual Studio and ASP.NET Core simply make it easier to interoperate with them. You are welcome to use whatever method you would like to add UI frameworks and tools to your application.

Q. Can I use NuGet to get jQuery, Bootstrap, and other frameworks into my ASP.NET application?

A. In older versions of ASP.NET, using NuGet was the preferred method to load these frameworks. It was more difficult to use `npm` and `bower` with older versions of ASP.NET. NuGet does not install these user interface frameworks for ASP.NET Core projects.

Q. There is a cool new JavaScript tool called `<foo>` that I want to use with Visual Studio instead of `npm` and `bower`. Is there a way I can use it?

A. Visual Studio and the JavaScript communities are very active in developing new tools and techniques to make web development easier. Check the Visual Studio Marketplace at https://marketplace.visualstudio.com to see if someone has written an extension that supports the tool you want to use. There is a high likelihood that someone is working on the integration already.

Workshop

The workshop contains quiz questions and exercises to help you solidify your understanding of the material covered. Try to answer all questions before looking at the "Answers" that follow.

Quiz

1. `npm` is installed with Visual Studio 2015 by default in what location?
2. What libraries are added by default through `bower` in a default website ASP.NET Core application?
3. What is the name of the tool in Visual Studio that allows you to bind compilation events to `npm` commands?
4. Where in Visual Studio can you find the configuration for the external web tools?
5. What is the purpose of the .bowerrc file?

Answers

1. C:\Program Files (x86)\Microsoft Visual Studio 14.0\Web\External
2. bootstrap, jquery, jquery-validation, jquery-validation-unobtrusive
3. Task Runner Explorer

4. Tools > Options > Projects and Solutions > External Web Tools

5. To configure how bower should interact with the current folder. In its simplest configuration, .bowerrc dictates the name of the directory to write bower packages into.

Exercise

In your ASPTravlerz project, you are going to use Angular 2 and the Bootstrap CSS framework to present your user interface. For practice, you can configure your project for npm to install Angular 2 packages and then add bower configuration options to install bootstrap. Take a look at the other packages that are available and add some that you might want to use to enhance the project in a way that you will find fun. The following are some packages to explore:

▶ font-awesome—Provides cool icon fonts

▶ Sharp—Allows resizing of PNGs, JPGs, and GIFs

▶ Moment.js—Manipulates and displays dates

▶ Moment Timezone—Handles those pesky time zones, which will be useful in your application when you may be traveling across time zones

▶ Os-locale—Allows you to get information about the locale of the executing system

HOUR 16
Introducing Angular

What You'll Learn in This Hour:

▶ What the Angular framework is

▶ Why Angular is so popular

▶ How to get started with the Angular command-line tool

▶ The simple component architecture of an Angular application

Since 2010, there has been a dramatic revolution in JavaScript development. Frameworks, technologies, runtimes, tools, terms, and architectures have been invented using open source technologies. These inventions have been shared, extended, built up, and reshared. The momentum of this JavaScript movement has been nothing short of spectacular to observe and participate in.

As a technology leader, Google organized the development framework for its applications and shared it for the community to learn from and build on. That framework was AngularJS. After a few years of public consumption, Google released a second version of the framework and decided to drop the JS from the name to indicate that it was more than just a user interface framework. Google also began supporting TypeScript as a first-class programming language to work with Angular.

Many developers have struggled with web page design and interactivity. Earlier versions of ASP.NET attempted to solve this problem with a rich server-side control ecosystem. You could easily drop a control into a web page, and at page-request time, ASP.NET would transform that control into some HTML, JavaScript, and style markup. Building user interfaces on the server can deliver a slow experience and fails to take into account any information about the client visiting your application. Is it a mobile device? Are you delivering content for a screen reader because your visitor is vision impaired? JavaScript user interface frameworks attempt to solve such issues by pushing more of these user interface decisions to the browser.

The Angular 4 version that you will learn about in this and the next few hours was published in March 2017 and provides a comprehensive framework for building applications with JavaScript and TypeScript. This lesson takes a brief break from ASP.NET Core to focus on how to use

Angular to build user interfaces. Hour 17, "Connecting Angular to ASP.NET Core," returns to ASP.NET Core and using Angular to work with your application.

Getting Started with Angular

Many JavaScript frameworks have a series of configuration steps, tools to install, and rules that you need to follow in order to get things started and write your first line of code. An open source team outside the main Angular team that wanted to make the experience simpler and easier for developers wrote a command-line tool that downloads and positions everything on your workstation so that you can get your first application running in minutes—or maybe even seconds.

NOTE

CLI Prerequisites

You should have Node.js 6.9.0 or later and npm version 3 or later installed on your system in order to use the Angular command-line interface (CLI).

You install the Angular CLI by executing this command at a command prompt:

```
npm install -g @angular/cli
```

Remember that npm is the Node Package Manager that you learned about in Hour 15, "npm and bower: Client-Side Package Managers." In this case, you are instructing it to install a package. The -g switch indicates that this package should be installed globally so that it can be used without being in the context of a project. The package to be installed is in the @angular organization and is called cli. All of the official packages and libraries built for and supported by the Angular team are prefixed with the @angular organization indicator.

With the CLI installed, you can start a new Angular application with this command:

```
ng new my-first-angular-app
```

The tool uses its internal templates to generate a boilerplate application and place it in the my-first-angular-app folder. You can start your application by using a development web server with the following command:

```
ng serve
```

By default, your application will be compiled and hosted on port 4200. Navigate to http://local-host:4200, and you should see a simple introductory website like the one shown in Figure 16.1.

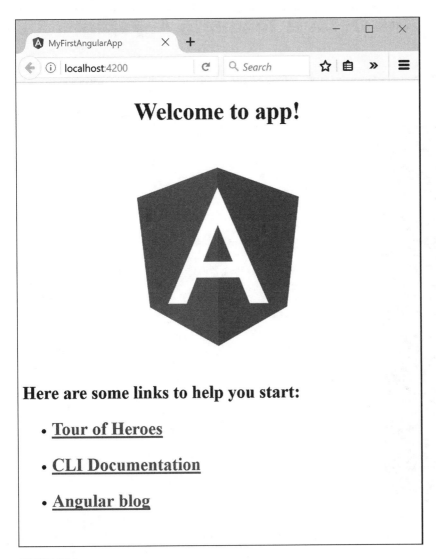

FIGURE 16.1
Default Angular CLI-generated website.

Notice that the only customization on this very simple website is the title displayed on the browser tab. The body of the page contains three simple links to a tutorial, documentation, and the Angular team's blog. Nonetheless, you have created this Angular website and run it in your browser. In the next section, let's take a peek under the hood and see what makes this website run.

Exploring the Default Template Angular Website

Figure 16.2 shows the folder layout for your first Angular website when viewed with Visual Studio Code.

FIGURE 16.2
Visual Studio Code Showing the Contents of the Default Generated Website.

There's a lot to see here, including some interesting file extensions that you may not have seen before. These are the folders, from the top:

- **e2e**—This folder contains end-to-end (hence e2e) tests for the application. You may also know them as integration tests.

- **node_modules**—This folder contains all the Node.js modules that are referenced by this project.

- **src**—This folder contains the source of the web application or the actual program that will be executed and served to visitors.

▶ **src/app**—This folder contains the Angular application that will be executed and served.

▶ **src/assets**—This folder contains static assets to be served to browsers are not to be executed or interpreted by the application. Stylesheets, images, and fonts are typically found here.

▶ **src/environments**—This folder contains configuration information that you may want to apply differently, depending on whether you are running in the development or production environment. This environment setting is maintained separately from the ASP.NET Core environment setting.

Next, you see a number of configuration files on the root of the application that end with a .json file extension. These files configure various services used in the compilation and delivery of the application:

▶ **angular-cli.json**—Configuration of how the Angular CLI should maintain the application

▶ **package.json**—npm configuration of packages to install and maintain in the application

▶ **tsconfig.json**—Configuration of the TypeScript compiler for this application

▶ **tslint.json**—Configuration of the TypeScript code-style checker, or "linter," that will be run against the application

As mentioned earlier, the preferred language for writing and interacting with Angular applications is TypeScript. TypeScript is an interpreted language that is a superset of JavaScript and compiles to JavaScript. All valid JavaScript that you know how to write is also valid TypeScript. There are additional keywords that you can use in TypeScript to drive functionality and build very large applications in a very object-oriented way. TypeScript also gives you type checking when you work with variables and parameters.

The Angular team recommends that you use TypeScript to develop Angular applications due to the number of files and references that you need to make from an application to Angular resources. By using TypeScript for these programming tasks, you will be assured that you are making accurate references, and your developer tools can better show you the features you are interacting with.

When you build and run your application, all of the .ts (TypeScript) files in your application are converted to JavaScript and formatted as directed in the tsconfig.json file. This should result in a smaller, more easily transportable application that your visitors can download and use.

The remaining two conf.js files in the project root folder, karma.conf.js and protractor.conf.js, are configuration files for unit-test frameworks. You will not be working with these test frameworks for your ASPTravlerz project.

Delivering Content to the Browser

The content shown in your browser (refer to Figure 16.1) starts with the index.html file in the src folder. This file contains standard HTML and is the first file served to visitors of your application. When your application is compiled, the CLI injects into the bottom of this page a set of references to the compiled JavaScript in your src folder. Take a look at the source delivered for index.html in Listing 16.1.

LISTING 16.1   Index.html Content Delivered to the Browser

```
<!doctype html>
<html lang="en">
<head>
  <meta charset="utf-8">
  <title>MyFirstAngularApp</title>
  <base href="/">

  <meta name="viewport" content="width=device-width, initial-scale=1">
  <link rel="icon" type="image/x-icon" href="favicon.ico">
</head>
<body>
  <app-root></app-root>
  <script type="text/javascript" src="inline.bundle.js"></script>
  <script type="text/javascript" src="polyfills.bundle.js"></script>
  <script type="text/javascript" src="styles.bundle.js"></script>
  <script type="text/javascript" src="vendor.bundle.js"></script>
  <script type="text/javascript" src="main.bundle.js"></script>
</body>
</html>
```

The head element and its contents are unchanged from the contents of the index.html file on disk. The body element, however, contains the same strange-looking app-root element, as well as five references to script files. The app-root element is the location where the Angular application will be presented within this HTML file, and the script elements are all of the references to Angular, its libraries, and the content of your application. You don't need to write a line of code in these files; rather, you maintain them when you compile your application.

By convention, your application actually starts at the src/main.ts file, whose initial contents are shown in Listing 16.2.

LISTING 16.2   The Default main.ts File in Your Application

```
import { enableProdMode } from '@angular/core';
import { platformBrowserDynamic } from '@angular/platform-browser-dynamic';
```

```
import { AppModule } from './app/app.module';
import { environment } from './environments/environment';

if (environment.production) {
  enableProdMode();
}


platformBrowserDynamic().bootstrapModule(AppModule);
```

You can immediately see some of the new keywords from TypeScript, along with some familiar JavaScript. The `import` statements bring into your application content from other TypeScript files. The first two statements bring in the `enableProdMode` tool and the `platformBrowser-Dynamic` features. `enableProdMode` configures the application to reduce the amount of rich logging information sent to the browser, and `platformBrowserDynamic` contains directions for Angular to work with a browser.

The next line brings in the first bits of your application that you will be maintaining from the `app/app.module` file. `AppModule` contains all the information about the application features and functionality that you are writing. This `main.ts` file bootstraps or starts up that functionality on the last line in the file.

An Angular module is a collection of related functionality that is similar to a .NET namespace. An Angular module can include components, directives, pipes, and services that you can use to compose and deliver related business functionality for your application. Every application contains at least one module to start and manage the application. For larger applications, you can add more modules to maintain other segments of the application. For the ASPTravlerz application, you will work with just the one app module. Listing 16.3 shows the initial contents of the app/app.module.ts file in your project.

LISTING 16.3   The Default app.module.ts in Your Application

```
import { BrowserModule } from '@angular/platform-browser';
import { NgModule } from '@angular/core';
import { AppComponent } from './app.component';

@NgModule({
  declarations: [
    AppComponent
  ],
  imports: [
    BrowserModule
  ],
  providers: [],
  bootstrap: [AppComponent]
})
export class AppModule { }
```

This TypeScript class is very simple, and you can easily read it. BrowserModule and NgModule are included at the beginning to give your application access to browser functionality and core Angular functionality. The third line includes AppComponent, a user interface and logic component for your application.

The @NgModule line is a TypeScript decorator, similar to a C# attribute, that decorates the class defined on the last line of this file. The declarations item inside the decorator defines the classes that are part of this module, like AppComponent. The imports item indicates what features to include in the module; in this case, BrowserModule is included to provide browser-targeted functionality. The providers item defines a collection of objects that should be instantiated and injected for use in your module. This simple module does not reference any providers. The bootstrap item occurs only in AppModule and defines the component to start when the application is first loaded. In this case, AppComponent will be started and presented to your visitors.

The next piece to load in your application is AppComponent, whose source code is provided in Listing 16.4.

LISTING 16.4 Initial app/app.component.ts Code in Your Application

```
import { Component } from '@angular/core';

@Component({
  selector: 'app-root',
  templateUrl: './app.component.html',
  styleUrls: ['./app.component.css']
})
export class AppComponent {
  title = 'app';
}
```

Now you're starting to see some references to HTML and CSS. You know what those are, but how do you get there?

The AppComponent class imports the Component object from Angular so that it can define itself as an Angular component object with the @Component decorator. This decorator can provide a number of values to define its behavior. In the case of this component, you see the following features defined:

- ▶ selector—The HTML element that will be replaced with the content of this component

- ▶ templateUrl—The HTML that will be formatted and output from this class

- ▶ styleUrls—An array of stylesheet files that should be used when this component is presented

This is a very convenient naming and organization scheme, as all templates and stylesheets are grouped together as a single component and loaded into your application as a single cohesive piece.

The final bit of this file shows the first code that is executed as part of a class definition, and it assigns the string 'app' to a title property of the AppComponent class. You can see that title property referenced in the HTML template source code shown in Listing 16.5.

LISTING 16.5   Initial app/app.component.html Template in Your Application

```
<!--The content below is only a placeholder and can be replaced.-->
<div style="text-align:center">
  <h1>
    Welcome to {{title}}!
  </h1>
  <img width="300" src="…">
</div>
<h2>Here are some links to help you start: </h2>
<ul>
  <li>
    <h2><a target="_blank" href="https://angular.io/tutorial">Tour of Heroes</a></h2>
  </li>
  <li>
    <h2><a target="_blank" href="https://github.com/angular/angular-cli/wiki">
CLI Documentation</a></h2>
  </li>
  <li>
    <h2><a target="_blank" href="http://angularjs.blogspot.ca/">Angular blog</a>
</h2>
  </li>
</ul>
```

NOTE

Formatting Content

In this case you drop the content of the img tag's src attribute because it is a full image in uuencoded format and unnecessary for this exploration. The title property from the AppComponent class is consumed on line 4 with the {{title}} markup. This double curly braces notation is sometimes referred to as a *moustache*, and its contents are executed against the root of the component class that references this template. There are other ways to format and use properties and methods of component classes, as you'll see in Hours 17, "Connecting Angular to ASP.NET Core," 18, "Routing Angular Requests Around ASP.NET Core," and 19, "Running Angular on the Server."

Is your application still running with that ng serve command from earlier in the hour? If not, run it again at the command line and open a browser to http://localhost:4200. Now you can start changing this application and see how the Angular application development process feels.

With the application running and visible in your browser, change the value of the title property in your app.component class from "app" to "My Cool Application". Save that file and watch your browser. (Don't reload it because the Angular CLI hosted server will do that for you.) You should see your new title at the top of the page, as shown in Figure 16.3.

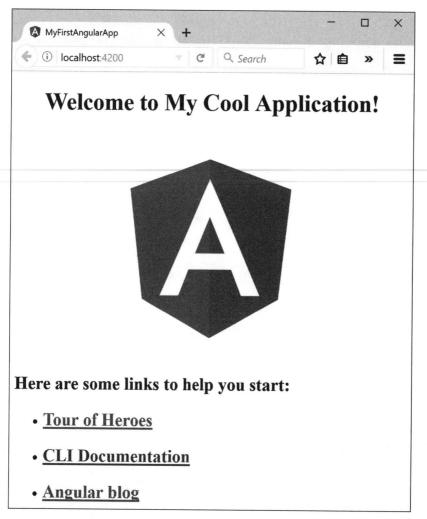

FIGURE 16.3
Your updated page after you change the `title` property.

This is a pretty simple change, but it's pretty neat to see it immediately reflected in your browser. What about the style of your content? You can add some style to the H1 that surrounds the title by adding the following markup in the app.component.css file:

```
H1 { color: green; text-decoration: underline; }
```

After you save that CSS file, the browser immediately updates with the applied style, as shown in Figure 16.4.

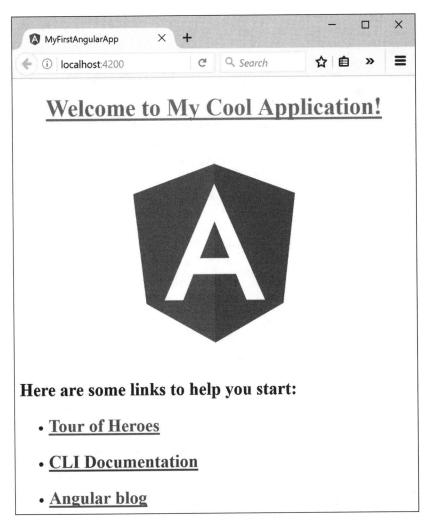

FIGURE 16.4
Your updated page after you update the header style.

Once again, it's pretty cool to see your page immediately reflect the code changes you make. Behind the scenes, the CLI tool is watching your application and recompiling any changes that are made. Any browser that is viewing the application has those changes pushed to it by using BrowserSync technology. You don't need to know how BrowserSync works, but it is interesting to know how your browser automatically updates with your changes.

Adding Some Real Code

You've done some simple variable changing and formatting, but now you're ready to actually add some code that mirrors a bit of what you have in the ASP.NET Core application. You can start by adding a Model class for your Trip object by executing the following command at the command line:

```
ng generate class Trip
```

If your server is still running from the last exercise, keep it running. You can add classes and functionality to the live site, and your browser will update as the features become available. The statement you just entered adds an empty TypeScript class named trip.ts to the top of your app folder. Enter the updated source for trip.ts that is shown in Listing 16.6 to add a few simple properties and a constructor so that you can create new Trip objects.

LISTING 16.6   A Simple Trip Object in the trip.ts File

```
export class Trip {
    Destination: string;
    DurationInDays: number;

    constructor(destination: string, durationInDays: number) {
        this.Destination = destination;
        this.DurationInDays = durationInDays;
    }

}
```

Notice the slight difference in declaring a TypeScript constructor compared to a C# constructor. TypeScript uses the constructor keyword to define the method executed when you call new Trip(). The properties Destination and DurationInDays are publicly accessible by default.

Say that you want to display some trips on your page. You can start by defining an array of Trip objects inside your AppComponent class, as shown in Listing 16.7.

LISTING 16.7   app.component.ts Constructor with the trips Array

```
export class AppComponent {
  title = 'My Cool Application';
  trips: Trip[] = [
    new Trip('New York City', 5),
    new Trip('Las Vegas', 2)
  ];
}
```

Two trips are identified: one to New York City for five days and one to Las Vegas for two days. The trips property is publicly accessible, and you can start to display the trips in your HTML template with a simple loop using the *ngFor attribute directive.

*ngFor is an attribute directive that indicates to Angular that the element should be repeated based on the collection defined inside the attribute. You can use the moustache notation in app.component.html to build a simple template for your trips with the syntax shown in Listing 16.8.

LISTING 16.8   Outputting Trip Information on Your Page

```
<ul>
  <li *ngFor="let trip of trips">
  {{trip.Destination}} for {{trip.DurationInDays}} days
  </li>
</ul>
```

The `let trip of trips` statement inside `*ngFor` defines the collection to loop over and assigns it to the `trip` variable, using the `let` command. You can then use the properties of the `Trip` object inside your moustache templates to report the destination and duration of the trip.

Now you're ready to add a little more formatting to your trip output. You can add a read-only property to the `Trip` object to indicate if the trip is longer than three days. Listing 16.9 shows the full listing of trip.ts, including this new property.

LISTING 16.9   A Trip with a New Property to Indicate if It Is Considered "Long"

```
export class Trip {
    Destination: string;
    DurationInDays: number;

    constructor(destination: string, durationInDays: number) {
        this.Destination = destination;
        this.DurationInDays = durationInDays;
    }

    public get longTrip(): boolean {
        return this.DurationInDays > 3;
    }

}
```

You can then update your template HTML to test whether the trip is long and apply a CSS class by adding a span and decorating it with the new attribute [class.longTrip], as shown here:

```
<span [class.longTrip]="trip.longTrip">  {{trip.Destination}} for {{trip.
DurationInDays}} days</span>
```

The square brackets around this attribute instruct Angular to execute the contents of the value of the attribute, and if the result is `true`, Angular should apply the `class` attribute and assign the value `longTrip`. The square bracket attribute notation in Angular indicates that the element should be updated with the content of the brackets, based on the output of the value of the attribute. You could write a similar attribute to set the color red or green with syntax like this:

```
[style.color]="trip.Duration>3 ? red : green"
```

Finally, define the `longTrip` style in app.component.css with the following entry at the end of that file:

```
.longTrip {  font-style: italic;  font-weight: bold;  color: red;  text-decoration: underline; }
```

After you save all your files, the browser should refresh automatically and look as shown in Figure 16.5.

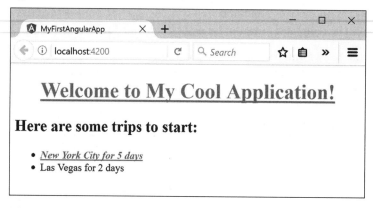

FIGURE 16.5
Reporting on some trips on your first page.

▼ TRY IT YOURSELF

Create a New FAQ Application

Follow these steps to create a new application to display some of the FAQ information that you've written in earlier lessons:

1. Navigate to a new folder in your command shell.

2. Execute `ng new ngFAQ` to create your new FAQ-serving application.

3. Create the `Faq` model by running `ng g class faq`.

4. Add `question` and `answer` properties to the `Faq` class.

5. Create an array of `Faq` objects in your `app_component` class.

6. Reformat app_component.html to use an `ngFor` loop to output your questions and answers.

7. Execute `ng serve` to start serving your application at http://localhost:4200.

Summary

This hour you have learned how to generate your first Angular content with JavaScript, TypeScript, CSS, and a little HTML templating. You have learned about the `ngFor` directive and how to build some very simple templates in Angular. As you have seen, TypeScript and the Angular CLI are very easy to get up and running. TypeScript is as simple as JavaScript, with just a few additional keywords, such as `class`, `export`, and `import`.

The Angular directive and component structures allow the community to create these classes and publish them to the `npm` registry for anyone to download and reference in their applications. Check out https://ng-bootstrap.github.io for a collection of directives that you can add to your project to enable the bootstrap CSS framework for your application.

Q&A

Q. Do I need to use the Angular CLI to use the Angular framework, or can I reference packages and features directly from `npm` or downloaded from the Angular website?

A. You can download and maintain the Angular tools yourself. The Angular CLI makes this maintenance a breeze and can be customized to meet your needs.

Q. `*ngFor` does not look like a valid HTML attribute. Doesn't that create a problem?

A. The attribute is parsed in the HTML template before your browser sees it as part of the page to display. Remember that the template is interpreted by Angular first.

Q. Are there other attribute directives that I should know about?

A. There are *lots* of attribute directives out there, and you can read the documentation about the current in-the-box directives on the Angular documentation site, at angular.io/api?type=directive. In particular, take a look at `ngIf` and `ngModel`, which you will learn about and use over the next few hours.

Q. Can I trust that Angular 4 will be supported for a long time?

A. Angular is an open source project, and you can therefore always find the source code available for the libraries. Very large teams of contributors are writing features and fixes that you can download and add to your project at any time. As long as there are still contributors who publish their updates, you will have support.

Workshop

The workshop contains quiz questions and exercises to help you solidify your understanding of the material covered. Try to answer all questions before looking at the "Answers" that follow.

Quiz

1. Where on the web can you find the Angular website, with a blog, documentation, and examples?

2. What does the *ngFor command do?

3. What is a component?

4. How can you start up your Angular application so that you can browse to it?

5. To where do you navigate in your browser in order to view your Angular application?

Answers

1. www.angular.io

2. *ngFor is an attribute directive that instructs Angular to repeat the current element based on a loop collection declared in the contents of the *ngFor attribute.

3. An Angular component is a collection of TypeScript, CSS, and an HTML template that can be referenced and executed, with the results painted onscreen.

4. You can start the Angular application by using the ng serve command in a terminal window.

5. By default, the Angular CLI presents your application at http://localhost:4200.

Exercise

You just started building a Trip object and formatting its information onscreen. Using the properties of the C# Trip object, write a TypeScript version of this object. With your new Trip object, enhance the trip list on the app.component.html page to contain a rich table like the table you previously built with ASP.NET in Hour 10, "Beginning MVC: Writing Your First View."

HOUR 17
Connecting Angular to ASP.NET Core

What You'll Learn in This Hour:

▶ How to use an Angular service

▶ How to connect Angular and ASP.NET Core project types

▶ How to build Angular and ASP.NET Core projects with one command

As you saw in Hour 16, "Introducing Angular," Angular delivers a great in-browser experience and makes it easy to deliver component-based user interfaces. You saw in Hour 16 that you can use an architecture in Angular that is very similar to the MVC techniques you use on the server with ASP.NET Core. This lesson will push your Angular knowledge further and help you start connecting Angular content to your existing ASPTravlerz project so that your Angular application can fetch and present your trip information onscreen. You will learn how to build two applications as though they were one application. This hour focuses on the Angular and ASP.NET Core applications as two distinct applications and shows you how to deliver a unified experience for your application users.

Connecting the Pieces

In Hour 16 you built a stand-alone project based on Node.js services using command-line tools that allow you to build and debug applications. In Hour 15, "npm and bower: Client-Side Package Managers," you built an ASP.NET Core application that, similarly, would run on its own from a command line and host an application for you to review and debug.

The project you created in Hour 16 shows on a simple screen the collection of trips stored in the TypeScript array that is hard-coded into your `AppComponent` class. In the ASP.NET Core application you created in Hour 15, an API service allows clients to manage trip information at a `/api/Trips` endpoint. This hour, you'll see how to connect the Angular application so that those trips are no longer hard-coded but rather are extracted from a database and presented through the ASP.NET Core application.

Creating and Using an Angular Service

You can start building a connection to the server-side ASP.NET Core application by generating an Angular service object for managing your `Trip` objects. An Angular service is an object that wraps your interactions with an external business service and applies any additional logic you may need in your application. In this case, it will make the HTTP requests to the server, translate, and present TypeScript `Trip` objects. You can take advantage of the Angular command line to generate a service for your `Trip` objects by executing the following code at the command line inside of your Angular app:

```
ng generate service trip
```

You should now see output similar to that shown in Figure 17.1.

```
C:\dev\my-first-angular-app>ng generate service trip
installing service
  create src\app\trip.service.spec.ts
  create src\app\trip.service.ts
  WARNING Service is generated but not provided, it must be provided to be used

C:\dev\my-first-angular-app>
```

FIGURE 17.1
Output of the `ng generate service` command.

Nice. You can see that Angular created a `trip.service.ts` file and a `trip.service.spec.ts` file to contain tests. (This book doesn't focus on the tests, but you can learn more about testing your Angular code at http://angular.io.) In Figure 17.1, note the line `Service is generated but not provided, it must be provided to be used`. The CLI is telling you that the service class is available, and it needs to be imported and requested by a component in order to be used. Listing 17.1 shows the initial contents of the `trip.service.ts` file.

LISTING 17.1   Initial trip.service.ts File Contents

```typescript
import { Injectable } from '@angular/core';

@Injectable()
export class TripService {

  constructor() { }

}
```

These contents appear very tame, but you should be aware that Angular generated two things for you:

▶ The class generated is named `TripService`, even though you asked Angular to generate a service named `trip`. This pattern of conversion to UpperCamelCase notation and ending with the term `Service` is common throughout the Angular CLI generators.

▶ The service class is decorated with an `Injectable` attribute. This indicates that `TripService` can be injected into other classes for processing, using the same dependency injection pattern you saw with ASP.NET Core in Hour 5, "Configuring the Service with the `Startup` Class."

Next, you'll migrate the array of trips that you had in your app.component.ts file to this service and review the enhancements you made to the `Trip` class at the end of Hour 16. The improved `Trip` class now matches the ASP.NET Core class with a few additional calculated properties for `DurationInDays` and `longTrip`. Listing 17.2 shows the source code.

LISTING 17.2   Improved TypeScript `Trip` Class to Match the ASP.NET Core `Trip` Class

```
export class Trip {
    id: number;
    name: string;
    description: string;
    startDate: Date;
    endDate: Date;
    segments: any;

    private MsPerDay = 24 * 60 * 60 * 1000;

    public constructor(id: number, name: string, desc: string, startDate: Date,
                       endDate: Date) {
        this.id = id;
        this.name = name;
        this.description = desc;
        this.startDate = new Date(startDate);
        this.endDate = new Date(endDate);
    }

    public get Destination(): string {
        return this.name;
    }
```

```
    public get DurationInDays(): number {
        return Math.floor( (this.endDate.valueOf() - this.startDate.valueOf())
            / this.MsPerDay);
    }

    public get longTrip(): boolean {
        return this.DurationInDays > 3;
    }


}
```

The properties of the C# class are defined using lowerCamelCase notation. The `DurationInDays` property is now calculated using the TypeScript `public get` notation for calculated properties. Because `DurationInDays` is the difference between two dates, you have also added the private `MsPerDay` to store the calculated number of milliseconds in a day. This number is used after the difference between `endDate` and `startDate` to convert the value into a number of days.

Finally, the `longTrip` property is a simple comparison to identify whether the duration is longer than three days.

You can now expand your two original `Trip` objects and add them to your service class so that they are returned from a `Get` method. Listing 17.3 shows how this initial simple service looks.

LISTING 17.3   Simple `TripService` Class Returning a Collection of Trips

```
import { Injectable } from '@angular/core';
import { Trip } from './trip';


@Injectable()
export class TripService {

  private trips: Trip[] = [
    new Trip(1, 'NYC', 'Trip to New York City',
      new Date(2017, 9, 2), new Date(2017, 9, 5)),

    new Trip(2, 'Las Vegas', 'Conference in Las Vegas',
      new Date(2017, 9, 30), new Date(2017, 10, 3))
  ];

  constructor() { }


  Get(): Trip[] {
```

```
        return this.trips;

    }


}
```

This is a very simple set of changes. You add a reference to the `Trip` object on line 2, move your `Trip` array to a private collection in the `TripService` object, and construct the `Get` method to return that collection of trips. You next need to wire up `AppComponent` so that it can work with the service and call the `Get` method to retrieve your trips. You can start by adding a reference to `TripService` and opening up the constructor of `AppComponent` to receive `TripService`, as shown in Listing 17.4.

LISTING 17.4 Adapting `AppComponent` **to Work with** `TripService`

```
import { Component } from '@angular/core';

import { Trip } from './trip';
import { TripService } from './trip.service';

@Component({
  selector: 'app-root',
  templateUrl: './app.component.html',
  styleUrls: ['./app.component.css']
})
export class AppComponent {

  title = 'My Cool Application';
  trips: Trip[];

  constructor(private service: TripService) {

    this.trips = service.Get();

  }

}
```

The constructor receives `TripService` with an argument named `svc` and immediately assigns the results of the `Get` method to the `trips` collection that the HTML template binds to. That's a fairly straightforward change. If you save these changes and attempt to load your page, you'll get an empty page in your browser and some truly ugly content dumped into the JavaScript console. You can access the JavaScript console in most browsers by pressing F12. The topmost errors in the Firefox console look as shown in Figure 17.2.

FIGURE 17.2
JavaScript errors reported in the Firefox console.

Yuck! The initial `Disconnected!` comment in the log comes from the Browsersync tool that is refreshing the browser for you. The second entry is the piece that you're interested in: `Error: No provider for TripService`. Remember from Hour 16 that `AppModule` had a definition for a `Providers` array. You need to add a reference to `TripService` in that array so that `AppModule` knows it should provide a new `TripService` to the `AppComponent` at construction time. You can add that reference in the `app.module.ts` `Providers` collection:

```
providers: [ TripService ],
```

After you save that change to app.module.ts, your browser should refresh and present the results shown in Figure 17.3.

FIGURE 17.3
Page with the correct `TripService` functioning.

Success! You have moved the logic for fetching your `Trip` objects to an external service component. The next step in integrating with your ASP.NET Core application is to start triggering HTTP fetch commands to get the trip data from the API you created previously.

Connecting to a Running ASP.NET Core Service

You can start your surgery on `TripService` by importing the `Http` object and allocating a private field for it on the constructor. You should also remove the `Trip` array and clear out the `Get` method, as shown in Listing 17.5.

LISTING 17.5 Introducing the `Http` **Object to** `TripService`

```
import { Injectable } from '@angular/core';
import { Http } from '@angular/http';
import { Trip } from './trip';
@Injectable(
)
export class TripService {

  constructor(private http: Http) { }

    Get():Trip[] {

      return null;

    }

}
```

If you save this change, your browser empties, and another nasty message appears in the JavaScript console. This time, it complains about a missing provider for `Http`. This parallels what you saw earlier, when `TripService` was not available. In this case, `HttpModule` needs to be imported into your module so that a series of resources and features that support the `Http` object are available throughout the Angular application. As shown in Listing 17.6, you should add an `import` statement and add `HttpModule` to the `imports` array of your `AppModule` class.

LISTING 17.6 Importing `HttpModule` **for Use in Server Communications**

```
import { BrowserModule } from '@angular/platform-browser';
import { NgModule } from '@angular/core';
import { HttpModule } from '@angular/http';
```

```
import { AppComponent } from './app.component';
import { TripService } from './trip.service';

@NgModule({
  declarations: [
    AppComponent
  ],
  imports: [
    BrowserModule,
    HttpModule
  ],
  providers: [ TripService ],
  bootstrap: [AppComponent]
})
export class AppModule { }
```

After you save this change, your browser will refresh, and the trips list will be empty. That's to be expected because you are returning null from your service's Get method. You can change that method to actually fetch the data from your ASP.NET Core service. To do so, you need to start the ASP.NET Core service, so at a separate command prompt, execute the following to start the service so that it is listening on port 5000:

```
dotnet run
```

You can then open a browser and navigate to http://localhost:5000/api/trips to verify that your trips collection is delivered to the browser. You can then start filling in the TripService Get method with the necessary code to return these Trip objects.

You're going to use the http.get method to connect to the ASP.NET Core service and fetch data in JSON format. The get method returns an Observable object. This object provides for the interaction with the external service to happen asynchronously. The request to the external service is started, the Observable object is immediately returned, and the Observable object is populated after the operation with the external service completes. You need to map your request from the raw JSON returned from ASP.NET Core into TypeScript-friendly Trip objects. You can update the source of your TripService.Get method with the contents of Listing 17.7 to start this conversion.

LISTING 17.7   Fetching Data by Using the Http Object

```
Get(): Observable<Trip[]> {

  return this.http.get('http://localhost:5000/api/trips')
    .map(response => response.json().map(item => {
      return new Trip(
        item.id,
```

```
      item.name,
      item.description,
      item.startDate,
      item.endDate
    );
  }));

}
```

The `Observable<Trip[]>` notation means that that you are changing the signature of the `Get` method to return an `Observable` object of a `Trip` array type. This supports the notion that the ASP.NET Core service may not return immediately, and the contents of the collection will be filled in when the process has completed. The address for the API is specified as an argument to the `http.get` method, and the response from that request is mapped into a new `Trip` object. You need to import these two lines at the top of the trip.service.ts file in order to get this to compile:

```
import 'rxjs/Rx';
import { Observable } from 'rxjs/Observable';
```

These are reactive extensions for Angular and contain the definition of the `Observable` object and the helper map method that you are using to handle the data returned from the service. With this update, your application no longer compiles properly because `AppComponent` was expecting a trip array to be returned. Next you will update your app.component.ts file to work with the new return type from this method. You don't want this heavy asynchronous operation to occur during the construction of `AppComponent` but rather after the framework has initialized it for use. You can implement the `OnInit` interface to indicate to the Angular framework that this code should execute after the component is initialized. Listing 17.8 shows these updates.

LISTING 17.8   Updated app.component.ts File to Support the Returned `Observable Object`

```
import { Component } from '@angular/core';
import { OnInit } from '@angular/core';

import { Trip } from './trip';
import { TripService } from './trip.service';

@Component({
  selector: 'app-root',
  templateUrl: './app.component.html',
  styleUrls: ['./app.component.css']
})
export class AppComponent implements OnInit {
```

```
title = 'My Cool Application';
trips: Trip[];

constructor(private service: TripService) {}

ngOnInit(): void {
  this.service.Get().subscribe(trips => this.trips = trips);
}

}
```

Notice that the class declaration now includes the terms `implements OnInit`, and you have imported the `OnInit` object. This inclusion gives your class the `ngOnInit` method and identifies to the Angular framework that this method is available for use. It is here that you now call the service's `Get` method and use the resulting `Observable` object's `subscribe` keyword to assign the output to the `trips` property on your `AppComponent`. The `subscribe` method declares code that should be executed when the `Observable` object's content changes. In this case, when the `Http` method completes and populates the `Observable` object inside the service's `Get` method, the `trips` property on the `AppComponent` is populated.

You should now see your server-side trips reported in the browser, right? Well, not quite. You should actually see an error message similar to the one in Figure 17.4 in your browser.

FIGURE 17.4
Error fetching data from localhost:5000.

`Cross-Origin Request Blocked` is an error raised by the ASP.NET Core application as a security precaution to prevent requests to your application from external domains, using a standard called CORS.

NOTE

Introducing the CORS Standard

Web server operators use CORS, which stands for Cross-Origin Resource Sharing, to grant or block access to the contents of the server when requested by an application. Web browsers and ASP.NET Core have a default policy called Same-Origin Policy that prevents JavaScript (such as your Angular application) from being executed against the server from a different host and port combination.

To work around this issue, you need to tell Angular to configure a proxy for requests to the ASP. NET Core server and route them appropriately. Your final configuration of the application will host these two resources on the same host, so this is a valid use of the proxy-config option for the Angular CLI while in development mode. You can write a file called proxy-config.json into the root of the Angular project and populate it with the contents of Listing 17.9.

LISTING 17.9   proxy-config.json File Contents

```
{
    "/api": {
        "target": "http://localhost:5000",
        "secure": false,
        "logLevel": "debug"
    }
}
```

This file defines the locations on the Angular server that should instead be routed to other locations if they allow the request. `target` specifies the location of the service to forward requests to, `secure` indicates that no TLS connection is required, and `logLevel` indicates that the requests forwarded to another server should be logged on the command line. This additional logging information will help in the future if you want to observe when the requests are actually forwarded to ASP.NET Core from Angular.

ASP.NET Core by default allows the request from another localhost resource, such as your Angular CLI hosted web page, but the browser will block the request because it is going to another web server. You can activate this proxy configuration by restarting your Angular server with this command:

```
ng serve --proxy-config proxy-config.json
```

Finally, you have to change the request address in `TripService` to point to /api/trips instead of the full URL of the service:

```
return this.http.get('/api/trips')
```

This should result in the data from your ASP.NET Core service being returned in the browser and displayed as the list of trips, as shown in Figure 17.5.

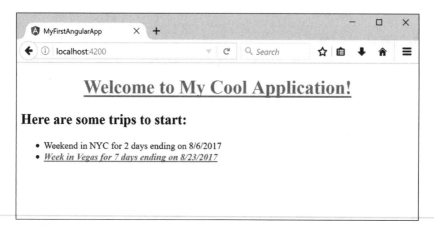

FIGURE 17.5
Data fetched from ASP.NET Core and presented on the Angular website.

You've done it! You have your Angular application querying and presenting your ASP.NET Core content.

Combining the Projects: Merging Angular and ASP.NET Core

At this point, you have two projects that know how to talk to each other, and they're not really a combined single application that could be published easily to a web server for visitors. You need to simplify things by making the Angular application the front end to the ASP.NET Core application so that you can browse to one location and get all the content from your combined application.

You can start by copying the contents of your Angular application into a new folder off the root of your ASPTravlerz application called ClientApp. This folder will have its build triggered as part of the overall build process for your ASP.NET Core application.

Next, you need to edit the AspTravlerz.csproj file and make some modifications to enable this child build process. You need to tell MSBuild to ignore the new TypeScript files that you added into the ClientApp folder, and you can do that with the `TypeScriptCompileBlocked` element. Insert this element in the first `PropertyGroup` with a value of `true`, as shown here:

```
<TypeScriptCompileBlocked>true</TypeScriptCompileBlocked>
```

Next, you need to tell MSBuild and Visual Studio to ignore the node_modules folder inside the ClientApp folder by using a new `ItemGroup` that excludes this folder and all child folders. Add the `ItemGroup` shown in Listing 17.10 to the bottom of the file, just inside the closing `Project` tag.

LISTING 17.10 Using `ItemGroup` to Exclude ClientApp/node_modules

```
<ItemGroup>
  <Compile Remove="ClientApp\node_modules\**" />
  <Content Remove="ClientApp\node_modules\**" />
  <EmbeddedResource Remove="ClientApp\node_modules\**" />
  <None Remove="ClientApp\node_modules\**" />
</ItemGroup>
```

You need to add the task to trigger the Angular command line to build the application. You can do that by inserting a new `Target` element below the previous `ItemGroup`. This `Target` element will be triggered before the `Build` step and will execute the `ng build` command for you inside the ClientApp folder. Listing 17.11 shows how easy it is to do this in the csproj file.

LISTING 17.11 Using `Target` to Build the Angular ClientApp Folder

```
<Target Name="BuildAngular" BeforeTargets="Build">
  <Exec Command="ng build" WorkingDirectory="ClientApp" />
</Target>
```

Now you can try it out by executing `dotnet build` at the command line. As shown in Figure 17.6, you see the same build information you saw when you built your ASP.NET Core application combined with the Angular build information you remember from Hours 15 and 16.

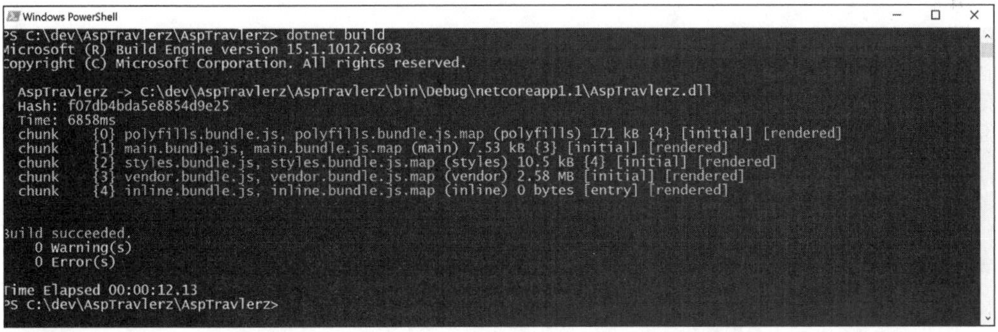

FIGURE 17.6
Building both applications with the `dotnet` tool.

Now with one build process, you have two projects and one output. There's just one slight problem: The Angular build created a child folder under ClientApp called dist and placed its content in there. That's not where you need your static content for the front end of the application to be placed; you need it in the wwwroot folder. You need to move the current contents of the wwwroot folder into the ClientApp/assets folder because that's where all static assets outside Angular are placed. Next, you need to edit the ClientApp/.angular-cli.json configuration file to tell it where you would like your Angular application deployed. You need to update the `outDir` setting in this file to point to the wwwroot folder as shown here:

```
"outDir": "../wwwroot",
```

You need to include the "parent folder" notation (. .) to indicate that the wwwroot folder resides as a sibling to the ClientApp folder. Now if you run the build process, your wwwroot folder contents are replaced with the contents of your Angular application. Perfect! Now you can start your application with `dotnet run` and browse to your application at http://localhost:5000/index.html to see your Angular application connecting to the API and returning properly (see Figure 17.7).

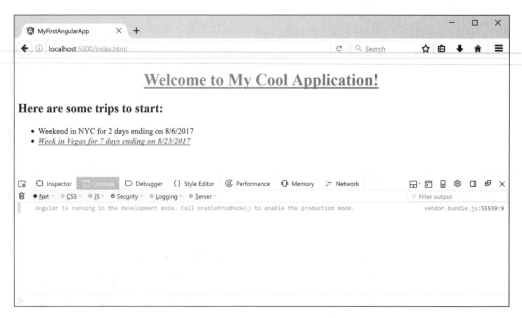

FIGURE 17.7
ASP.NET Core application hosting your Angular content.

Now your applications build together and can be deployed together.

CAUTION

Two Separate Development Environments

While the applications will build together, they can negatively affect each other. If you build and debug with the `dotnet` application, you will not be able to edit and get the live response to your Angular code that you experienced in Hours 15 and 16. When you're actively developing Angular content, I recommend that you start and run your Angular development server separately at the command line using the proxy configuration arguments, as shown earlier this hour. However, every time you make a change to your Angular code, the live-reload will clear the contents of the wwwroot folder and not replace it.

▼ TRY IT YOURSELF

Add an FAQ Service

At the end of Hour 16, you created a simple FAQ application. Now you can extend it with an FAQ service that returns your collection of questions. In Hour 18, "Routing Angular Requests Around ASP.NET Core," you will combine it with your Angular and ASP.NET Core ASPTravlerz app. Follow these steps to add the FAQ service:

1. Generate the `Faq.service` class by navigating in a command shell to your ngFAQ application and running `ng g service faq`.

2. Migrate the `faqs` array from `app.component` to the new `Faq.service` class.

3. Add a method called `Get()` to the `Faq.service` class that returns the array of FAQs.

4. Add a constructor to the `app.component` class that accepts the input parameter `private service: FaqService`.

5. Inside the constructor, assign the results of `service.Get()` to a `faqs` property on the `app.component` class.

6. Update `app.module` to include the `Faq.service` class in the list of providers for the module.

7. Start the application with `ng serve`, navigate to http://localhost:4200, and observe the list of your FAQs coming from a service now instead of from the component class.

Summary

In this hour, you have connected your Angular application to the ASP.NET Core APIs for your trip application. You now have an Angular browser application that queries and returns data from ASP.NET Core. In addition, you have merged the two applications so that they can be managed as a single project. You have learned how to build Angular and ASP.NET Core components with a single build process.

Q&A

Q. The Angular build process drops some very large files into the wwwroot folder. Is this really what I should deploy to my production web space?

A. No. This is a development configuration with extra assets deployed so that you can receive debug information in your browser console. In Hour 22, "Deploying to Production," you will learn the steps to deploy an optimized configuration to your production space.

Q. How does this configuration work on a continuous integration service like TeamCity, Jenkins, or Visual Studio Team Services?

A. You need `npm`, the Angular CLI, and the .NET SDK installed on those services just as you would if you were building an Angular application or a .NET Core application. The combination of the two project types should be configured as an ASP.NET Core application being built with the command-line `dotnet` tool.

Q. I can read data and present it with Angular in the browser. Now how do I start writing that data as well?

A. Spoiler alert: You'll learn the answer to this question in Hour 18.

Q. Are there extensions to Visual Studio 2017 I should install to more easily manage my Angular project?

A. For Visual Studio 2017, I recommend that you install Web Essentials 2017, which includes a number of extensions to improve your web development experience. Angular developers have flocked to Visual Studio Code, and I recommend that you work on your Angular code with this slimmer editor that has some amazing extensions, including the following:

▶ **Angular Language Service**—This extension teaches the Visual Studio Code IntelliSense how to navigate the Angular application so that you get IntelliSense when referencing component properties and tag attributes in HTML templates.

▶ **vscode-icons**—This nifty little icon package assigns different icons to your files in the project list.

▶ **TSLint**—This TypeScript linter automatically inspects your TypeScript files for code style issues.

▶ **AutoImport**—This extension automatically scans your TypeScript files and adds the import statements for you as you are coding.

Workshop

The workshop contains quiz questions and exercises to help you solidify your understanding of the material covered. Try to answer all questions before looking at the "Answers" that follow.

Quiz

1. Where do you have to define the list of Angular services that you would like injected into your components?

2. What do you need to import in order to enable AJAX interactions with an HTTP server?

3. In order to facilitate an asynchronous request to an HTTP server, what type is returned from the service's `Get` operation?

4. What method does the `OnInit` interface provide, and when is this method executed?

5. What does CORS stand for?

6. What is the default CORS policy in browsers, and what does it prevent?

Answers

1. You define services and other components to be injected in the `Providers` array of your Angular module's `NgModule` decorator.

2. `HttpModule` needs to be in the `@NgModule Imports` array.

3. `Observable<Trip[]>` is returned to allow the `Trip` array to be populated when the request for data is completed.

4. `OnInit` provides the `ngOnInit` method that is executed each time the component is initialized for presentation onscreen.

5. CORS stands for Cross-Origin Resource Sharing and refers to the capability for web applications to share resources with other domains.

6. The Same-Origin Policy prevents the browser from accessing resources on a different scheme (HTTP or HTTPS), host, and port from the page they are currently displaying.

Exercise

Now that you have moved your layout and interactions into Angular, update the ClientApp/src/index.html file to use the bootstrap layout with the menu bar and CSS from the original ASP.NET Core template. You will enhance this layout in Hour 18, as you add more features to the Angular application.

HOUR 18
Routing Angular Requests Around ASP.NET Core

What You'll Learn in This Hour:

▶ How to configure and use the server-side ASP.NET Core router
▶ How to use the Angular client-side router
▶ How to use multiple Angular components in an application
▶ How to mix and match the use of both router technologies

Way back in Hour 5, "Configuring the Service with the `Startup` Class," you saw a snippet of configuring the `Startup` class in your application with a statement that contained the `MapRoute` function call. This hour, you will learn about the server-side routing configuration options in ASP.NET Core, the client-side routing options with Angular, and how you can mix and match these features to deliver a cohesive application to your visitors.

What Is Routing?

Basically, routing is a technique for mapping URLs requested from your application to functionality that should be delivered to the browser. The application maintains a routing table that contains a list of templated URLs and the destination functionality to provide. The routing functionality of the ASP.NET Core or Angular framework uses this table to determine which functionality to serve based on how the templated URLs match the URL requested of the application. In addition, routing can be used to generate a URL for desired functionality that you'd like your visitor to access.

Configuring ASP.NET Core Routing

Listing 18.1 shows an entry in the `Startup.Configure` method that adds a very simple routing table entry to your application.

LISTING 18.1 Adding MVC and Configuring the Default Route

```
app.UseMvc(routes =>
{
  routes.MapRoute("default", "{controller=Home}/{action=Index}/{id?}");
});
```

This initial route provided in the ASP.NET Core template is called the default route, and it is the pattern typically used for URLs in ASP.NET MVC applications. The "default" parameter is the name of the route and can be used later in your C# code to reference this route. The second parameter is the template URL to match against. Let's look at this piece by piece:

▶ {controller=Home} is a token that should be captured and used as the controller route parameter. You know this because this element is surrounded by curly braces. This token captures the controller class that ASP.NET Core should use to serve the request. The =Home segment indicates that if the initial segment of the URL is missing, it should default to HomeController.

▶ The forward slash indicates that there should be a slash in the URL if there is more content present. This makes the URL look like a folder and file requested from disk.

▶ The next token, {action=Index}, captures the action route parameter. This parameter defines which method within the controller class should be triggered for this request. If there is no action element captured in this URL, the Index action will be used by default.

▶ Another forward slash does the same thing as the first one. (See a pattern here?)

▶ The last element attempts to capture a final token called id that will be passed to the route parameters. This is helpful when you want to navigate to a URL such as Trips/Details/1. The id, if present, will be passed in as an argument to the action identified in the previous segment. The question mark indicates that the id parameter is optional, and a null value will be passed if there is an id parameter in the method chosen by the router.

Table 18.1 shows the various requests that match this route, how they map to actual route parameter values, and what method will be triggered.

TABLE 18.1 URLs That Match the Default Route and Executed Code

URL	Method Executed
/	HomeController.Index()
/Home	HomeController.Index()
/Home/About	HomeController.About()
/Trips	TripsController.Index()
/Trips/Details	TripsController.Details(default(int?))
/Trips/Details/1	TripsController.Details(1)

Notice with the /Trips/Details URL that when an id is not passed as a final segment of the URL, no argument value is passed in to the Details method. This could be a problem if your Details method expects to always have an integer id argument. How can you improve this?

The default controller with Entity Framework templates in ASP.NET Core generates a nullable int (int?) as the parameter type for the Details method. This allows a default value of null to be submitted as the id argument. The template populates the Details method with two checks to ensure that valid data is handled:

▶ An initial validation that the id is not null

▶ A check that a search for the model—in this case a Trip object—locates an object with the key submitted

In both validations, the default error handling is to return a NotFound() result to the visitor. With the standard error handling in ASP.NET Core, this returns an empty page and an HTTP 404 status code indicating that "Not Found" is presented for the browser or HttpClient to handle. This doesn't provide a great user experience.

You can improve this slightly by still returning an HTTP 404 status code but including some HTML with a helpful link to return the visitor to the trips index page. Listing 18.2 shows how you can update the Details method to make this happen.

LISTING 18.2 Updated Details **Method with a Friendly** NotAvailable **Message**

```
public async Task<IActionResult> Details(int? id)
{

  if (id == null)
  {
    Response.StatusCode = (int)HttpStatusCode.NotFound;
    ViewBag.Id = id;
    return View("NotAvailable");
  }

  var trip = await _context.Trips.SingleOrDefaultAsync(m => m.ID == id);
  if (trip == null)
  {
    Response.StatusCode = (int)HttpStatusCode.NotFound;
    ViewBag.Id = id;
    return View("NotAvailable");
  }

  return View(trip);
}
```

In this code, you set the `ViewBag.Id` property to the value of the `id` submitted. `ViewBag` is a dynamic object that allows you to assign any values you would like to carry into your view to any property that you name. You conjured up the `Id` property on `ViewBag`, but you could name it anything you like, as long as you know how to refer to that property in your `View` method.

The `View` method returned in the validation checks is passed the name "NotAvailable", indicating the name of the view to use as the output. You can create a simple razor view in your / Views/Trips folder named NotAvailable.cshtml and paste in the code shown in Listing 18.3.

LISTING 18.3 The NotAvailable.cshtml File Content

```
@{
  ViewData["Title"] = ViewBag.Id == null ?
    "No Trip Selected" : "Trip Not Found";
}

<h2>@ViewData["Title"]</h2>

<p>Unable to locate the requested trip with id (@ViewBag.Id).</p>

<a asp-action="index">Back to the list of Trips</a>
```

Here you simply format the information about the trip requested and give a link at the bottom so the visitor can return to the complete list of trips on the index page.

Say that you also want your visitors to be able to navigate to a URL such as /Trips/Details/ Weekend in NYC in the application, This would seem to fit your route template, but Weekend in NYC is not an integer, so how can you provide this functionality?

You can start by adding a second `Details` method to your `TripsController` class that accepts a string parameter and finds that trip, as demonstrated in Listing 18.4.

LISTING 18.4 Added `Details` Method That Accepts the Name of a Trip

```
public async Task<IActionResult> Details(string name)
{

  if (name == null)
  {
    Response.StatusCode = (int)HttpStatusCode.NotFound;
    ViewBag.Id = null;
    return View("NotAvailable");
  }

  var trip = await _context.Trips.SingleOrDefaultAsync(m => m.Name == name);
  if (trip == null)
```

```
{
   Response.StatusCode = (int)HttpStatusCode.NotFound;
   ViewBag.Id = name;
   return View("NotAvailable");
}

   return View(trip);
}
```

The only real changes from the previous `Details` method is the input parameter changing from an integer named `id` to a string named `name` and the query searching on the Name field of the trip. If you try to navigate to the `/Trips/Details/Weekend in NYC` page now, you get routed to the `NotAvailable` page, with a null value reported. In this case, you need to add an additional routing table rule to instruct the router to use this method when the third segment of the URL is a string (containing letters, numbers, and special characters) is matched. You can add this rule to your controller by adding an `HttpGet` attribute above the method.

The `HttpGet` attribute instructs the router to use the decorated method when the GET verb is used to request content. The first (optional) parameter of the attribute is the route template to be matched for this method. Consequently, you can craft a more constrained route template for this method:

```
[HttpGet("Trips/Details/{name:regex([[\\w\\W]]+)}")]
```

This template contains the explicit URL elements that you want to match, `Trips/Details/`, and then you see the curly braces with the name parameter that you want to capture. The `:regex(...)` content is new. These elements instruct the router to apply a constraint that the captured parameter must satisfy the regular expression enclosed in parentheses in order to be matched. The regular expression has some escaped characters from a standard expression because it is being used in a .NET string as part of this constraint:

▶ The square brackets (`[]`) are duplicated to escape their usage as part of the route table, where they can be used in other routing notation.

▶ Backslashes (`\\`) are duplicated in order to escape the standard .NET string backslash escape character.

This regular expression matches any word that has a mixture of numbers, letters, and special characters with a length greater than one. This should work great for your new `Details` method, but it will also match the integers that you want to use with your previous `Details` method. You need to add a second `HttpGet` attribute to that method, with the following syntax:

```
[HttpGet("Trips/Details/{id:int}")]
```

This time, the id parameter has the constraint int applied to it. As you might guess, it restricts the usage of this method to only URLs that contain an integer in the third segment. With these two attributes in place, your new routes work properly.

Table 18.2 lists the other constraints you can apply to your routes in the route table.

TABLE 18.2 Available Route Constraints in ASP.NET Core

Constraint	Example	Matches
int	{id:int}	1234
bool	{active:bool}	True
datetime	{startdate:datetime}	2017-08-01
decimal	{cost:decimal}	5.00
double	{distance:double}	300.2
float	{weight:float}	300.2
guid	{id:guid}	12b86598-de84-4877-85de-37831ec779e5
long	{ticks:long}	123456789
minlength(value)	{destination:minlength(2)}	New York
maxlength(value)	{name:maxlength(20)}	Weekend in NYC
length(value)	{filename:length(12)}	thisfile.htm
length(min,max)	{name:length(2,20)}	Weekend in NYC
min(value)	{duration:1}	2
max(value)	{duration:30}	20
range(min,max)	{duration:range(1,30)}	14
alpha	{name:alpha}	Jeff
regex(expression)	{flightnum:regex([a-z]+-\d+)}	AA-123
required	{name:required}	Weekend in NYC

Your configuration still feels strange because now you have three rules that could all apply to the /Trips/Details/1 URL. It certainly matches the default rule, but it also matches your integer constraint and your regular expression constraint. How does the router choose which method to apply in this scenario?

First, the ASP.NET Core router identifies that you have specified a route as an attribute on the method. The attributes take top precedence over any routes specified in the Startup class's configuration of the router. Second, the integer constraint and the regular expression constraint are higher precedence than an unconstrained parameter, but you already eliminated the unconstrained parameter in the first step. Next, if there is an Order property set on the route, which you can define in the attributes or in the MapRoute statements in Startup.cs, the matching routes are sorted in ascending order, based on the `Order` property. Finally, the matching routes are ordered alphabetically, and the `id` parameter comes before the `name` parameter, so it takes precedence if a number is submitted. The order of route-matching precedence is summarized in Figure 18.1.

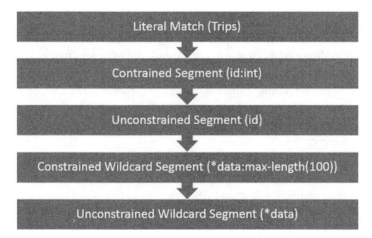

FIGURE 18.1
Routing match precedence before sorting by ascending order and finally by ascending name.

The last two items in Figure 18.1 are items we have not discussed. You can craft your route parameters to capture any text (including no text) at the end of the URL by prefixing it with an asterisk (*). These values can either be ignored or passed in as an argument value to a method for further analysis.

Generating URLs from ASP.NET Core

Routing in ASP.NET Core is a two-way street: You can also use the route table to generate URLs for a given method and controller combination. Do you remember using the anchor tag helper with the `asp-controller` and `asp-action` attributes in Hour 14, "Introducing Reusable User Interface Components"? Now you can see that those are segments of the route that should be used to generate the URL. You could also use the `asp-route-*` attributes to add a reference to the other elements of the captured route parameters for which you need to generate a URL. For example, you could use your `Details` route to generate a route with the name of your weekend in NYC trip with the following markup:

```
<a asp-action="Details" asp-controller="Controller" asp-route-name="Weekend in
NYC">Weekend in NYC</a>
```

There is also an HTML helper that triggers this same functionality, but I recommend using the tag helper for clarity and ease of seeing exactly what format will be delivered to the browser.

In addition, you can use these route parameters when redirecting as part of the `Redirect` method inside a controller. Simply return `RedirectToAction` as follows:

```
return RedirectToAction("Details", "Trips", new { name = "Weekend in NYC" });
```

Routing in Angular

On the client side, when your visitors are clicking through your Angular application, they can be routed between various client-side components without making additional trips to the server for user interface components. This client-side routing capability is another module for you to configure in your Angular application, using the `Routes` object exposed by the `@angular/router` module. You can generate a module to contain the information about your routing with the following command in the command shell:

```
ng g module app-routing -flat
```

This gives you a bare module to start adding the routing features to, but you also need to include it in your application. You can add `AppRoutingModule` to your `imports` attribute in app.module.ts as shown in Listing 18.5.

LISTING 18.5   Importing `AppRoutingModule` into app.module.ts

```
import { AppRoutingModule } from './app-routing.module';
@NgModule({
  declarations: [
    AppComponent
  ],
  imports: [
    AppRoutingModule,
    BrowserModule,
    FormsModule,
    HttpModule
  ],
  providers: [ TripService ],
  bootstrap: [AppComponent]
})
export class AppModule { }
```

Now you can start writing the directions for Angular to route requests to additional components on the client side with `AppRoutingModule`. You can start with a very simple route for your AppComponent, as shown in Listing 18.6.

LISTING 18.6 Routing in `AppRoutingModule` in app-routing.module.ts

```
import { NgModule } from '@angular/core';
import { RouterModule, Routes } from '@angular/router';
import { AppComponent } from './app.component';
const appRoutes: Routes = [
  { path: '**', component: AppComponent }
];
@NgModule({
  imports: [
    RouterModule.forRoot(appRoutes)
  ],
  exports: [ RouterModule ]
})
export class AppRoutingModule { }
```

You import a set of modules at the start that give you the ability to build a module that defines routing information. `AppComponent` is imported as well because you are going to route all requests to it. The `appRoutes` variable defines the collection of paths to match and the corresponding component to trigger when that path is identified. This concept is identical to the routing concepts in ASP.NET Core: Match a path that was requested and trigger functionality based on that string matching some information.

The assignment of the routes to your application happens in the `RouterModule.forRoot` statement. This statement is triggered when the module is included and applies the routing configuration to `AppModule`. You could eliminate this module altogether and just include these few statements to define `appRoutes` and import `RouterModule` directly into `AppModule`, but keeping the configuration of the router here means that you do not need to change `AppModule` when adding routes to the application.

The only route that is defined in your collection at this point matches all paths with the double-asterisk (**) notation and triggers `AppComponent`, which is where your application is at this point. However, you already have your application configured to render `AppComponent` when a visitor first navigates to your application; this is your root component. You should update `AppComponent`'s HTML template to indicate where the results of the router should be placed, but doing so creates a circular reference, and you're starting to add too many things to the single `AppComponent`.

You can use a second component, `TripComponent`, that is specific to displaying the trip objects. You can generate a set of files for this component with the following Angular command:

```
ng g component trip -flat
```

You can now move all the contents of app.component.ts, app.component.html, and app.component.css that relate to your trips user interface into the corresponding trip.component.ts,

trip.component.html, and trip.component.css. Listing 18.7 shows the new contents of the trip.
component.ts file.

LISTING 18.7   Relocated Contents of trip.component.ts

```
import { Component, OnInit } from '@angular/core';

import { Trip } from './trip';
import { TripService } from './trip.service';

@Component({
  selector: 'app-trip',
  templateUrl: './trip.component.html',
  styleUrls: ['./trip.component.css']
})
export class TripComponent implements OnInit {

  trips: Trip[];
  selectedTrip: Trip = null;

  constructor(private service: TripService) { }

  ngOnInit(): void {
    this.service.Get().subscribe(trips => this.trips = trips);
  }

  onSelect(trip: Trip) {
    this.selectedTrip = trip;
  }

}
```

In order to use `TripComponent`, you need to add an `import` statement and an entry in the
declarations of `app.module`, as shown in Listing 18.8.

LISTING 18.8   Additional References in app.module for TripComponent

```
import { TripComponent } from './trip.component';
@NgModule({
  declarations: [
    AppComponent,
    TripComponent
  ],
```

Now you can change `app-routing.module` to point to `TripComponent` for all requests
instead of to `AppComponent`. Don't forget to include `TripComponent` as shown in Listing 18.9.

LISTING 18.9   Adding `TripComponent` **to** `AppRoutingModule`

```
import { TripComponent } from './trip.component';
const appRoutes: Routes = [
  { path: '**', component: TripComponent }
]
```

Finally, you need to clear up that impending circular reference by replacing the trips content in your app.component.html file with a simple `router-outlet` tag that instructs the router where to place its content:

```
<router-outlet></router-outlet>
```

In a real application, you would have multiple components and route requests between those components. To better understand this functionality, you can move the path for `TripComponent` to listen for the /mytrips path and to route all requests for the root URL to that path. You can update your Routes constant in app-routing.module.ts with the content of Listing 18.10 to achieve this.

LISTING 18.10   Modifying the Routes to Respond to the `mytrips` Path

```
const appRoutes: Routes = [
  { path: 'mytrips', component: TripComponent },
  { path: '', redirectTo: '/mytrips', pathMatch: 'full' }
];
```

Notice the new rule that matches the root path and indicates that it should redirect to the /mytrips path. The `pathMatch` argument instructs the router to trigger this rule only if the path matches completely.

This change drops support that you previously had, where any requested URL would deliver the list of trips in the application. You should re-introduce that but instead route to a friendly message indicating that no page was found. You can start by generating a `PageNotFound` component:

```
ng g component PageNotFound -flat
```

Notice that the Angular CLI generates the file named page-not-found.component.ts and still names the component `PageNotFoundComponent`. This ensures that you get the case intended for your components in code and that all files generated are lowercase for simplicity in referencing.

You can delete page-not-found.component.html and page-not-found.component.css and instead embed your simple message in page-not-found.component.ts directly. The contents of this file are shown in Listing 18.11.

LISTING 18.11   Contents of the Simple page-not-found.component.ts File

```
import {Component} from '@angular/core';

@Component({
    template: '<h2>Page Not Found</h2><a routerLink="/mytrips" >Back to the list
of trips</a>',
})
export class PageNotFoundComponent {
}
```

Don't forget to add references to the PageNotFoundComponent in app.module.ts just as you did with TripComponent in Listings 18.8 and 18.9. Then you can add the PageNotFound entry to the routes collection:

```
{ path: '**', component: PageNotFoundComponent }
```

Now if you browse to http://localhost:4200/ThisPageDoesntExist, you should be greeted with the simple Page Not Found message.

This section quickly skipped over an interesting snippet in the template embedded in page-not-found.component.ts: the routerLink attribute. Angular parses this attribute and generates an appropriate JavaScript call to trigger the router to present the contents of the matching path.

Merging Projects: The Final Steps

Up to this point, you may have felt as though you've had two projects, with one nested inside the other and no real way to use the Angular project by itself. You will now merge these two applications so that a request to the root of the ASP.NET Core application returns the content of the Angular application.

First, you need to pull some trickery to get Angular to deliver content that an ASP.NET Core view can consume. To do that, start by creating an empty text file in ClientApp/src called index.cshtml. You will use this file as the new static file that Angular will build its script resources into.

Next, modify the ClientApp/.angular-cli.json configuration file and change the index entry from index.html to index.cshtml.

Finally, modify Views/Home/Index.cshtml so that it now includes the content generated in your new index.cshtml file and provide the app-root element that the Angular framework will look for to begin the application. This file is shown in Listing 18.12.

LISTING 18.12   Contents of the Updated Views/Home/Index.cshtml File

```
<app-root></app-root>

@section scripts {
    @Html.Partial("~/wwwroot/index.cshtml")
}
```

Your angular application now renders on the server the home page of the application by including your _Layout.cshtml from ASP.NET Core and the scripts generated by the Angular build process (Figure 18.2). It's very cool . . . but not yet complete.

Here are some trips to start:

Name	Description	Start Date	End Date	Duration
Weekend in NYC	Train to New York City for the weekend	10/6/2017	10/8/2017	2
Week in Vegas	*Trip with friends to Las Vegas*	*10/14/2017*	*10/21/2017*	*7*

ASP Travlerz Website - Some Rights Reserved by Contributors

FIGURE 18.2
Your combined Angular index page displayed as part of the ASP.NET Core home page.

What happens when someone clicks a link from outside your application and attempts to access the /mytrips path without first running the Angular application? ASP.NET Core does not know how to present that content, but you need to route those requests back to the Angular application so that it can inspect and handle the requests appropriately.

To route the requests, you can add a catch-all route to your ASP.NET Core application's Startup class, as shown in Listing 18.13.

LISTING 18.13   **Additional SPA Catch-all Route to Force Requests into the Angular App**

```
app.UseMvc(routes =>
{

  routes.MapRoute("default", "{controller=Home}/{action=Index}/{id:int?}");

  routes.MapRoute(
    name: "spa-fallback",
    template: "{*url}",
    defaults: new { controller = "Home", action = "Index" });

});
```

You add this code after the default route so that any attempt by the router to locate ASP.NET Core content that doesn't exist gets routed to the Index.cshtml file that you just updated. This means your `PageNotFound` component will also handle any requests for content that does not exist and frame them in your ASP.NET Core layout.

Debugging and Building Your App

Things have changed a bit in the structure of your app, so how do you build it and debug it now?

You have already embedded into your project file a call to build the Angular components when you publish the application, and you need to now do something to build the Angular components as you are actively working on them.

I recommend that you open a command shell window and navigate to the ClientApp folder while you are working in your favorite text editor on the Angular content. Inside the command shell, execute the following:

```
ng build
```

This causes the Angular resources to build and deploy all content to the wwwroot folder. While you are actively working, you can add a watch parameter to that command, and Angular will watch for any changes to your files and republish changes to the wwwroot folder:

```
ng build -watch
```

If you couple this with running the `dotnet watch` command, you can be actively editing any file that should be executed server side or client side, and your application will be automatically rebuilt for you while you are actively working on the code.

▼ TRY IT YOURSELF

Bring Your FAQ to the Merged Application

Follow these steps to introduce `FaqComponent` to display your FAQ from the Angular application:

1. Copy the faq.service.ts and faq.ts files into the ClientApp\src\app folder.

2. Generate `FaqComponent` in ASPTravlerz at the command line with the `ng g component Faq -flat` command.

3. Copy the contents of your app.component.ts file that activated and queried `FaqService` for questions into the new faq.component.ts file.

4. Copy your HTML from the app.component.html file that formatted questions into the faq.component.html file.

5. Add `FaqService` as a provider in the app.module.ts file.

6. Add a route to the routes collection in the app-routing.module.ts file that will route requests for /faq to the new `FaqComponent`.

7. Add a hyperlink in the navbar defined in /Views/Shared/_Layout.cshtml to /faq with the text FAQ so that visitors can access your FAQ.

8. Build the Angular application with `ng build`.

9. Start the ASP.NET Core application and navigate to your application's new FAQ page.

Summary

This hour you have configured routing—the ability to define what functionality is triggered on each request to your application—for both your Angular application and your ASP.NET Core application. You have completed the final integration of those two applications into one mega-application that looks nice, feels very responsive, is easy to maintain, and was fun to develop.

Q&A

Q. Do I need to configure routes for static content?

A. No. Routing is configured for functionality that should be executed by the server (ASP.NET Core) or on the client (Angular).

Q. Can I use ASP.NET Core routing to validate URL parameters?

A. No. You should validate URLs by using routing constraints. Use the constraints to determine which method to execute and perform validation inside that method.

Q. Can I have ASP.NET Core instead of Angular handle the HTTP 404 Page Not Found errors?

A. Yes. It's possible to add some middleware at the top of the ASP.NET Core HTTP pipeline to inspect whether the 404 error is being returned for something that is not static content and determine whether it should be routed to Angular or use the server-side error handler.

Q. Can I still use the Angular CLI server to run my Angular application while developing?

A. Yes. You can continue to run in this manner by publishing to index.html as you did previously, but you will lose the frame of the ASP.NET Core application.

Q. I've heard of a concept called Angular Universal that executes Angular JavaScript code on the server. Can that be used here?

A. Spoiler alert: You're going to learn about this in Hour 19, "Running Angular on the Server."

Workshop

The workshop contains quiz questions and exercises to help you solidify your understanding of the material covered. Try to answer all questions before looking at the "Answers" that follow.

Quiz

1. What purpose does routing serve in an application?

2. Where do you configure routing in an ASP.NET Core application?

3. What Angular module do you use to configure Angular routing?

4. What syntax can you use in an Angular route to capture any nonmatching URL?

5. What is the purpose of the ClientApp/src/index.cshtml file?

Answers

1. Routing defines the functionality that should be triggered for a given URL. In ASP.NET Core, it can also be used in reverse to generate URLs for requested functionality.

2. You configure ASP.NET Core routing in the `Startup.Configure` method and, by default, inside the `UseMvc` statement.

3. The Angular routing functionality is in `@angular/routing`.

4. You can use a double asterisk (**) for the path as a wildcard to capture a path that did not match another route.

5. The index.cshtml file receives the compiled Angular scripts that should be injected into Razor views by using the `@Html.Partial` statement.

Exercise

Go back into the FAQ component that you have been building in the Try It Now segments and add the font-awesome glyphs to the HTML template in the same way you added them in your ASP.NET Core view. Should you leave your ASP.NET Core view for FAQ, or should you remove it in favor of the Angular `FaqComponent`?

You've built out your application now and merged Angular and ASP.NET Core into a cohesive application. Try using `dotnet publish` to generate a folder with your composite application and run the application from that published folder.

HOUR 19
Running Angular on the Server

What You'll Learn in This Hour:

▶ What is Angular Universal?

▶ How to add more templates to the .NET SDK

▶ How SpaServices works

JavaScript-rendered web pages are amazing. Interactive and very responsive, these sites are just as good as applications written for native platforms. However, not all browsers see them the same way. In fact, search engines and embedded references from sites like Twitter and Facebook don't see rendered JavaScript content at all. How do you address that? You render JavaScript as HTML on the server.

Introducing Angular Universal

JavaScript is typically executed in the browser after it has been delivered from a server. Thanks to Node.js, you can now consider running JavaScript code in lots of other places: at the command line, in desktop applications, and on the server. The trick is always the same: Use JavaScript to access some APIs exposed by the environment through a platform-specific framework and interact with them using standard JavaScript constructs. But what if you could use JavaScript on the server to render code that is standard HTML and JavaScript that the browser could pick up and start presenting immediately, without having to interpret and execute any initial code?

That is exactly what Angular Universal does. It is a server-side architecture specification for working with Angular code. It has three distinct advantages:

▶ **Better perceived performance**—Because the output of Angular on the server is rendered HTML and JavaScript, there is no waiting for a server to paint the first Angular component.

▶ **Optimization for search engines**—Rendered HTML can be consumed easily by every search engine, whereas JavaScript execution and interpretation are not handled very well by search engines other than Google or Bing.

▶ **Working site previews**—Social media services like Twitter and Facebook include a default screenshot of your site when someone references it in a tweet or post. The rendered HTML delivered by an Angular Universal application guarantees that there is content for these services to take a screenshot of without executing code in the browser.

Many different server-side programming languages and frameworks deliver the Angular Universal architecture and promise, but this hour focuses on the ASP.NET Core SpaServices templates.

Acquiring SpaServices

For ASP.NET Core, the general feature of server-side JavaScript frameworks are included in SpaServices. These services support the Angular, Aurelia, and React JavaScript frameworks so that you can get the same sort of server-side interaction with your JavaScript code and also write some C# and ASP.NET Core features to run on the server.

You can add the SpaServices templates to your ASP.NET Core development environment by executing the following code at the command line:

```
dotnet new --install Microsoft.AspNetCore.SpaTemplates::*
```

This command downloads the latest version of SpaTemplates from NuGet.org, the public package repository for .NET software. SpaTemplates installs quickly on your workstation, and you can find the new templates available when you execute dotnet new without specifying a template name. Figure 19.1 shows the results you should see after installing these templates.

```
Templates                                   Short Name     Language     Tags
-------------------------------------------------------------------------------------
Console Application                         console        [C#], F#     Common/Console
Class library                              classlib       [C#], F#     Common/Library
Unit Test Project                          mstest         [C#], F#     Test/MSTest
xUnit Test Project                         xunit          [C#], F#     Test/xUnit
ASP.NET Core Empty                         web            [C#]         Web/Empty
ASP.NET Core Web App                       mvc            [C#], F#     Web/MVC
MVC ASP.NET Core with Angular              angular        [C#]         Web/MVC/SPA
MVC ASP.NET Core with Aurelia              aurelia        [C#]         Web/MVC/SPA
MVC ASP.NET Core with Knockout.js          knockout       [C#]         Web/MVC/SPA
MVC ASP.NET Core with React.js             react          [C#]         Web/MVC/SPA
MVC ASP.NET Core with React.js and Redux   reactredux     [C#]         Web/MVC/SPA
MVC ASP.NET Core with Vue.js               vue            [C#]         Web/MVC/SPA
ASP.NET Core Web API                       webapi         [C#]         Web/WebAPI
Solution File                              sln                         Solution
```

FIGURE 19.1
The new list of templates available after installing SpaTemplates.

You can then start a new Angular with ASP.NET Core application in the current folder by simply executing this command:

```
dotnet new angular
```

You must then restore your .NET packages with the following command:

```
dotnet restore
```

Finally, you need to install the JavaScript content by executing the following:

```
npm install
```

With your .NET and JavaScript packages all installed and configured for your application, you can start this application with the following command:

```
dotnet run
```

The website listens on http://localhost:5000, and you will see a significantly different template from the standard Bootstrap templates you're familiar with the ASP.NET team delivering. It should look similar to the site shown in Figure 19.2.

Hello, world!

Welcome to your new single-page application, built with:

- ASP.NET Core and C# for cross-platform server-side code
- Angular and TypeScript for client-side code
- Webpack for building and bundling client-side resources
- Bootstrap for layout and styling

To help you get started, we've also set up:

- **Client-side navigation.** For example, click *Counter* then *Back* to return here.
- **Server-side prerendering.** For faster initial loading and improved SEO, your Angular app is prerendered on the server. The resulting HTML is then transferred to the browser where a client-side copy of the app takes over.
- **Webpack dev middleware.** In development mode, there's no need to run the webpack build tool. Your client-side resources are dynamically built on demand. Updates are available as soon as you modify any file.
- **Hot module replacement.** In development mode, you don't even need to reload the page after making most changes. Within seconds of saving changes to files, your Angular app will be rebuilt and a new instance injected is into the page.
- **Efficient production builds.** In production mode, development-time features are disabled, and the webpack build tool produces minified static CSS and JavaScript files.

FIGURE 19.2
The initial appearance of an ASP.NET Angular template.

As you can see in Figure 19.2, you have a menu as a left-side bar and content on the right side. There are a few simple pages linked from the left that show some JavaScript functionality running on the client but that can be executed from the server.

TRY IT YOURSELF ▼

Explore the Fetch Data Sample

Follow these steps to see what's going on in the Fetch Data sample on the menu bar:

1. Open your browser's web developer tools and watch the network traffic for the website.

2. Click the Fetch Data link in the menu bar. Notice that the only request to the server is for the weather forecast.

3. Click the Counter link in the menu. Notice that no data is fetched from the server. This is because Angular renders the complete contents of the Counter page, which is already loaded in your browser.

4. Click Fetch Data again and notice that the only data fetched this time is the weather forecast.

5. Refresh your browser by pressing Ctrl+R on the Fetch Data page.

6. Inspect the HTML document that was returned from the /fetchdata request. It has the forecast embedded in it as fully rendered HTML.

Listing 19.1 shows the source code for the fetchdata Angular TypeScript component at /ClientApp/app/components/fetchdata/fetchdata.component.ts.

LISTING 19.1   fetchdata **TypeScript Component**

```
import { Component, Inject } from '@angular/core';
import { Http } from '@angular/http';

@Component({
    selector: 'fetchdata',
    templateUrl: './fetchdata.component.html'
})
export class FetchDataComponent {
    public forecasts: WeatherForecast[];
    constructor(http: Http, @Inject('ORIGIN_URL') originUrl: string) {
        http.get(originUrl + '/api/SampleData/WeatherForecasts').subscribe(result
=> {
            this.forecasts = result.json() as WeatherForecast[];
        });
    }
}

interface WeatherForecast {
    dateFormatted: string;
    temperatureC: number;
    temperatureF: number;
    summary: string;
}
```

This should look very familiar, as it is just another Angular component like the ones you worked on in Hours 16, "Introducing Angular," 17, "Connecting Angular to ASP.NET Core," and 18, "Routing Angular Requests Around ASP.NET Core." There is a new concept here, though: an injected parameter using the @Inject decorator inside the constructor statement. This injects the location of the website so that the subsequent request from the SampleData API can be properly located. The HTML that goes along with this is just as simple, as shown in Listing 19.2.

LISTING 19.2 `Fetchdata` **HTML Template**

```
<h1>Weather forecast</h1>
<p>This component demonstrates fetching data from the server.</p>
<p *ngIf="!forecasts"><em>Loading...</em></p>
<table class='table' *ngIf="forecasts">
    <thead>
        <tr>
            <th>Date</th>
            <th>Temp. (C)</th>
            <th>Temp. (F)</th>
            <th>Summary</th>
        </tr>
    </thead>
    <tbody>
        <tr *ngFor="let forecast of forecasts">
            <td>{{ forecast.dateFormatted }}</td>
            <td>{{ forecast.temperatureC }}</td>
            <td>{{ forecast.temperatureF }}</td>
            <td>{{ forecast.summary }}</td>
        </tr>
    </tbody>
</table>
```

Just as you would expect, this template formats the collection of forecast objects that were retrieved from the ASP.NET Core service. Even more cool, the application is configured for hot module reloading when in the development environment, just as you configured your Angular CLI project in Hour 16. Try adding some HTML to the bottom of this template and saving it. The browser should automatically refresh and show the new content you added.

The referenced service is a standard API controller that renders randomized weather information just to show what it looks like to fetch some complex data from a server. Listing 19.3 shows the `SampleDataController` source code.

LISTING 19.3 `SampleDataController` **Source Code**

```
[Route("api/[controller]")]
public class SampleDataController : Controller
{
    private static string[] Summaries = new[]
    {
        "Freezing", "Bracing", "Chilly", "Cool", "Mild", "Warm", "Balmy", "Hot",
"Sweltering", "Scorching"
    };

    [HttpGet("[action]")]
    public IEnumerable<WeatherForecast> WeatherForecasts()
    {
```

```
        var rng = new Random();
        return Enumerable.Range(1, 5).Select(index => new WeatherForecast
        {
            DateFormatted = DateTime.Now.AddDays(index).ToString("d"),
            TemperatureC = rng.Next(-20, 55),
            Summary = Summaries[rng.Next(Summaries.Length)]
        });
    }
}
```

This is not too magical; it's just random data being generated on the fly for the template. You've seen how the Angular works, and you've seen that it's the same as what you used previously. You've also seen how the data is generated, and you've seen that, also, is the same as what you worked with previously. But how are the two pieces put together and allowed to render on the server? Let's take a look at the home page Razor template in /Views/Home/Index.cshtml, whose contents are showing in Listing 19.4.

LISTING 19.4   Home Page Razor Template

```
[@{
    ViewData["Title"] = "Home Page";
}

<app asp-prerender-module="ClientApp/dist/main-server">Loading...</app>

<script src="~/dist/vendor.js" asp-append-version="true"></script>
@section scripts {
    <script src="~/dist/main-client.js" asp-append-version="true"></script>
}
```

Here is the glue that puts together the two pieces. The asp-prerender-module tag is a special tag helper that is delivered as part of the SpaServices package. You can see a reference to SpaServices in the /Views/_ViewImports.cshtml template to support this tag. Behind the scenes, this tag runs Node.js and injects the results of the Angular application requested for the URL specified.

There is a final place that you'll see the configuration of SpaServices: a route in the Startup class. Listing 19.5 shows the routes configured by default in this template.

LISTING 19.5   SpaServices Default Routing

```
app.UseMvc(routes =>
{
    routes.MapRoute(
        name: "default",
        template: "{controller=Home}/{action=Index}/{id?}");

    routes.MapSpaFallbackRoute(
```

```
        name: "spa-fallback",
        defaults: new { controller = "Home", action = "Index" });
});
```

That final bit, `MapSpaFallbackRoute`, is added just as in Hour 18, to handle URLs that ASP.
NET does not have controllers to respond to. In this case, it hands off control to the Angular
application that resides in `HomeController`'s `Index` view, just like you saw in Hour 18.

There is some extra code added to the .csproj file to configure the node process for executing the
code and preparing it for publication when you are ready to publish the application.

Migrating Your Application to SpaServices

Due to the complex configuration of the Angular template, it's much easier to migrate your
application into an existing Angular Universal application from an ASP.NET Core application.
Follow these steps to migrate your application from the source folder of your ASP.NET Core application to the source folder of the Angular Universal application you created earlier:

1. Copy the entire contents of the Controllers, Data, Migrations, Models, TagHelpers, Views,
   and wwwroot/assets folders into the Angular application.

2. Copy the appsettings.json file into the new application, overwriting the existing file.

3. Update the `Startup.cs` class by replacing the content of the `ConfigureServices` method with your existing content. Also add the following to the `Configure` method above the
   `app.UseMvc` statement:

   ```
   SampleData.InitializeData(app.ApplicationServices, loggerFactory);
   ```

4. Replace the stylesheet references in the head of the _Layout view with the following:

   ```
   <link rel="stylesheet" href="~/dist/vendor.css" asp-append-version="true" />
   <link href="~/assets/site.css" rel="stylesheet" />
   ```

5. Replace the contents of the Views/Home/Index.cshtml with the code shown in Listing 19.6.

LISTING 19.6   Updated Index.cshtml View

```
@{
    ViewData["Title"] = "Home Page";
}


<app asp-prerender-module="ClientApp/dist/main-server">Loading...</app>

<script src="~/dist/vendor.js" asp-append-version="true"></script>
@section scripts {
    <script src="~/dist/main-client.js" asp-append-version="true"></script>
}
```

6. Delete the contents of the ClientApp/app/components folder.

7. Copy the contents of your ClientApp/src/app folder from ASPTravlerz into the new project's ClientApp/app/components folder.

8. The app.module.shared.ts file is the new `AppModule` for your Angular application, and it is included in the client and server versions, called app.module.client and app.module. server. You need to update the contents of this module to reflect the contents of your former app.module.ts, as shown in Listing 19.7.

LISTING 19.7   Updated app.module.shared.ts

```
import { NgModule } from '@angular/core';

import { AppComponent } from './components/app.component'
import { FaqComponent } from './components/faq.component';
import { PageNotFoundComponent } from './components/page-not-found.component';
import { TripComponent } from './components/trip.component'

import { AppRoutingModule } from './components/app-routing.module';

import { FaqService } from './components/faq.service';
import { TripService } from './components/trip.service';

export const sharedConfig: NgModule = {
    bootstrap: [ AppComponent ],
    declarations: [
        AppComponent,
        TripComponent,
        FaqComponent,
        PageNotFoundComponent
    ],
    imports: [
        AppRoutingModule
    ],
    providers: [
        TripService,
        FaqService
    ]
};
```

9. To update app.module.server.ts and app.module.client.ts to also import the providers you declared in your shared module, add the following `providers` line after the imports statement in both files:

```
, providers: [ ...sharedConfig.providers ]
```

10. In the app.component.ts file, change `selector` from `app-root` to just `app`.

11. Update the trip.service.ts file to inject the URL of the site by adding this parameter to the constructor:

```
, @Inject('ORIGIN_URL') private originUrl: string
```

Then add the `originUrl` value to the front of the address requested in the `http.get` method call.

12. Restart your application to rebuild all JavaScript dependencies.

That should do it. You should now be able to restart your ASP.NET Core web application and see the same content that you had previously, but now the Angular content is rendered and handled on the server as needed. If you'd like to add the hot module reloading feature to your application, you can update the `Startup.Configure` method to instruct it to enable the Webpack middleware:

```
app.UseWebpackDevMiddleware(new WebpackDevMiddlewareOptions {
  HotModuleReplacement = true
});
```

You would typically add this inside a block of code that executes only in development environments. You wouldn't want to enable this feature in a production environment.

Summary

In this hour you have pulled together your Angular and ASP.NET Core applications as a unified development experience, behind the SpaServices capabilities. Doing so allows you to deliver a universal Angular application that can be rendered on the server or the client.

Q&A

Q. Do I really need to use this SpaServices approach with my application?

A. No. If your application is going to live on a company intranet, you may want to stay with a pure Angular solution, like the one you completed in Hour 17. However, if you are publishing an application on the Internet for the public to visit, you may want to use the SpaServices approach as it can deliver a better experience for a first click into the application.

Q. Hot module reloading works great with my TypeScript file and HTML templates in the ClientApp folder. Can I get a similar experience with the Razor templates (.cshtml files)?

A. If you are using Visual Studio 2017, you can turn on the BrowserLink feature, and these templates will update for you automatically in the browser as you update them in the editor.

Q. Can I use the `dotnet watch` command with hot module reloading to have my application reload as I make changes to my C# code?

A. Yes. You can use this technique, and hot module reloading should continue to work for you. However, you are working on two different areas of the application and may want to focus on one area at a time to improve your productivity.

Workshop

The workshop contains quiz questions and exercises to help you solidify your understanding of the material covered. Try to answer all questions before looking at the "Answers" that follow.

Quiz

1. Angular Universal architecture delivers on three promises. What are they?

2. What JavaScript frameworks are supported by the SpaTemplates that you installed?

3. How do you configure hot module reloading in an ASP.NET Core application?

4. What does the `@Inject` decorator in `TripService` do?

Answers

1. Better perceived performance, optimization of your application for search engines, and site previews for social media sites

2. Angular, Aurelia, Knockout, React.js, React.js, Redux, and Vue.js

3. Add an entry in the `Startup.Configure` method that runs when in the development environment only and calls `UseWebpackDevMiddleware` to set `WebpackDevMiddlewareOptions.HotModuleReplacement` to `true`.

4. It injects the text value for the base URL of the application. This helps configure the loading of HTTP-served resources on the server by indicating exactly where the HTTP client needs to communicate.

Exercise

This hour you migrated your application to a new format and structure to support the three promises of Angular Universal. Take some time now to tune your FAQ features so that they continue to work in this new environment, following the TripService example shown this hour. You should be able to review your FAQ content easily and quickly in the application when you have completed this task. Finally, add a link to the menu bar to make it easy to get to your improved FAQ.

HOUR 20
Authenticating Your Users

What You'll Learn in This Hour:

▶ How to configure ASP.NET Core authentication
▶ How to configure an application to register new users
▶ How to require a user to be logged in to access features of your application

Authentication is typically confused with authorization in discussing security configuration of an application. *Authentication* is the process of verifying that the person requesting access is who he or she claims to be, and it is typically achieved through a username and password exchange. *Authorization* is the process of verifying that you are allowed access to the feature you are requesting. In this hour, you will learn how to configure authentication for your application using a local datastore and third-party services like Azure Active Directory. You'll then use your new configuration to prevent anonymous, or non-logged-in users, from accessing segments of the application.

Starting a New Application

Way back in Hour 3, "Exploring the New Project Templates," when you started a new application, you had an option to set an authentication option in the Visual Studio New Project template dialog. To remind you, Figure 20.1 shows that New Project template dialog in Visual Studio.

When you choose Web Application from this screen, the Change Authentication button on the right side becomes accessible. If you click that button, you are presented with the options for configuring security in an ASP.NET Core application, as shown in Figure 20.2.

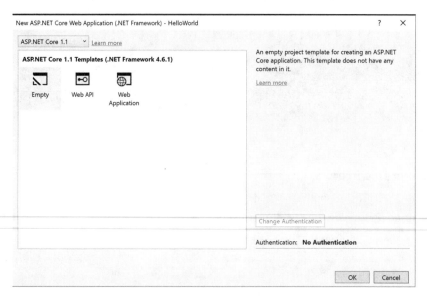

FIGURE 20.1
The New Project template dialog in Visual Studio with the Change Authentication button.

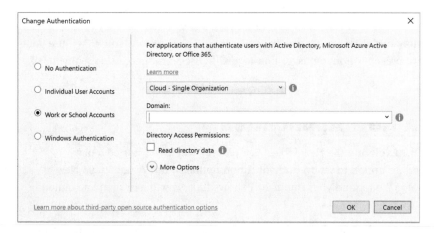

FIGURE 20.2
Authentication configuration options.

There are four options on this screen, each serving a unique purpose:

▶ **No Authentication**—Adds no security to your application and is a good choice if you do not need to restrict access.

▶ **Individual User Accounts**—Creates a local datastore for you to maintain users and their access credentials using Entity Framework.

▶ **Work or School Accounts**—Connects to a cloud authentication service such as Azure Active Directory to delegate maintenance of user accounts and credentials to that service.

▶ **Windows Authentication**—Delegates access control to Windows user management when running on a Windows machine. You may have also heard this referred to as Active Directory or integrated authentication. In order to use this effectively, you must host your service on a Windows web server.

If you are not using Visual Studio, you can also choose to use one of these configuration options when you build a new application from the command line. You can execute the following command to get a list of valid options that you can use:

```
dotnet new mvc --help
```

TRY IT YOURSELF ▼

Build a Sample Application with Azure Active Directory

Follow these steps to explore Azure Active Directory configuration of a new application. You will need a Microsoft Azure account to try this sample.

1. Click Web Application in the Visual Studio New Project template dialog to open the Change Authentication window (refer to Figure 20.2). If you already have an Azure account, the Domain box will already be filled out with the name of your default Azure Active Directory. You can create other directories on Azure, but this one will do for your sample.

2. Select the Read Directory Data check box and click OK. Visual Studio adds your application to the Azure Active Directory and acquires access keys for your application to be able to communicate with the service.

3. Open the appsettings.json file. Examine the new Authentication section that was added; it contains information about where Azure Active Directory resides, your domain, `ClientId`, and `TenantId`. These are key pieces of information that your application uses to interact with the service.

4. Open the Startup.cs file and navigate to the `Configure` method. Notice the calls to `UseCookieAuthentication` and `UseOpenIdConnectAuthentication`. These are the two pieces that connect your application to the authentication service, and no other configuration is required. You will restrict access to components of the application later.

Because you started your application from a very simple empty application, you need to reintroduce authentication to your application by hand; this is a very effective way to learn all the places these services affect your website. To add configuration for individual user accounts using the Microsoft Identity package, add the following line to your list of referenced packages in the .csproj file:

```
<PackageReference Include="Microsoft.AspNetCore.Identity.EntityFrameworkCore"
Version="1.1.2" />
```

This adds the authentication and authorization capabilities to your application and provides a storage mechanism using Entity Framework. After you save your .csproj file, Visual Studio automatically restores the packages you need from nuget.org. If you are working outside Visual Studio, you need to execute `dotnet restore` before proceeding.

Configuring Authentication

Next, you need to define how your users are configured and stored in the database. Just as you did with your trip objects, you need to add a class that will contain the information that defines what a user is. You can add a new class called `ApplicationUser` to the Models folder and give it the simple content shown in Listing 20.1.

LISTING 20.1 `ApplicationUser` **Class Source Code**

```
public class ApplicationUser : IdentityUser
{

 public string FirstName { get; set; }

 public string LastName { get; set; }

}
```

This seems a little too simple to be a complete definition of a user, but there's a lot more hiding under the `IdentityUser` base class that it inherits from. The `IdentityUser` object has the following properties:

- ▶ `Email`—The email account for this user

- ▶ `PasswordHash`—A one-way hash of the user's password

- ▶ `UserName`—The ID to be used to log in to the application

- ▶ `Roles`—The collection of roles assigned to this user

- ▶ `Claims`—The collection of claims about this user

Other fields on the `IdentityUser` object assist with the mechanics of authentication—for example, `AccessFailedCount` and `LockoutEnabled`. These fields are not for you to work with

but are for the identity system to work with. When you add `FirstName` and `LastName` properties to your `IdentityUser` object, these fields are also captured and stored in the database for
each user.

Next, you need to configure the Entity Framework context `TripDbContext` to be able to
store and interact with the identity tables in the database. Fortunately, this enhancement
is as simple to implement as changing the class that `TripDbContext` inherits from, as
follows:

```
Public class TripDbContext : IdentityDbContext<ApplicationUser>
```

No other changes to your data context class are necessary; the tables are added to your database
automatically.

Next, you need to add the identity features to the dependency injection framework. You need
to add the lines in Listing 20.2 after the `AddDbContext` statement in the `Startup` class's
`ConfigureServices` method.

LISTING 20.2   Adding Identity Services to the Dependency Injection Framework

```
services.AddIdentity<ApplicationUser, IdentityRole>()
  .AddEntityFrameworkStores<TripDbContext>()
  .AddDefaultTokenProviders();
```

The final item to complete in adding identity to your application is to add the identity services
into the HTTP pipeline inside the `Startup Configure` method. To do so, add the following
statement after the `AddStaticFiles` statement in the `Startup Configure` method:

```
app.UseIdentity();
```

It's important to add this statement after the static files are configured. If you add it before the
static files are configured, the application will check a user's authentication status before granting that user access to the static files of your website, which creates unnecessary delay and extra
work for your website.

Adding the Registration Feature

Your application can now authenticate users, but you need a way to sign up new users to the
application and allow them to log in. You can do this by adding `AccountController` to the
Controllers folder with the initial contents shown in Listing 20.3.

LISTING 20.3   Initial `AccountController` **Source Code**

```
[Authorize]
public class AccountController : Controller
{
  private readonly UserManager<ApplicationUser> _userManager;
  private readonly SignInManager<ApplicationUser> _signInManager;
  private readonly ILogger _logger;
  private readonly string _externalCookieScheme;

  public AccountController(
    UserManager<ApplicationUser> userManager,
    SignInManager<ApplicationUser> signInManager,
    IOptions<IdentityCookieOptions> identityCookieOptions,
    ILoggerFactory loggerFactory)
  {
    _userManager = userManager;
    _signInManager = signInManager;
    _externalCookieScheme = identityCookieOptions.Value.
      ExternalCookieAuthenticationScheme;
    _logger = loggerFactory.CreateLogger<AccountController>();
  }
}
```

This initial constructor collects from the `Identity` module the information to manage users, sign them in, and log information as needed. `identityCookieOptions` is the one parameter that looks a little strange; it contains information about the cookie used to maintain the logged in user's state. You'll use it later to create a logout action.

The `Authorize` attribute at the top of the controller indicates that you want to ensure that users are logged in before they can access the features of this controller. You'll override this configuration for those features where you are expecting non-logged-in users to access this controller. The first of those features is the register action. You can add this feature to the `AccountController` class by including the source shown in Listing 20.4.

LISTING 20.4   **Registering Methods to Add to** `AccountController`

```
[HttpGet]
[AllowAnonymous]
public IActionResult Register()
{
  return View();
}


[HttpPost]
[AllowAnonymous]
[ValidateAntiForgeryToken]
```

```
public async Task<IActionResult> Register(RegisterViewModel model)
{
  ViewData["ReturnUrl"] = returnUrl;
  if (ModelState.IsValid)
  {
    var user = new ApplicationUser {
      FirstName = model.FirstName,
      LastName = model.LastName,
      UserName = model.Email,
      Email = model.Email
    };
    var result = await _userManager.CreateAsync(user, model.Password);
    if (result.Succeeded)
    {
      await _signInManager.SignInAsync(user, isPersistent: false);
      _logger.LogInformation(3, "User created a new account with password.");
      return Redirect("/")
    }
    foreach (var error in result.Errors)
    {
      ModelState.AddModelError(string.Empty, error.Description);
    }
  }

  return View(model);
}
```

The first method in Listing 20.4 displays the new user registration form. It is marked with an HttpGet attribute to ensure that it can be viewed only by users who navigate to it. The AllowAnonymous attribute indicates that all users including anonymous users, or those who have not logged in, are allowed access to that page.

The second method accepts anonymous users and can be triggered only by an HTTP Post, such as clicking a submit button on a form. The final attribute on this method, ValidateAntiForgeryToken, ensures that the form that was presented to the user was not tampered with before it is processed on the server. This method defines a new user and creates that user by using the UserManager from Identity that you captured in the constructor of this class. If the user was created successfully, you authenticate that user and return him or her to the front page of the site.

The RegisterViewModel class is not defined, and this is a good practice that I want to highlight. This class contains all the information necessary to register a user, but you don't want to expose your data storage object, ApplicationUser, directly to your web visitors. The RegisterViewModel class resides in the Models folder and contains a few properties with some decorators to help with validation of your new user's information, as shown in Listing 20.5.

LISTING 20.5   `RegisterViewModel` **Source Code**

```
public class RegisterViewModel
{

  [StringLength(20)]
  public string FirstName { get; set; }

  [StringLength(20)]
  public string LastName { get; set; }

  [Required]
  [EmailAddress]
  [Display(Name = "Email")]
  public string Email { get; set; }

  [Required]
  [StringLength(100, MinimumLength = 6)]
  [DataType(DataType.Password)]
  public string Password { get; set; }

  [DataType(DataType.Password)]
  [Display(Name = "Confirm password")]
  [Compare("Password", ErrorMessage = "The password and confirmation password do
not match.")]
  public string ConfirmPassword { get; set; }
}
```

A lot of attributes on this simple class assist in enforcing validation criteria:

▶ `StringLength`—Enforces a minimum and maximum length for a property.

▶ `Required`—Requires a value to be submitted.

▶ `EmailAddress`—Validates that the value captured is formatted as an email address.

▶ `DataType`—Provides a more specific type for the string captured. In this case, you're indicating that this value should be treated as a password.

▶ `Display`—Defines what text a label for this property should contain.

▶ `Compare`—Provides a validation check by comparing for equality with another property and displaying the error message listed if the values are not equal.

With these attributes configured on `RegisterViewModel`, you can quickly scaffold a view for the Register page by creating a folder under Views called Account. Right-click that folder and choose Add View to bring up the Add View dialog, shown in Figure 20.3.

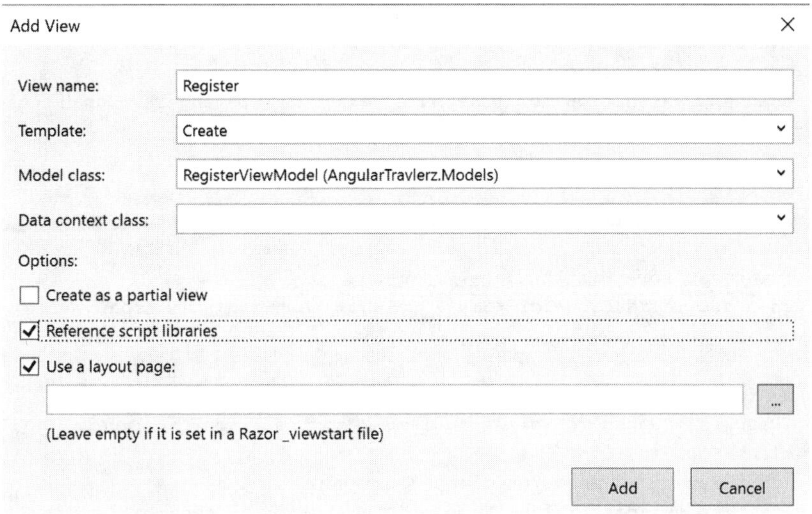

Add View   ✕

View name:	Register
Template:	Create ⌄
Model class:	RegisterViewModel (AngularTravlerz.Models) ⌄
Data context class:	⌄

Options:

☐ Create as a partial view

☑ Reference script libraries

☑ Use a layout page:

[   ] [...]

(Leave empty if it is set in a Razor _viewstart file)

                                                    [Add]   [Cancel]

FIGURE 20.3
The Add View dialog for the new Register view.

With the configuration shown, you don't need to write any additional code to enable your users to register to use the application. The code this dialog generates is shown in Listing 20.6.

LISTING 20.6   The Generated Register.cshtml View Template

```
@model AngularTravlerz.Models.RegisterViewModel

@{
    ViewData["Title"] = "Register";
}

<h2>Register</h2>

<form asp-action="Register">
    <div class="form-horizontal">
        <h4>RegisterViewModel</h4>
        <hr />
        <div asp-validation-summary="ModelOnly" class="text-danger"></div>
        <div class="form-group">
            <label asp-for="FirstName" class="col-md-2 control-label"></label>
            <div class="col-md-10">
                <input asp-for="FirstName" class="form-control" />
                <span asp-validation-for="FirstName" class="text-danger"></span>
            </div>
        </div>
        <div class="form-group">
```

```
            <label asp-for="LastName" class="col-md-2 control-label"></label>
            <div class="col-md-10">
                <input asp-for="LastName" class="form-control" />
                <span asp-validation-for="LastName" class="text-danger"></span>
            </div>
        </div>
        <div class="form-group">
            <label asp-for="Email" class="col-md-2 control-label"></label>
            <div class="col-md-10">
                <input asp-for="Email" class="form-control" />
                <span asp-validation-for="Email" class="text-danger"></span>
            </div>
        </div>
        <div class="form-group">
            <label asp-for="Password" class="col-md-2 control-label"></label>
            <div class="col-md-10">
                <input asp-for="Password" class="form-control" />
                <span asp-validation-for="Password" class="text-danger"></span>
            </div>
        </div>
        <div class="form-group">
            <label asp-for="ConfirmPassword" class="col-md-2 control-label">
</label>
            <div class="col-md-10">
                <input asp-for="ConfirmPassword" class="form-control" />
                <span asp-validation-for="ConfirmPassword" class="text-danger">
</span>
            </div>
        </div>
        <div class="form-group">
            <div class="col-md-offset-2 col-md-10">
                <input type="submit" value="Create" class="btn btn-default" />
            </div>
        </div>
    </div>
</form>

<div>
    <a asp-action="Index">Back to List</a>
</div>

@section Scripts {
    @{await Html.RenderPartialAsync("_ValidationScriptsPartial");}
}
```

You need to do some minor cleanup: Remove the extra lines for RegisterViewModel and change the link at the bottom to return to the home page instead of to the list. Otherwise, this page allows a new user to sign up easily with some friendly validation built in and no extra code needed from you.

Adding the Login and Logout Features

Listing 20.7 shows how to add the Login and Logout methods to AccountController.

LISTING 20.7   Login and Logout **Methods in** AccountController

```
[HttpGet]
[AllowAnonymous]
public async Task<IActionResult> Login(string returnUrl = null)
{

  ViewData["ReturnUrl"] = returnUrl;
  return View();
}


[HttpPost]
[AllowAnonymous]
[ValidateAntiForgeryToken]
public async Task<IActionResult> Login(LoginViewModel model,
                                    string returnUrl = null)
{
  ViewData["ReturnUrl"] = returnUrl;
  if (ModelState.IsValid)
  {

    var result = await _signInManager.PasswordSignInAsync
                (model.Email, model.Password, model.RememberMe);
    if (result.Succeeded)
    {
      _logger.LogInformation(1, "User logged in.");
      return Redirect(returnUrl ?? "/");
    }
    else
    {
      ModelState.AddModelError(string.Empty, "Invalid login attempt.");
      return View(model);
    }
  }

  // If you got this far, something failed, redisplay form
  return View(model);
}
```

```
[HttpPost]
[ValidateAntiForgeryToken]
public async Task<IActionResult> Logout()
{
  await _signInManager.SignOutAsync();
  _logger.LogInformation(4, "User logged out.");
  return RedirectToAction("Index", "Home");
}
```

The first `Login` method is the same as what you saw with `Register`: You are allowing anonymous users to navigate to this method. If they were sent here because they were not authorized to access a page, then they will carry a `returnUrl` destination that you should redirect them to after they complete the login process.

The second `Login` method processes the username and password information submitted through another view model object with the `SignInManager` to verify whether the user should be granted access. If a user succeeds, he or she is returned to the desired destination; if not, the user is returned to the login page with an appropriate error message.

Finally, the `Logout` method uses the `SignInManager` object to log the user out of the application and return him or her to the home page.

You can build the `LoginViewModel` object in the Models folder with the source shown in Listing 20.8.

LISTING 20.8   `LoginViewModel` to Support User Login Capabilities

```
public class LoginViewModel
{
  [Required]
  [EmailAddress]
  public string Email { get; set; }

  [Required]
  [DataType(DataType.Password)]
  public string Password { get; set; }

  [Display(Name = "Remember me?")]
  public bool RememberMe { get; set; }
}
```

Much as with `RegisterViewModel`, here you're defining the properties you need to capture in order to authenticate the user, and you're also defining the initial simple validation you would like the page to do for you before you check for a valid password. You can generate a Login view in the Views/Account folder, using the same technique you used for `RegisterViewModel` and the Register view. Listing 20.9 shows the source code from that process.

LISTING 20.9   Login.cshtml Generated View Template

```
@model AngularTravlerz.Models.LoginViewModel

@{
    ViewData["Title"] = "Login";
}

<h2>Login</h2>

<form asp-action="Login">
    <div class="form-horizontal">
        <h4>LoginViewModel</h4>
        <hr />
        <div asp-validation-summary="ModelOnly" class="text-danger"></div>
        <div class="form-group">
            <label asp-for="Email" class="col-md-2 control-label"></label>
            <div class="col-md-10">
                <input asp-for="Email" class="form-control" />
                <span asp-validation-for="Email" class="text-danger"></span>
            </div>
        </div>
        <div class="form-group">
            <label asp-for="Password" class="col-md-2 control-label"></label>
            <div class="col-md-10">
                <input asp-for="Password" class="form-control" />
                <span asp-validation-for="Password" class="text-danger"></span>
            </div>
        </div>
        <div class="form-group">
            <div class="col-md-offset-2 col-md-10">
                <div class="checkbox">
                    <input asp-for="RememberMe" />
                    <label asp-for="RememberMe"></label>
                </div>
            </div>
        </div>
        <div class="form-group">
            <div class="col-md-offset-2 col-md-10">
                <input type="submit" value="Create" class="btn btn-default" />
            </div>
        </div>
    </div>
</form>

<div>
```

```
    <a asp-action="Index">Back to List</a>
</div>

@section Scripts {
    @{await Html.RenderPartialAsync("_ValidationScriptsPartial");}
}
```

Once again, this is pretty close to what you need for your application. You can clean up the header and the `Back to List` link at the bottom as there is no list to return to.

Finally, you need to add some links to the header to take users to the next registration, login, and logout features. To do so, you can create a new view in the Views/Shared folder called _LoginPartial.cshtml that contains these links, as shown in Listing 20.10.

LISTING 20.10 _LoginPartial.cshtml with Links to Register, Login, and Logout Features

```
@using Microsoft.AspNetCore.Identity
@using AspTravlerz.Models

@inject SignInManager<ApplicationUser> SignInManager
@inject UserManager<ApplicationUser> UserManager

@if (SignInManager.IsSignedIn(User))
{
  <form asp-area="" asp-controller="Account" asp-action="Logout" method="post"
        id="logoutForm" class="navbar-right">
    <ul class="nav navbar-nav navbar-right">
      <li>
        <a asp-area="" asp-controller="Manage" asp-action="Index"
           title="Manage">Hello @UserManager.GetUserName(User)!</a>
      </li>
      <li>
        <button type="submit" class="btn btn-link navbar-btn navbar-link">Log out
</button>
      </li>
    </ul>
  </form>
}
else
{
  <ul class="nav navbar-nav navbar-right">
    <li><a asp-area="" asp-controller="Account" asp-action="Register">Register
</a></li>
    <li><a asp-area="" asp-controller="Account" asp-action="Login">Log in</a></li>
  </ul>
}
```

This template uses `SignInManager` to check whether the user is currently logged in to your application. If so, you want to display a friendly Hello message and a button to post to the logout action on `AccountController`. If the user is not logged in, you want to present the register and login links so that the user can join your application. You can add these links to your layout by inserting the following line into the _Layout.cshtml page, just after the closing `ul` tag for the navbar:

```
@Html.Partial("_LoginPartial")
```

With this piece in place, a guest can now register, login, and navigate around your application easily as an authenticated user. In the next hour, you'll start to add constraints on who is allowed access to various features of the application.

Summary

In this hour you have added authentication capabilities to your website. Users can register, log in, and log out from the application.

Q&A

Q. Is it possible to use social authentication providers like Twitter or Facebook or Twitter to have users log in to my application?

A. Yes. There are templates and links with up-to-date instructions on how to connect to these ever-changing services in the .NET templates.

Q. How do I get the user ID of the currently logged in user so that I can mark that person's data as belonging to him or her?

A. You can inject `UserManager<ApplicationUser>` as shown in Listing 20.10 and get the user ID with `UserManager.GetUserId()`.

Q. The `AllowAnonymous` and `Authorize` attributes are too simple for my needs, and I need more fine-grained control over who has access to different functions. What should I use?

A. This is the subject of the next hour. Read on!

Q. Do I need to build login, register, and logout pages if I use Windows Authentication or Azure Active Directory?

A. No. Those services have their own registration and authentication pages. In the case of Azure Active Directory, your ASP.NET Core application will show the login page for your directory to users who are not logged in. When your users log out of Active Directory, they are logged out of your application as well.

Workshop

The workshop contains quiz questions and exercises to help you solidify your understanding of the material covered. Try to answer all questions before looking at the "Answers" that follow.

Quiz

1. What is the difference between authentication and authorization?

2. What are the four types of authentication that can be configured from Visual Studio?

3. What deployment requirement must be met to use integrated Active Directory authentication in an application?

4. What is the name of the authentication services in ASP.NET Core?

Answers

1. Authentication validates who the user is; authorization validates if the user is allowed to access a resource.

2. No Authentication, Individual User Accounts, Work or School Accounts, Windows Authentication

3. Integrated Active Directory authentication or Windows Authentication must be deployed to a Windows web server.

4. ASP.NET Core Identity

Exercise

Now that you know how to configure authentication in your application, you can clean up the login and register pages so that they look a little nicer. Format the headers and add some more friendly error messages to the `RegisterViewModel` and `LoginViewModel` objects when the validation criteria for their properties are not properly met.

Try configuring some of the options for user passwords by adding a call in the `Startup.ConfigureServices` method with this syntax:

```
services.Configure<IdentityOptions>(options =>
{
 // Password settings
 options.Password.RequireDigit = true;
})
```

Experiment with the features you can enable and disable by using the `IdentityOptions` class.

HOUR 21
Granting Access to Users

What You'll Learn in This Hour:

▶ How to configure authorization for your application
▶ How to construct authorization policies
▶ How to write more complex custom authorization requirements

Once you have authenticated users to your application, you know who they are. To complete the picture of securing your application from unauthorized users, you need to write some code to verify that your users have been granted access. In ASP.NET Core, you can configure authorization policies to enforce requirements that users must pass in order to use your application's features. ASP.NET Core gives you a very flexible authorization system utilizing users, roles, claims, and policies. In this hour, let's learn about how to use these features together to secure our application.

Defining Roles, Claims, and Policies

When it comes to qualifying users for access to features, there are three security capabilities that you need to understand before proceeding to writing code: roles, policies, and claims. You can use these three capabilities to group and qualify users to be able to access features. In this hour you'll look at each of these capabilities to ensure that you understand the purpose of each one.

You may be familiar with the concept of a role or a user role—a collection of users that all have the same access capabilities to features in the system. In some applications or operating systems, users can be assigned to more than one role. In the case of ASP.NET Core, users are allowed to be assigned to multiple roles.

A *security claim* is a property of the user that can be used to help judge whether that user is allowed access to a feature. On a web application for a liquor manufacturer, for example, the age of the visitor is an important security claim as the site is required to restrict access based on age (21 in the United States). You as a system designer can determine what information about a user is qualified as a claim.

A security policy is a collection of information used to qualify access to a feature. In the example of a liquor manufacturer, the policy might be called "Americans 21 and Older," and it might verify the residence and age of the visitor. Simpler policies are possible, too, like "Administrators Only" to check the roles assigned to a user and verify that the user is assigned the Administrator role. In addition to a policy verifying roles and claims for a user, they can also execute arbitrary code that is defined as part of a requirement class. We'll look at more complex requirements later in this hour.

The relationship between users, roles, claims, and requirements is illustrated in figure 21.1.

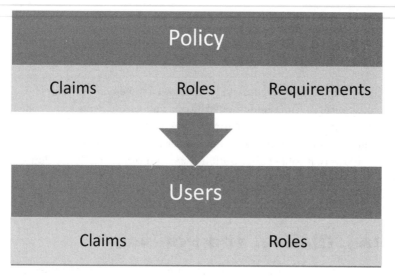

FIGURE 21.1
Relationship between users, roles, claims, and requirements.

Adding Claims to Your Users

In Hour 20, "Authenticating Your Users," you defined your application user object to contain information about the first name and last name of a user. This hour you'll enhance the storage of these properties so that they are assigned as claims in the repository.

You can start assigning these properties as claims by modifying the AccountController. Register method that handles the HttpPost verb. Listing 21.1 shows the code you need to add right after the UserManager.Create method.

LISTING 21.1   Adding Claims for New Users

```
var result = await _userManager.CreateAsync(user, model.Password);
if (result.Succeeded)
{

  await _userManager.AddClaimsAsync(user, new Claim[]
    {
      new Claim(ClaimTypes.GivenName, user.FirstName),
      new Claim(ClaimTypes.Surname, user.LastName),
      new Claim(ClaimTypes.Email, user.Email)
    });
await _signInManager.SignInAsync(user, isPersistent: false);
```

With this configuration, you are adding information into the user repository about the user, and you're converting these user properties into security claims that can be later checked and have policies enforced against them. The ClaimTypes object is a class that contains a set of string constants that you can use to create a set of standard claims in your application. (Table 21.1 lists some of those claims.) These constants resolve to a URI that defines the standard for a claim.

TABLE 21.1   Standard Claims in System.Security.Claims.ClaimTypes

Claim	Description
GivenName	The first name of the user
SurName	The last name of the user
Email	The user's email address
DateOfBirth	The birthdate of the user
HomePhone	The user's home telephone number
Gender	The user's gender, as a string
Country	The user's country of residence
StateOrProvince	The user's home state or province

Some of these claims are very valuable for enforcing regional laws and custom rules. All of them have their values stored as strings, and it's up to you to format and interpret the string as needed. This is of particular note with the DateOfBirth claim, as you need to format the date into a string.

With the name and email added as claims for your user, you can update the _LoginPartial.cshtml view to now present the first name of the user by simply reading the appropriate claim. You can update the greeting segment of this template as shown in Listing 21.2.

LISTING 21.2   Greeting Users with Claims in _LoginPartial.cshtml

```
@if (SignInManager.IsSignedIn(User))
{
    <form asp-area="" asp-controller="Account" asp-action="Logout" method="post"
        id="logoutForm" class="navbar-right">
      <ul class="nav navbar-nav navbar-right">
        <li>
          <a href="#">Hello @User.Claims.First(c => c.Type == ClaimTypes.GivenName)
                             .Value</a>
        </li>
        <li>
          <button type="submit" class="btn btn-link navbar-btn navbar-link">Log out
</button>
        </li>
      </ul>
    </form>
}
```

The claims collection on the User object can be traversed with LINQ methods, and this code finds the GivenName claim and outputs the value assigned. You can use this trick in other places where you want to consume claim information. However, you really want to use the claims as part of authorization enforcement.

Adding a Sample Administrator User

You can extend your SampleData class to add an administrator user that you can use to test some of the new authorization features you will be adding to the application. To start with, add a call to a new CreateUsers method inside the SampleData.InitializeData method that looks as follows:

```
CreateUsers(serviceScope).GetAwaiter().GetResult();
```

This calls your new asynchronous CreateUsers method and proceeds when the method has completed. Listing 21.3 shows the content of this method.

LISTING 21.3   Creating a Sample Administrator User

```
private static async Task CreateUsers(IServiceScope serviceScope)
{

  var userManager = serviceScope.ServiceProvider.GetService
    <UserManager<ApplicationUser>>();
  var roleManager = serviceScope.ServiceProvider.GetService
    <RoleManager<IdentityRole>>();
```

```
if (!roleManager.Roles.Any(role => role.Name == "Administrator"))
{
  await roleManager.CreateAsync(new IdentityRole("Administrator"));
}

if (!userManager.Users.Any(u => u.UserName == "admin@example.com"))
{

  var user = new ApplicationUser
  {
    FirstName = "Admin",
    LastName = "Admin",
    UserName = "admin@example.com",
    Email = "admin@example.com"
  };
  var result = await userManager.CreateAsync(user, "Passw0rd!");
  if (result.Succeeded)
  {

    await userManager.AddClaimsAsync(user, new Claim[]
    {
      new Claim(ClaimTypes.Name, $"{user.FirstName}, {user.LastName}"),
      new Claim(ClaimTypes.GivenName, user.FirstName),
      new Claim(ClaimTypes.Surname, user.LastName),
      new Claim(ClaimTypes.Email, user.Email)
    });
    await userManager.AddToRoleAsync(user, "Administrator");

  }
 }
}
```

This code starts by getting the currently registered UserManager and RoleManager, the components that the Identity system uses to manage users and the security roles available in the system. Just as you inherited ApplicationUser from IdentityUser, there is a default IdentityRole available that you could enhance as well. For this simple application, there is no need to do that, though; you can use the default IdentityRole with your users. If the Administrator role does not exist, you create it by using the roleManager.CreateAsync method call.

After the user is defined and created with the password Passw0rd!, the default claims you used in AccountController in Hour 20 are added. Finally, the user is registered with the new Administrator role.

Configuring Authorization

You have already configured authentication for your application, and now you need to modify the `Startup` class to add features to configure the ASP.NET identity system to handle authorization requests. You need to define where to route folks if they attempt to access a location while they are logged in but not allowed access. Such an error page is known as a "forbidden page" and can be configured as shown in Listing 21.4.

LISTING 21.4   Configuring a Forbidden Page

```
services.Configure<IdentityOptions>(options =>
{
   options.Cookies.ApplicationCookie.AccessDeniedPath = "/Account/Forbidden";
});
```

This entry should be placed inside the `ConfigureServices` method, and it clearly routes requests to the `AccountController.Forbidden` method. That method, shown in Listing 21.5, is a simple return of a view and is marked to allow anonymous.

LISTING 21.5   `AccountController's` Forbidden Method

```
[AllowAnonymous]
public async Task<IActionResult> Forbidden()
{
   return View();
}
```

Next, put some boilerplate text into a /Views/Account/Forbidden.cshtml page to indicate that the user is not allowed access. Try adding something like the code shown in Listing 21.6.

LISTING 21.6   The Forbidden Page Template

```
@{
    ViewData["Title"] = "Forbidden";
}

<h2>Forbidden</h2>

<p>You do not have access to this page</p>

<a asp-action="Index" asp-controller="Home">Return to the Home Page</a>
```

At this point, you could add a global filter to the MVC configuration to require that users be authenticated to access any action. Remember how in Hour 20 you added the `Authorize` attribute to `AccountController`? You can now programmatically add that to every controller with a global filter defined in the `ConfigureServices` method, as shown in Listing 21.7.

LISTING 21.7 A Global `AuthorizeFilter` **Requirement**

```
services.AddMvc(config =>
  {
    var policy = new AuthorizationPolicyBuilder()
      .RequireAuthenticatedUser()
      .Build();
    config.Filters.Add(new AuthorizeFilter(policy));
  })
```

This filter is effective at blocking access to all users unless they are authenticated, and it shows a new feature that you are going to explore this hour: `AuthorizationPolicyBuilder`. Listing 21.7 shows a feature to it: `RequireAuthenticatedUser`. At this point, do not add the contents of Listing 21.6 to your application; in the following sections, you will configure slightly different policies.

Defining Security Policies

You can start defining more granular and focused security policies by adding a call to `AddAuthorization` in the `ConfigureServices` method. Inside the arguments of this method, you define the various policies that you will apply to your application. First you will add a policy called `AdministratorsOnly` that requires the role `Administrator`, as shown in Listing 21.8.

LISTING 21.8 Creating Your First Security Policy, Called `AdministratorsOnly`

```
services.AddAuthorization(configure =>
{
  configure.AddPolicy("AdministratorsOnly", policy =>
    policy.RequireRole("Administrator"));
});
```

The code in Listing 21.8 adds your new policy to the authorization capabilities of the application. You can then enforce this requirement on controllers or controller methods by decorating them with an `Authorize` attribute, the same way you did previously, but now with an added parameter to indicate the policy to enforce. You will see three syntaxes for this attribute in use:

▶ `[Authorize("AdministratorsOnly")]`—Enforces the `AdministratorsOnly` policy.

▶ `[Authorize(Policy="AdministratorsOnly")]`—Explicitly enforces the AdministratorsOnly policy.

▶ [Authorize(Roles="Administrator")]—Enforces a requirement of the role(s) listed. Multiple roles are separated by commas, and a user participating in any of the roles grants the roles access.

In this case you will decorate the Edit action of TripsController with the Authorize attribute specifying the AdministratorsOnly policy, as follows:

```
[Authorize(Policy="AdministratorsOnly")]
public async Task<IActionResult> Edit(int? id)
```

This prevents anonymous users and non-administrators from accessing the Edit screen for trips. If a user is not logged in and attempts to access the Edit page, the code shown above routes the user the Login screen. If a user is logged in but not as an administrator, he or she should see the forbidden page. The presence of the Edit link on the MyTrips page seems out of place and really shouldn't be there for users who don't have access.

Enforcing Authorization Policies in Content

Inside Razor templates, you can use the authorization service to check whether policies are met and whether to include content in the output. You can add to the top of the Views/Trips/Index.cshtml template an inject directive for the authorization service:

```
@inject Microsoft.AspNetCore.Authorization.IAuthorizationService
AuthorizationService
```

This makes the authorization service available to the view, and you can query it whenever you plan to verify if a user should have access to content you want to present on screen. You can wrap the Edit and Delete buttons in the rightmost column of this screen with validation checks as shown in Listing 21.9.

LISTING 21.9   Enforcing the AdministratorsOnly Policy in a Razor Template

```
<td>
  @if (await AuthorizationService.AuthorizeAsync(User, null, "AdministratorsOnly"))
{
    <a asp-action="Edit" asp-route-id="@item.ID">Edit</a> @:|
  }
  <a asp-action="Details" asp-route-id="@item.ID">Details</a>
  @if (await AuthorizationService.AuthorizeAsync(User, null, "AdministratorsOnly"))
{

  @:| <a asp-action="Delete" asp-route-id="@item.ID">Delete</a>
  }
</td>
```

The `AuthorizeAsync` method checks the user for access to the `AdministratorsOnly` policy and returns a `true` value if he or she is allowed access. By wrapping the Edit and Delete buttons with this check, you tell the application to show those links only if the user is granted access.

Make Policies Descriptive and Apply Them Liberally

The `AdministratorsOnly` policy may be overreaching and may not describe what you are truly protecting with the edit and delete capabilities for trips. Follow these steps to create a more focused policy and apply it to your trip views and controller:

1. Inside the `Startup.ConfigureServices` method, add a new policy beneath the `AdmininstratorsOnly` policy, like this:

```
configure.AddPolicy("TripMaintainers", policy => policy.
RequireClaim(ClaimTypes.Surname, "YourLastName"));
```

   This new policy restricts access to users with your same last name. You could create a custom claim type name in your application, but if you want your family to be able to see and edit your trips, this works.

2. Decorate the `TripsController Edit` and `Delete` methods with `Authorize` for the new `TripMaintainers` policy created in step 1.

3. Update the `Index` and `Details` views in the Trips folder to show the edit and delete links only if the user is authorized with the `TripMaintainers` policy.

Creating More Complex Policies

The standard methods of checking for the presence of a role or a claim may not be enough to meet the security needs for your application. You can create policies that check the value of a claim against a list of possible values, or you can write more code into the policy validation.

If you want your `TripMaintainers` policy to check for the presence of one of several roles you can use code like this:

```
configure.AddPolicy("EditorsAndAdmins", policy => policy.
RequireRole("Administrator", "Editor"));
```

Similarly, you can check for the presence of one of several values of a claim by using the following code:

```
configure.AddPolicy("NorthAmerica", policy =>
policy.RequireClaim(ClaimTypes.Country, "USA", "Canada", "Mexico");
```

What if you want to combine these policies and allow users who are administrators *or* are located in Canada? You can use `RequiresAssertion`, which uses an action syntax to string together authorization requirements, like this:

```
configure.AddPolicy("CanadianOrAdmin", policy => policy.RequireAssertion(context =>
  {
    return context.User.IsInRole("Administrator") ||
      context.User.HasClaim(claim => claim.Type == ClaimTypes.Country &&
                                     claim.Value == "Canada");
  }));
```

In addition, you can write your own custom requirements and move some of this code into its own class, as shown in Listing 21.10.

LISTING 21.10   A Custom Requirement Class to Check for Canadians

```
public class CanadianRequirement : AuthorizationHandler<CanadianRequirement>,
IAuthorizationRequirement
{
  protected override Task HandleRequirementAsync(
                     AuthorizationHandlerContext context,
                     CanadianRequirement requirement)
  {

    if (context.User.IsInRole("Administrator"))
    {
      context.Succeed(requirement);
    }

    if (context.User.HasClaim(claim => claim.ValueType == ClaimTypes.Country &&
                                       claim.Value == "Canada"))
    {
      context.Succeed(requirement);
    }

    return Task.CompletedTask;

  }
}
```

This class defines the requirement and returns a check for that requirement, marking `AuthorizationHandlerContext` as successful if the user is an administrator or if the user is from Canada. Notice that the context is never marked as `Failed`, as that is the default state when the user has failed this requirement check. You can enforce this requirement as a policy by using the following code:

```
configure.AddPolicy(
  "CanadianRequirement",
  policy => policy.AddRequirements(new CanadianRequirement())
);
```

Summary

In this hour, you have learned how to add authorization requirements to components of your ASP.NET Core application. You have created policies, defined claims, checked for the presence of security roles, and even written your own custom security requirements.

Q&A

Q. This hour shows how to use the `RequiresAssertion` policy allows to logically OR together several checks. Is there an easy way to logically AND these requirements?

A. Yes. You can simply chain together your checks like this:

```
policy.RequiresRole("Role1").RequiresRole("Role2").RequiresClaim("ClaimA")
```

Q. I'm using Azure Active Directory to manage users. Will it check the claims I've added to those users?

A. Yes! If you are sharing claims with Azure Active Directory, you can write authorization policies against those claims.

Q. Is there an easy administrative interface I can use to manage my users?

A. No such interface comes as part of ASP.NET Core, but you can use a third-party solution like IdentityServer to manage users.

Q. If I create a `Requirement` class, can I use constructor dependency injection to inject other services?

A. The policy is created as part of the `ConfigureServices` method and is not created using the dependency injection container. You should be able to pass in concrete references to anything you need as the services would be configured as part of that method.

Workshop

The workshop contains quiz questions and exercises to help you solidify your understanding of the material covered. Try to answer all questions before looking at the "Answers" that follow.

Quiz

1. How do you prevent any non-logged-in user from accessing an `Edit` action?
2. How do you only grant access to users in the `Administrator` role to an `Edit` action?
3. What is an authorization policy?

4. What abstract class should a custom requirement inherit from?

5. How can you write a policy to check whether a user belongs to the `Admin` or `Editor` role?

Answers

1. Add a plain `[Authorize]` attribute above the `Edit` method.

2. Add an `[Authorize(Role="Adminstrators")]` attribute above the `Edit` method.

3. An authorization policy is a series of checks against a user's identity to validate access to a feature.

4. `AuthorizationHandler`

5. `configure.AddPolicy("AdminOrEditor", policy => policy.` `RequireRole("Admin", "Editor"));`

Exercise

This hour shows several policies that can be used across your application. Try creating a new policy for your manager, who belongs to the `Managers` role, that allows her to see how long you are traveling but does not allow her to see your trip destinations or details. In addition, ensure that your manager cannot modify your trips. You don't want your manager to shorten your vacation on you!

HOUR 22

Deploying to Production

What You'll Learn in This Hour:

▶ What "production" means with ASP.NET Core?
▶ How to configure a production web space securely
▶ Deploying to a production Windows server
▶ Deploying to a production Linux server

You've finished writing your application, and you're ready to welcome the world to it. What are the next steps? This hour takes a look at what you need to do to make your application available for production use. What does *production* mean to you? ASP.NET Core has a very clear definition of *production*, and you should know what it is prior to deploying your application.

What Is This "Production" You Speak Of?

Production is typically a term you hear in enterprise environments to refer to a "live" site where an application will run. Typically, this location is an isolated web server that an operations team manages to ensure the uptime and stability of the application. When I refer to an *isolated location*, I mean a data center. In some organizations, that facility could be on-site, or it could be at a co-location vendor that has high-speed access to the Internet, or it could even be a cloud vendor like Azure, Amazon, or Google Compute.

Within your ASP.NET Core application, you may recall from Hour 6, "Configuring Your Application," that there is an Environment setting. By default, it is set to Production, but Visual Studio overrides it to the setting Development. The Production setting is very important here because it triggers different behaviors in some of the middleware you are using with your application.

You may recall that the Startup.cs file's Configure method includes the default section of code in Listing 22.1.

LISTING 22.1 `Configure` Method Snippet That Tests for the Development Environment

```
if (env.IsDevelopment())
{

  app.UseDeveloperExceptionPage();
  app.UseBrowserLink();

} else {

  app.UseExceptionHandler("/Home/Error");

}
```

This example clearly shows that the `DeveloperExceptionPage` middleware is available only in the development environment. What happens if you run this middleware in a designated production environment? Visitors see the same white screen error page that you see in Development mode that shows all the internals of a stack trace. Is that what you want your application users to see? To savvy security analysts or hackers, such information is a treasure trove that tells a *lot* about your application, including some vectors with which they can start attacking now that they know you didn't properly configure your ASP.NET Core application for production use.

The lesson here is that you shouldn't expose development information or logs to anyone exception technical support personnel who are managing your application. These folks can take actions to repair or remediate problems and are the only ones who should see "internal" information about your application.

Hosting ASP.NET Core Behind Another Server

You have a really cool new server called Kestrel that runs with your ASP.NET Core application. It is very fast, and you have full control over it from inside of your application. However, the ASP.NET team has not yet certified it for open-Internet use. It has not been hardened against hacking attempts, and the team is actively working toward improving it.

To circumvent any problems that may crop up before Kestrel is fully hardened, the ASP.NET Core team recommends hosting the Kestrel service behind another server: IIS or Apache or nginx on Linux. This is a common configuration for Rails and Node.js, which are often configured to run on these servers with a reverse proxy into the process that handles the server-side executable part of the application.

If you've used older versions of ASP.NET, you may remember the W3SVC process for managing ASP.NET applications. This process ran in isolation from the IIS web server on Windows and had traffic requests routed to it for processing by the application. This is a similar configuration to what you are using with ASP.NET Core, except that instead of W3SVC managing the requests, the executable you have built hosts the Kestrel server.

Preparing Production Web Space

When you consider a location to deploy your application to, you need to take into consideration the access levels granted to the users who will be running your web application. The following are several best practices about the service account that you should use for your web application:

▶ The service account should not be able to log in to the server directly.

▶ The service account should not be able to write to disk. If your application needs to write to a location on disk, that location should be isolated and the only place the service account is allowed to write.

▶ The service account should not have read access to sensitive areas on disk.

▶ The service account is only allowed to execute the executable files that are delivered with your application.

When deploying to a Windows server, the IUSR_MACHINENAME account is automatically created for Internet Information Server (the Windows web server) to use for running processes. I recommend that you add an additional service account for each application that you run and restrict that service account to running only the individual application the service is assigned to.

On a Linux server, I recommend a similar approach: Create a service account with a name similar to your application (perhaps asptravlerz_worker) and configure that user to be able to run and read your application.

When in doubt while configuring a server for deploying your application, consult your server administrators.

Deploying Your Application to a Windows Server

When your production server runs Windows, much of the configuration of the application is already prepared for you. All those mentions of IISIntegration that you have seen while working with the application are now going into effect for you. The IISIntegration package and IISIntegration commands inside Program.cs, as shown in Listing 22.2, trigger the Kestrel web server to listen for and receive interactions from the ASP.NET Core web module that runs inside IIS and interacts with Kestrel.

LISTING 22.2   Default Configuration of IISIntegration Inside Program.cs

```
var host = new WebHostBuilder()
  .UseConfiguration(config)
  .UseKestrel()
  .UseContentRoot(Directory.GetCurrentDirectory())
  .UseIISIntegration()
  .UseStartup<Startup>()
  .Build();
```

The configuration of the ASP.NET Core module lives inside that pesky web.config file that was created for your project that you thought you wouldn't have to deal with. Take a quick look at the contents of that file in Listing 22.3 to learn more about how ASP.NET Core is hosted from IIS.

LISTING 22.3   web.config Configuration for Hosting ASP.NET Core

```
<system.webServer>
  <handlers>
    <add name="aspNetCore" path="*"
        verb-"*" modules="AspNetCoreModule"
        resourceType="unspecified" />
  </handlers>
  <aspNetCore processPath="%LAUNCHER_PATH%"
              arguments="%LAUNCHER_ARGS%"
              stdoutLogEnabled="false"
              stdoutLogFile=".\logs\stdout"
              forwardWindowsAuthToken="false" />
</system.webServer>
```

There's a lot of configuration of your service going on in this little block. Let's analyze the pieces to better understand what's happening here.

First, this is a template file that will be transformed when the `publish` action is taken with the project. This means those %LAUNCHER% markers will be replaced with information about the true location and arguments to use when calling the ASP.NET Core web server. Typically, they are replaced with the `processPath dotnet` and an argument that contains the name of the DLL corresponding to the project. (You'll learn about some different options for this later this hour, when we discuss self-contained deployments.)

The `stdoutLogEnabled` attribute defines whether the console logging that you saw earlier will be written to a file on disk. With the default setting `false`, the console log of Kestrel will not be captured. You can use other loggers for ASP.NET Core, such as Serilog, which have better performance and allow you to log the data with a more flexible configuration.

The `stdoutLogFile` attribute is the name of the file that will be written to if the `stdoutLogEnabled` value is set to `true`. The . at the beginning of the configuration indicates a path relative to the topmost folder of the application.

The `forwardWindowsAuthToken` attribute indicates whether the Windows Authentication token will be forwarded to the process as a header called `MS-ASPNETCORE-WINAUTHTOKEN` on each request. If you are using Windows Authentication with your application and need to interact with those credentials, you will want to set this value to `true`.

The following are some of the other options you may want to configure for `aspNetCoreModule`:

- **startupTimeLimit**—An optional integer that sets the direction in seconds that the module should wait for the executable to start listening. The default value is 120 seconds.

- **shutdownTimeLimit**—An optional integer that sets the direction in seconds that the module should wait for the executable to gracefully shut down if an app_offline.htm file is detected. The default value is 10 seconds.

- **rapidFailsPerMinute**—An optional integer that indicates the maximum number of times the executable process is allowed to crash per minute. If this limit is exceeded, the module will stop launching the process for the remainder of the minute. The default value is 10 failures.

- **requestTimeout**—A time span that specifies the amount of time the ASP.NET Core module waits for a response from the process. The default value is `00:02:00`, or 2 minutes.

- **disableStartUpErrorPage**—A value of `true` or `false` that indicates whether the 502.5 process failure page will be prevented from being displayed and a 502 status page defined in your web.config should be shown instead. The default value ASP.NET Core uses is `false`, and the standard 502.5 error page from ASP.NET Core will be shown if there is a failure in launching the process. We will use the false value in our application as well

If you would like to configure environment variables specific to your IIS deployment of ASP.NET Core, you can add a child element to the `aspNetCore` section called `environmentVariables`, as demonstrated in Listing 22.4.

LISTING 22.4   Environment Variables Defined in web.config

```
<aspNetCore processPath="%LAUNCHER_PATH%"
            arguments="%LAUNCHER_ARGS%"
            stdoutLogEnabled="false"
            stdoutLogFile=".\logs\stdout"
            forwardWindowsAuthToken="false">
  <environmentVariables>
    <environmentVariable name="ASPNETCORE_ENVIRONMENT" value="Staging" />
    <environmentVariable name="MyCustomVariable" value="true" />
  </environmentVariables>
</aspNetCore>
```

This simple configuration sets these environment variables only for the running process defined in the `processPath` attribute.

The shutdownTimeLimit option references the presence of the app_offline.htm file. This feature was available in previous versions of ASP.NET and has been brought to ASP.NET Core. If you deploy a file called app_offline.htm to the root of your web application, IIS will gracefully shut down the ASP.NET Core process and serve your app_offline.htm file to all requests of your application. The process will be restarted when IIS detects that this file has been removed from your folder. One practice is to keep a copy of this file in the folder with an alternate file extension or a slightly different filename so that you can quickly and easily rename it and shut down the application.

With this simple configuration, your application is almost ready to deploy to a Windows server. You need to prepare the Windows server by installing the ASP.NET Core module. You deploy it either by installing the .NET Core Windows Server Hosting bundle on the server or installing the WindowsHosting option from the DotNetCore SDK, as discussed in the following sections.

.NET Core Windows Server Hosting

If your server is going to host multiple .NET Core applications, you will want to have one copy of the .NET Core runtime, library, and ASP.NET Core module available in a shared configuration. You can get a copy of this bundle from the Microsoft site, at https://go.microsoft.com/fwlink/?linkid=837808.

ASP.NET Core Module Install Only

If you plan to host only self-contained deployments and not provide a shared .NET Core runtime or library, you can use the same link to download the bundle and install only the ASP.NET Core module with this command at the command prompt:

```
DotNetCore.1.0.5_1.1.2-WindowsHosting.exe OPT_INSTALL_LTS_REDIST=0 OPT_INSTALL_FTS_
REDIST=0
```

The filename may vary, as Microsoft updates the name of the file to indicate which specific versions of .NET Core it covers.

Shared and Self-Contained Deployments

Up to this point, you have only built your application and run it from a local development folder. When you are ready to publish your application, you can either use the publishing tool within Visual Studio or you can execute the dotnet publish command at the command line. Under the covers, the Visual Studio publishing tool uses the same dotnet publish action from the command-line tool.

When you published web applications in older versions of ASP.NET, you could safely assume that the target server had ASP.NET installed because that server was Windows, and all Windows versions have the base framework required to run ASP.NET installed in the global assembly cache of the machine. With ASP.NET Core, those foundation pieces are not necessarily in the global assembly cache. There are two approaches to deploying your application: shared mode and self-contained mode.

If the destination server is configured with the full .NET Core Windows Server Hosting option, as described above, then it is available for "shared hosting" because there is a common .NET Core or .NET Framework available on the machine that can be shared across all applications. With the currently configured project file as you wrote it in Hour 4, "Defining ASP.NET Core Configuration," you can easily copy the output of a `dotnet publish` command and place it in a folder on the destination web server. The shared components will be consumed by your application, and it will run happily behind the IIS web server.

On the other hand, if you are deploying to a server that you are not sure has the .NET Core runtime and libraries that match your application, you can bundle all references appropriate for the target runtime on that server and deliver them in the same folder as your application. This requires the addition of a `RuntimeIdentifiers` property in your project file that includes the runtime of the platform you are targeting, as shown in Listing 22.5.

LISTING 22.5   `RuntimeIdentifiers` **Property Inside the Project File**

```
<PropertyGroup>
  <Version>0.4.0</Version>
  <TargetFrameworks>net461;netcoreapp1.1</TargetFrameworks>
  <RuntimeIdentifiers>win7-x64;osx.10.11-x64;ubuntu.16.04-x64</RuntimeIdentifiers>
</PropertyGroup>
```

Your code should contain at least the runtime identifier for the development environment you are operating on. The `win7-x64` identifier dictates that Windows versions 7, 8, 8.1, and 10 can all run this application if they are 64-bit. The `osx.10.10-x64` identifier provides a runtime for OS X 10.10 Mavericks. `ubuntu.16.04-x64` indicates Ubuntu v16.04 on a 64-bit machine. Table 22.1 show some of the other runtime identifiers that are available.

Other currently supported runtime identifiers are listed in the RID catalog documentation for .NET Core at https://docs.microsoft.com/en-us/dotnet/articles/core/rid-catalog.

With a runtime defined for your project, you can now publish a self-contained deployment that includes the necessary runtime libraries for your application on the destination system.

TABLE 22.1   Runtime Identifiers Supported and Available for .NET Core

Windows	Mac	Linux
Windows 7/Server 2008 R2	**OS X Mavericks**	**Red Hat Enterprise Linux**
win7-x64	osx.10.10-x64	rhel.7-x64
win7-x86	**OS X El Capitan**	rhel.7.0-x64
Windows 8 / Server 2012	osx.10.11-x64	rhel.7.1-x64
win8-x64	**Mac OS Sierra**	rhel.7.2-x64
win8-x86	osx.10.12-x64	rhel.7.3-x64
win8-arm		rhel.7.4-x64
Windows 8.1/Server 2012 R2		**Ubuntu**
win81-x64		ubuntu.14.04-x64
win81-x86		ubuntu.14.10-x64
win81-arm		ubuntu.15.04-x64
Windows 10/Server 2016		ubuntu.15.10-x64
win10-x64		ubuntu.16.04-x64
win10-x86		ubuntu.16.10-x64
win10-arm		**Debian**
win10-arm64		debian.8-x64
		Fedora
		fedora.23-x64
		fedora.24-x64

CAUTION

You May Need to Restore Packages

If you are publishing to a system that is not the same runtime as your current system, you need to run `dotnet restore` in order to add the packages for that runtime to your machine so that they can be included in your deployment package.

You can publish a self-contained application for your target system by executing the following at the command line:

```
dotnet publish -r <RUNTIME_ID> -c Release
```

This command publishes your application in release configuration, which omits any debug information from the output and includes only libraries for the `<RUNTIME_ID>` specified. By default, this command creates a folder called publish under the bin\Release folder of your application with the complete contents of your application. The key to making this a self-contained deployment is the -r switch; without this switch, the application is published in shared framework mode, which requires.NET Core or .NET Framework to be installed (depending on the framework chosen) on the target machine.

You can also use the -o switch to output the contents of the publish task to a different folder.

At this point, you can copy your output to a folder on your Windows web server that can host the application. Configure that folder as a web application inside the IIS console and set ApplicationPool to not run any .NET managed code, as shown in Figure 22.1.

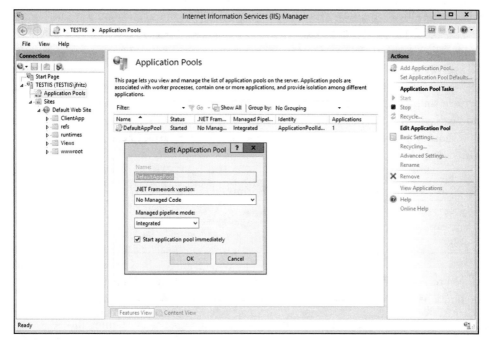

FIGURE 22.1
ApplicationPool configuration for IIS.

With this configuration, you should now be able to navigate to your server's hosted site (the sample in Figure 22.1 was hosted at http://testiis) and see your application running.

Deploying Your Application to a Linux Server

If you are publishing your application to a Linux server, you need to ensure that the application is targeting the .NET Core framework. I recommend that you do a self-contained deployment when publishing to a Linux server because there is a lower chance of users having the .NET Core framework installed. You should also have an appropriate runtime identifier marked in your project file, as shown earlier this hour, in Listing 22.5. You should trigger your `publish` command with the same command as above, specifying an appropriate runtime identifier that matches your target Linux server. For this deployment, you should notice that there is an ASPTravlerz application in the publish target folder that does not have a file extension. This is the executable for your web application, and the `dotnet` command-line tool is unnecessary.

The interesting part of this process is configuring the Linux server to host your application. The following configuration directions were written based on Ubuntu 16, and your configuration may be slightly different on a different Linux distribution. You can use the Apache web server to proxy requests to the Kestrel server that's serving the ASP.NET Core application. For this deployment, place the application in /var/AspTravlerz and mark the ASPTravlerz file as executable with the following:

```
chmod +x AspTravlerz
```

I like to write a simple script file to ensure that an application is being executed from the correct folder and I can add any additional environment setup details to that script as needed. You can save such a simple script, called `StartAspTravlerz` as shown in Listing 22.6, in the same /var/AspTravlerz folder.

LISTING 22.6 A Simple StartAspTravlerz Script

```
#!/bin/sh
cd /var/AspTravlerz
./AspTravlerz
```

If needed, you can add a call to set the ASP.NET Core environment variables inside this script before the final line, and that configuration will be in place every time the application starts.

Next, you need to ensure that the proxy module is installed for Apache by running the following:

```
a2enmod proxy
```

With the proxy module in place to redirect requests from outside visitors to your ASP.NET Core application, you can write a configuration file for those requests and save it as /etc/apache2/asptravlerz.conf. Listing 22.7 shows the contents of this configuration file.

LISTING 22.7 Apache Configuration for Proxying Requests to ASP.NET Core

```
<VirtualHost *:80>
  ProxyPreserveHost On
  ProxyPass / http://127.0.0.1:5000
  ProxyPassReverse / http://127.0.0.1:5000/
  ErrorLog /var/log/apache2/asptravlerz.log
  CustomLog /var/log/apache2/asptravlerz.log common
</VirtualHost>
```

This configuration creates a host listening on port 80, the default web port, and passes all requests through to the server listening on port 5000. Remember that the Kestrel web server listens on port 5000. Logs are then configured to capture information about those requests and errors in the /var/log/apache2/asptravlerz.log folder. After writing this configuration, restart Apache by using this command from the command line:

```
sudo systemctl restart apache2
```

This has all been easy so far, and Apache is configured. Next, you need to configure the ASP.NET Core application as a service that starts and restarts appropriately with the server. You can do this by writing a service configuration file into /etc/system called asptravlerz.service and placing the contents of Listing 22.8 in that file.

LISTING 22.8 AspTravlerz.service Configuration for an Ubuntu Server

```
[Unit]
    Description:  AspTravlerz Application

    [Service]
    ExecStart=/var/AspTravlerz/StartAspTravlerz
    Restart=always
    RestartSec=10
    SyslogIdentifier=asptravlerz
    User=apache
    Environment=ASPNETCORE_ENVIRONMENT=Production

    [Install]
    WantedBy=multi-user.target
```

This configuration defines the service, names the service, tells how to start the service, says how to log activity for the service, and specifies under which system configurations the service should run. It's a very simple configuration, and once it is written, you should enable the new service and start it with the following two commands:

```
systemctl enable myapp.service
systemctl start myapp.service
```

Then open a browser and navigate to http://localhost:5000, and you should see your website. Then navigate to http://localhost, and you should still see your website. Don't worry about folks navigating directly to the Kestrel server on port 5000, as that port is blocked from outside access by the default firewall configuration.

▼ TRY IT YOURSELF

Build an Application on Windows or Mac and Deploy It to an Ubuntu Server

Follow these steps to get your application running on an Ubuntu 16.04 Linux server after you build it on a Windows machine or a Mac:

1. Update your application's .csproj file to contain a `RuntimeIdentifiers` property that contains the following runtime IDs:

   ```
   win7-x64;osx.10.11-x64;ubuntu.16.04-x64
   ```

2. Restore the necessary packages to support the additional runtimes by executing `dotnet restore`.

3. Compile and publish the application with this command at a terminal window:

   ```
   dotnet publish -r ubuntu.16.04-x64 -c Release
   ```

4. Copy the contents of the \bin\Release\netcoreapp1.1\ubuntu.16.04-x64\publish folder to your Linux server's /var/AspTravlerz folder by using SCP, FTP, or another copy strategy that works for you. You could even share your application folder to OneDrive or Dropbox and download it from there to your server.

5. Make your application executable by running the following command:

   ```
   chmod +x /var/AspTravlerz/AspTravlerz
   ```

6. Navigate to the /var/AspTravlerz folder and run the application by executing the following:

   ```
   ./AspTravlerz
   ```

7. Open a browser and navigate to http://localhost:5000 to verify that your application works on your Linux server.

Summary

In this hour, you have packaged and deployed your application to Windows and Linux servers. This is an easy process that kicks off with use of the `dotnet` command-line tool.

Q&A

Q. Can I run my ASP.NET Core application on Azure, AWS, and Google Compute?

A. Yes. ASP.NET Core support is terrific with all these cloud environments. In fact, you can run an ASP.NET Core application on almost any hosting provider by delivering a self-contained deployment appropriate for the hosting platform.

Q. **Why would I want to use a shared framework deployment?**

A. On a server that hosts several ASP.NET Core applications, you should want to deploy several copies of the .NET Core framework and tools. A shared framework installation delivers a centrally managed copy of the most common features of the framework so that you only need to deploy the third-party libraries and your application. It also means that the shared framework can be precompiled for your platform, and you can deploy your application faster than is possible with a self-contained deployment.

Q. **Why are the contents of the publish folder different from the contents of the folder named for the targeted runtime?**

A. The targeted runtime folder contains just the output of the application compile process. The publish folder contains all the files that need to be delivered, including that compiled output, for a different computer to be able to run the application.

Workshop

The workshop contains quiz questions and exercises to help you solidify your understanding of the material covered. Try to answer all questions before looking at the "Answers" that follow.

Quiz

1. What `dotnet` command can you use to generate a folder containing the files needed to run your application on another computer?

2. What property must you configure in your project file to publish a self-contained deployment?

3. What switch must be configured when executing the command to publish your application as a self-contained deployment?

4. What is a runtime identifier?

5. Can you publish an ASP.NET Core application written on .NET Framework to Linux or to Windows?

Answers

1. `dotnet publish`

2. `RuntimeIdentifiers`

3. `-r` or `-runtime` defines the target runtime on which to deliver the application.

4. A *runtime identifier* is a shorthand notation for a target operating system that your application will run on. The appropriate .NET runtime for that operating system configuration will be used with an application so that it runs properly.

5. .NET Framework applications only work on Windows. In order to run an ASP.NET Core
    application on Linux, the project must be compiled with the .NET Core framework.

Exercise

You can configure continuous integration systems to call the `dotnet publish` command for you
and generate an appropriate package for deployment to your favorite server. Try using Jenkins,
TeamCity, VSTS, or your favorite continuous integration tool to build your application whenever you
commit a change to your source control provider and build a deployment package appropriate for
your target server.

Working with Docker Containers

What You'll Learn in This Hour:

▶ What containers are

▶ Why you should consider using containers to deploy an application

▶ How to install and run both Linux and Windows containers on Windows 10

▶ How to put your application in a container

▶ How to deploy a containerized application to Microsoft Azure

Containers are a very hot topic in DevOps circles these days. Teams that are building new applications are making a shift away from using "bare metal" servers—that is, deploying to servers hosted directly on hardware—to virtual machines and containers. What is the appeal of this strategy? What concessions must you as an application developer make? How can you take advantage of this trend to deploy your ASPTravlerz application? In this hour, you'll learn about containers and how to deploy your application in a container to Microsoft Azure.

What Is a Container?

A *container* is a lightweight stand-alone executable unit of software that includes everything needed to run it, from system tools, to application configuration, to code. Containers, which can be built on Linux and Windows operating systems, isolate the executable unit from the host operating system. Unlike a virtual machine, which is a complete operating system installed and running on a host machine, a container is defined using a software configuration file and hosted directly on the operating system. Figure 23.1 illustrates the architectural differences between virtual machines and containers.

You can stand up a container much more quickly than you can a virtual machine, as containers don't require a guest operating system to be started on the hypervisor. This means you can start multiple containers very quickly—within seconds—without impacting the overall performance of the host operating system.

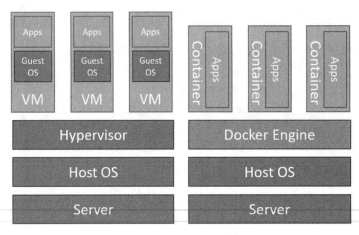

FIGURE 23.1
Architectural difference between virtual machines and containers.

Why Use Containers?

Perhaps you've had the terrible experience of writing code and deploying it to another machine and then finding that it just didn't work. The "it works on my machine" feeling certainly settled in. Every developer has had this problem, and containers give you a unit of deployment that is standard for every machine that you deploy them to. You can build a container on your developer workstation or a continuous integration system and run that application anywhere that the container hosting services are installed.

In the case of ASP.NET Core, the application framework has a docker container image available that you can build on. This image contains everything you need to get started using ASP.NET Core on Linux in about 300MB and will run on any system that has docker container services installed.

Installing Docker

The dominant container platform in the industry today is the open source and free Docker platform. On Windows 7 and later, you can install Docker Community Edition easily from www.docker.com. If you are using Windows 10, you have the option of hosting either Windows or Linux containers. All other Windows installs support only Linux containers. By default, after you install Docker for Windows, it hosts Linux containers. Docker for Windows is limited in that it hosts only Windows *or* Linux containers—not both at the same time. If you need to use both Windows and Linux containers, you need to use the Docker for Windows application to change back and forth between the operating systems.

You can install Docker on a Mac by navigating to the Docker Store at store.docker.com and installing the Docker Community Edition for Mac. Once it is installed, you will be able to run and manage Linux-based containers.

On Linux machines, you can install Docker a number of different ways. The Docker Store hosts installs for the most common Linux distributions, but it's even easier to install from the command line on Ubuntu. You can download, install, and run the Docker engine with the following three simple commands:

```
sudo apt-get update
sudo apt-get install docker-engine
sudo service docker start
```

On any of the three operating systems, you can open a console window and execute the following command to verify that your install is working properly:

```
docker version
```

You should be presented with some version information about the client and the server that are running on your system, similar to that in Figure 23.2.

```
C:\>docker version
Client:
 Version:       17.09.0-ce
 API version:   1.32
 Go version:    go1.8.3
 Git commit:    afdb6d4
 Built:         Tue Sep 26 22:40:09 2017
 OS/Arch:       windows/amd64

Server:
 Version:       17.09.0-ce
 API version:   1.32 (minimum version 1.12)
 Go version:    go1.8.3
 Git commit:    afdb6d4
 Built:         Tue Sep 26 22:45:38 2017
 OS/Arch:       linux/amd64
 Experimental:  true
```

FIGURE 23.2
Output of the `docker version` command to verify that Docker is installed.

You can further verify that your Docker install is running properly by executing the hello-world sample image. This very simple image built on Linux simply writes some sample output text to the screen to indicate that it is running properly. You can run this sample with the following command:

```
docker run hello-world
```

You probably don't have the hello-world image downloaded to your machine, but the Docker service will download it from the Docker hub for you. It's a very small image, and once it's downloaded, it will be started and show you the sample text in Figure 23.3 (or text similar to it) to prove that your workstation is running Docker containers properly.

```
C:\>docker run hello-world
Unable to find image 'hello-world:latest' locally
latest: Pulling from library/hello-world
5b0f327be733: Pull complete
Digest: sha256:07d5f7800dfe37b8c2196c7b1c524c33808ce2e0f74e7aa00e603295ca9a0972
Status: Downloaded newer image for hello-world:latest

Hello from Docker!
This message shows that your installation appears to be working correctly.

To generate this message, Docker took the following steps:
 1. The Docker client contacted the Docker daemon.
 2. The Docker daemon pulled the "hello-world" image from the Docker Hub.
 3. The Docker daemon created a new container from that image which runs the
    executable that produces the output you are currently reading.
 4. The Docker daemon streamed that output to the Docker client, which sent it
    to your terminal.

To try something more ambitious, you can run an Ubuntu container with:
 $ docker run -it ubuntu bash

Share images, automate workflows, and more with a free Docker ID:
 https://cloud.docker.com/

For more examples and ideas, visit:
 https://docs.docker.com/engine/userguide/
```

FIGURE 23.3
Output of the Docker hello-world container.

As mentioned earlier, the reference to `hello-world` is a Docker image, or a recipe for how a container should be configured. When you execute the `docker run` command, Docker instantiates an instance of that image, called a container, and runs the instructions inside the container. Those instructions write the text to the screen, as seen in Figure 23.3.

Packaging Your Application

You need to get a fresh copy of Microsoft's ASP.NET Core image for use on your workstation by executing the following command:

```
docker pull microsoft/aspnetcore:1.1
```

With a local copy of the Linux-based image for packaging ASP.NET Core applications, you can start preparing your application to be delivered as a container.

Packaging on Linux

Before you package your application into a container, you need to build your application as a release configuration so that all your content is prepared and optimized for delivery to a production location. Execute the following command to build your application and publish the contents into a Docker folder under the obj folder in your project folder:

```
dotnet publish -c Release -o obj/Docker/publish
```

The -c switch requests the release configuration of the application, and the -o switch indicates the output folder to which the contents of your ready-to-publish application should be written.

Next, you need to construct a file that contains instructions for Docker to package the application. By default, this file is called Dockerfile, and it is typically stored in the root folder of the application you are bundling. Add to your application the Dockerfile shown in Listing 23.1. This file uses some of the standard Dockerfile commands to reference your base image and add your application to it. You can find a complete reference for the Dockerfile syntax on Docker's website, at https://docs.docker.com/engine/reference/builder/.

LISTING 23.1   A Dockerfile for Packaging the ASPTravlerz Application

```
FROM microsoft/aspnetcore:1.1
WORKDIR /app
EXPOSE 80
COPY obj/Docker/publish .
ENTRYPOINT ["dotnet", "AspTravlerz.dll"]
```

Here's what each line of this file does:

- ▶ The FROM statement indicates the base image to which you are adding your application. In this case, you are referencing and building on top of the standard Microsoft aspnetcore image for ASP.NET Core 1.1.

- ▶ The WORKDIR command indicates that Docker should create a directory called app off the root of the hosted Linux filesystem. It then makes the app folder the current working directory.

- ▶ The EXPOSE command declares that your application is listening on port 80, and the host machine can use this to communicate with the container.

- ▶ COPY starts the action of taking the published source of your application in your obj/Docker/publish folder and inserting it into the container's current working directory, /app.

- ▶ ENTRYPOINT tells Docker how to start the application when you ask for the container to be started. In this case, it will execute the dotnet command with a single argument: the name of the project DLL file that was created by your publish operation.

You can now use this configuration file to instruct Docker to build an image with your application hosted inside it. When that container runs, it will start the web server and listen on port 80 for incoming requests. You can build the image with the following command from the root folder of your application:

```
docker build -t asptravlerz:1 -t asptravlerz:latest
```

This command builds a new image based on the configuration in the current folder. It then assigns two tags or names to the image: `asptravlerz:1` and `asptravlerz:latest`. The text after the colon (:) is a version number that you can use when running your application. `latest` is a convenience indicator that allows you to run that version of the container if you do not specify a version number when referencing the container.

You can start a new instance of your web application container with the following command:

```
docker run -d -p 80:80 --name web asptravlerz
```

The `-d` argument indicates that the container should run in the background and not stop unless it is explicitly halted. The `-p 80:80` argument instructs Docker to route requests for the host machine's network port 80 to the container's port 80. The format of the port mapping is the host port followed by the container port. You could map port 5000 on your workstation to port 80 of the container by using the `-p 5000:80` argument.

The `--name web` argument names this container web. Finally, `asptravlerz` is the name of the container image to run.

▼ TRY IT YOURSELF

Navigate and Monitor the Running Container

Now that you've learned how to start a container, you can navigate to the container and explore some monitoring tools provided by Docker. Follow these steps:

1. Navigate your web browser to http://localhost, and you should see your application running.

2. Execute `docker logs web` to view the log messages that are being written to the console of the running container.

3. Execute `docker logs web -f` to view the log messages and follow them as new messages are logged. While this command is running, click some links in the application and watch how the logs are updated in your console window. Use the Ctrl+C key combination to exit the log following operation in the console.

4. Run `docker stats web` to see the processor and memory utilization of the application. Try navigating around the application in your browser and watch how the statistics are affected. Use the Ctrl+C key combination to exit this mode.

5. Stop and remove the running container instance with the following command:

   ```
   docker rm -f web
   ```

Packaging on Windows

If you are developing and planning to deploy to a Windows operating system, you can optionally build and deploy by using a Windows-based container. Fortunately, the Microsoft team has
built the `aspnetcore` container using a multi-architectural approach that will recognize on
which operating system Docker is hosting containers. You can use the same command as you
used earlier with Linux containers to package your application for Windows:

```
docker build -t asptravlerz:1 -t asptravlerz:latest .
```

The same Dockerfile works for both Linux and Windows, and each hosted operating system
maintains its own catalog of Docker images on disk. You can run your application inside the
Windows container with the same command you use for Linux:

```
docker run -d -p 80:80 --name web asptravlerz
```

This time, a Windows container is started and hosts your application. Try navigating to it, and
you should see very little difference between the previously running Linux application and the
currently running Windows application.

Running Multiple Containers

You can run multiple instances of your containers with a load balancer very easily in the Linux
operating system configuration. The recommended way to do this is to use the docker-compose.
yml file to declare how the containers should be structured. To do this, create a file named docker-
compose.yml in the root folder of your application and add the contents of Listing 23.2 to that file.

LISTING 23.2   Docker-Compose Configuration for Running Multiple Containers

```
version: '3'

services:
  web:
    image: asptravlerz
    build:
      context: .
      dockerfile: Dockerfile

  loadbalancer:
    image: dockercloud/haproxy
    links:
      - web
    volumes:
      - /var/run/docker.sock:/var/run/docker.sock
    ports:
      - "80:80"
      - "1936:1936"
```

This configuration defines two services: web and loadbalancer. The web service is a pointer to your application, and the loadbalancer service uses the haproxy software-based load balancer to connect to your web server and present its content. The links under the loadbalancer service indicate that there should be a network link between the loadbalancer and web services. In addition, the volumes entry indicates that the Docker sockets of the host machine and the load balancer should by shared at the location specified. Finally, the network ports 80 and 1936 are shared to the host machine.

The haproxy image chosen here has some automatic configuration built into it such that it will handle load balancing for any ports exposed by those containers. The port 80 entry under loadbalancer grants the host machine and external machines access to the web service port 80. The 1936 port is a monitoring port where you can view information about the load balancing service.

You can start the service with this command:

```
docker-compose up -d --scale web=4
```

This command creates one instance of your load balancer, four instances of your web container, and an appropriate internal network to connect those five containers. If you navigate your browser to your http://localhost location, you should quickly see your web application. You can review the load balancer configuration by navigating to http://localhost:1936 and using the default user ID and password combination stats and stats. You should see a dashboard console similar to the one shown in Figure 23.4.

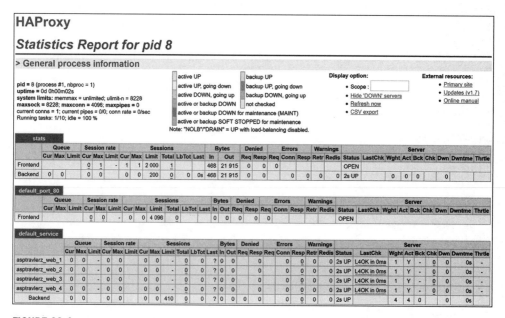

FIGURE 23.4
The haproxy statistics dashboard.

Deploying to Azure

On Microsoft Azure, you can create a private container registry, similar to the public registry at hub.docker.com, where you can grab premade Docker images. In your private registry, you can store images for your applications, and they will be secured from the public. You can deploy instances of those images with an appropriate user ID and password combination to any service that is able to connect to your registry.

If you start creating a registry from the Azure portal by using the New > Container Registry menu option from the left side, you will be presented with options similar to those in Figure 23.5. In this case, name the registry 24hoursContainerRegistry.azurecr.io.

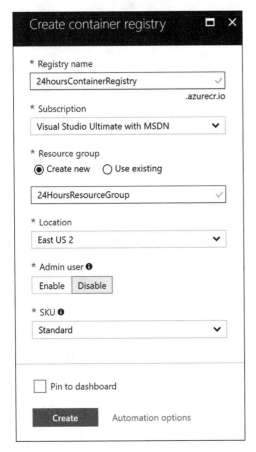

FIGURE 23.5
Configuring an Azure container registry.

You should configure the registry as shown in Figure 23.5, except you should choose to enable an admin user to prevent unauthorized access to your applications. Once the registry is provisioned by Azure, you can enter the access keys configuration, shown in Figure 23.6, of the registry and copy out the user ID and password associated with your registry.

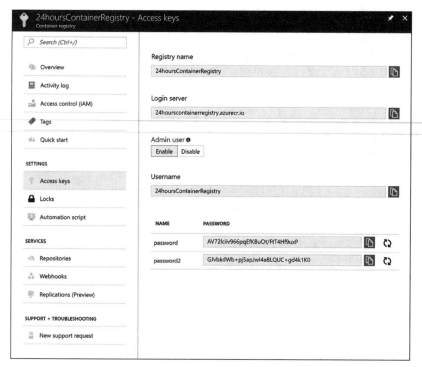

FIGURE 23.6
Access keys for a container registry on Azure.

Next, you can configure your developer workstation to push your new `asptravlerz` image to the Azure registry by following these steps:

1. Log in to the registry on your workstation's command line with this statement and the user ID/password combination shown in Figure 23.6:

```
docker login 24hourscontainerregistry.azurecr.io
```

2. Add a local tag to your `asptravlerz` image by using this statement:

```
docker tag asptravlerz
24hourscontainerregistry.azurecr.io/asptravlerz
```

3. Push your `asptravlerz` image to the registry with this command:

```
docker push 24hourscontainerregistry.azurecr.io/asptravlerz
```

Now, you can install and run your ASPTravlerz application on any hosting service that's able to install images from your registry. The easiest way to do this is to open the Azure cloud shell, using the button at the top of the Azure portal. Figure 23.7 indicates the button to use to activate the cloud shell.

Activate the cloud shell

FIGURE 23.7
Activating the cloud shell in the Azure portal.

With the shell opened in the bottom half of the screen, you can configure the resource group and app service plan for your new application. A *resource group*, if you don't have one already provisioned, is a collection of related resources that are managed together and not necessarily running on the same physical hardware. It can be considered a nice grouping of resources for billing purposes. You can allocate a new resource group with a command similar to the following:

```
az group create --location "East US" --name 24HourResourceGroup
```

An *app service plan* is a grouping of application services that all run on the same physical machine. You can allocate a new app service plan with the following command:

```
az appservice plan create --name myServicePlan
    --resource-group 24HoursResourceGroup --is-linux
```

It is important that you include the `is-linux` argument on this command, as the container services on Azure only run on Linux. Finally, you can create and use your container with the following command, which allocates the web application:

```
az webapp create -g 24HourResourceGroup -p myServicePlan -n asptravlerzwebapp
```

Next, you can configure the web app to install and use the container in the registry with this command:

```
az webapp config container set --name asptravlerzwebapp
    --resource-group 24HoursResourceGroup
    --docker-custom-image-name asptravlerz
    --docker-registry-server-url https://24hourscontainerregistry.azurecr.io
    --docker-registry-server-user <docker-id>
    --docker-registry-server-password <password>
```

At this point, the container image should be acquired by the Azure app service instance and deployed. Try navigating to your application, and you should see the contents of your image.

Summary

In this hour you have learned about containers and placed your application into a container for easy deployment to Microsoft Azure or any other hosting service. Containers are a great distribution unit, as you can deliver your entire web application in a pre-configured image that runs exactly the way you configured it. You have also learned how to use `docker-compose` to run multiple copies of your application behind a software-based network traffic load balancer.

Q&A

Q. Can the Windows container version of my application be run on Azure?

A. Yes. However, currently the only Azure service that supports this type of deployment is Azure Service Fabric. App service should support Windows containers in the future.

Q. Is there a way to reduce the size of the container that my application is deployed in?

A. No. The ASP.NET team works to keep the base image size as small as possible. Future updates to the image may use a smaller distribution of Linux called Alpine, and that could reduce your footprint.

Q. Can I configure sticky sessions in the software load balancer?

A. Yes! The load balancer image that was demonstrated in this hour is called haproxy, and you can configure it by passing in any number of environment variables. For this configuration, you can add an environment block to your web service to assign the `BALANCE` configuration to `source`, like this:

```
web:
  image: asptravlerz
  build:
    context: .
    dockerfile: Dockerfile
  environment:
    - BALANCE: source
```

Other configuration options can be found on the container image page, at https://hub. docker.com/r/dockercloud/haproxy/.

Q. Can I instruct `docker-compose` to start with three web servers by default instead of remembering to include that argument when starting the containers?

A. You can't do this with `docker-compose`, but this is possible with other Docker orchestration tools, like `docker swarm`.

Workshop

The workshop contains quiz questions and exercises to help you solidify your understanding of the material covered. Try to answer all questions before looking at the "Answers" that follow.

Quiz

1. How is a Docker container image configured?

2. What operating systems can Docker images contain as a guest operating system?

3. On what host operating systems can Windows images be run?

4. What does `docker-compose` allow you to do?

5. Why should you use a private container registry on a service such as Microsoft Azure?

Answers

1. Image configuration is written into a Dockerfile.

2. Docker images can contain Linux or Windows operating system-based images.

3. Windows images can be run only on Windows operating systems.

4. It creates multiple instances of related Docker containers at once.

5. The private container registry allows you to secure your application images that should not be public and deploy them to any publicly accessible hosting service.

Exercise

Now that you have learned how to configure and run ASPTravlerz in a container, try running the service in Microsoft Azure as shown in this hour. Microsoft offers a free service level that requires no credit cards and allows you to start exploring the service. Give it a try and see how your application runs in the cloud. When you're done exploring, delete the service from Microsoft Azure.

Looking to the Future and .NET Standard

What You'll Learn in This Hour:

▶ What .NET Standard is

▶ How to write code that works with .NET Framework and .NET Core

▶ Future updates for ASP.NET Core

▶ How to stay connected to the ASP.NET Core community and learn about planned features

As an open source project, ASP.NET Core receives hundreds of lines of code committed to the various libraries, templates, and projects every day. With more than 450 contributors registered on the ASP.NET GitHub organization, the framework is evolving quickly, and new features are published every three to six months. In this hour, you will learn about the .NET Standard concept and how this feature allows your existing code to keep up with the changes in the .NET community.

What Is .NET Standard?

Way back in Hour 3, "Exploring the New Project Templates," you learned that there are two different frameworks on which you can build ASP.NET Core: .NET Framework and .NET Core. .NET Framework has been actively maintained since 2002 and runs on Windows only. .NET Core was released with ASP.NET Core and provides support for running applications on Windows, Mac, and Linux. How can you write shared libraries that can be used regardless of the .NET framework type you are using?

In 2013, Microsoft's .NET team faced this problem, with the rising challenges of a Windows Phone distribution of .NET Framework that was distinctly different from the Windows desktop version of the framework. In addition, Silverlight's Flash-like experience used yet another version of the .NET Framework. To solve this problem, the team invented the Portable Class Library (PCL). The goal of the PCL was to deliver a development experience that could be compiled and run on any of the frameworks it targeted and allowed use of all the features that were common to those chosen frameworks.

The problem with this approach was that you had to select specific frameworks and versions at project creation time, and you were constrained to using only features common to those frameworks. Consequently, as you added more target frameworks to your library, you reduced the APIs that were available to you. Figure 24.1 shows a Venn diagram illustrating this situation with frameworks and features.

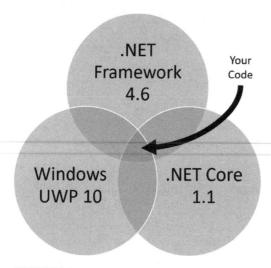

FIGURE 24.1
Targeting multiple frameworks with PCLs meant you could write code targeting the intersection of their common features.

To project maintainers of existing code this was a stumbling block rather than a gateway to code reuse. The reduced footprint of available APIs to code against was a significant barrier, and with the entry of .NET Core into the mix, as many as 10 different .NET Frameworks could be utilized. This growth of .NET could not be sustained, and the team took steps to rein in the issues with PCLs.

.NET Standard is the answer to those issues with PCLs and provides a way out of the mire of managing interactions and APIs exposed by different frameworks. .NET Standard accomplishes this by providing the following:

▶ A set of immutable versioned framework contracts that define the common APIs exposed by each version of the .NET Standard contract.

▶ Compiler and packaging rules that allow you to code against a .NET Standard set of APIs that will be swapped out at build time for a project in a supported framework. For example, when a .NET Standard library is referenced by a .NET Core project, the references in the .NET Standard library are redirected to the .NET Core implementations. When that same library is referenced by a .NET Framework project, the .NET Framework implementations are swapped in at build time.

▶ A clear set of APIs that you are familiar with. In addition, each version of .NET Standard includes additional APIs and does not modify previous contract versions.

.NET Standard defines the common APIs that all framework versions need to implement in order to be called ".NET." In addition, as new .NET Frameworks are invented and implemented, they will declare which version of the .NET Standard APIs they support, and your code that supports the same .NET Standard version or lower will just work when included in a project for that platform.

The .NET Standard Versions

There are several versions of .NET Standard that define the various sets of APIs and versions that implement those APIs. When you write code targeting one of the .NET Standard versions, you develop with confidence that it will work on the framework versions associated with it. Table 24.1 provides a helpful grid of .NET Standard versions and .NET framework versions.

TABLE 24.1 .NET Standard Versions and Supported Frameworks

Framework	.NET Standard Version						
	1.0	**1.1**	**1.2**	**1.3**	**1.4**	**1.5**	**1.6**
.NET Framework	4.5	4.5	4.5.1	4.6	4.6.1	4.6.1	4.6.1
.NET Core	1.0	1.0	1.0	1.0	1.0	1.0	1.0
Mono	4.6	4.6	4.6	4.6	4.6	4.6	4.6
Xamarin iOS	10.0	10.0	10.0	10.0	10.0	10.0	10.0
Xamarin Mac	3.0	3.0	3.0	3.0	3.0	3.0	3.0
Xamarin Android	7.0	7.0	7.0	7.0	7.0	7.0	7.0
Universal Windows Platform	10.0	10.0	10.0	10.0	10.0	10.0.16299	10.0.16299
Windows	8.0	8.0	8.1	—	—	—	—
Windows Phone	8.1	8.1	8.1	—	—	—	—
Windows Phone Silverlight	8.0	—	—	—	—	—	—

For the frameworks listed in the leftmost column of Table 24.1, at a minimum you can use the version indicated in the middle with the .NET Standard version at the top of the column. For example, you can use .NET Framework 4.6.1 with .NET Standard 1.0 if you prefer. However, you cannot use .NET Framework 4.5 with .NET Standard 1.6.

This is an exciting opportunity for .NET developers, as your code can now be used to deliver web applications with ASP.NET Core, Windows applications using the Universal Windows Platform, and mobile applications for iOS and Android with Xamarin.

The .NET team recommends that for maximum future compatibility, you should build your projects using the lowest possible version of .NET Standard. Visual Studio comes with a portability analyzer that you can use to inspect your class library projects to determine which versions of .NET Standard you could re-target your project to support. In addition, the Visual Studio compiler reports when you are using APIs that are not available in the version of .NET Standard that your project is targeting.

Building and Using a .NET Standard Library

You can get started building a .NET Standard project for use with the ASPTravlerz application very easily by using the `dotnet new` command and templates. In this section, you'll use these templates to build a simple weather client that will fetch the current conditions for a particular city. For this example, you will connect to the free openweathermap.org service to acquire forecast data. To use the openweathermap API, you need to navigate to openweathermap.org and sign up for a free account and request an API key. Be sure to make note of that API key assigned to you, as you will use it in this project.

Create a new Weather project in a folder next to your ASPTravlerz project by using this command:

```
dotnet new classlib -f netstandard1.1 -o Weather
```

The Weather.csproj file that this command generates is pretty empty, and you need to add a reference to the Newtonsoft.Json package so that you can parse output from the public API you will read from. Therefore, update the content of the project file to match that of Listing 24.1.

LISTING 24.1   **Weather Project File Contents**

```
<Project Sdk="Microsoft.NET.Sdk">

  <PropertyGroup>
    <TargetFramework>netstandard1.1</TargetFramework>
  </PropertyGroup>

  <ItemGroup>
    <PackageReference Include="Newtonsoft.Json" Version="10.0.1" />
  </ItemGroup>

</Project>
```

Next, rename the class1.cs file that was generated to the new name WeatherProxy.cs and add the content of Listing 24.2 to that file.

LISTING 24.2 `WeatherProxy` **Object to Fetch Weather Conditions**

```
public class WeatherProxy
{

  const string myApiKey = "<< YOUR API KEY >>";

  public static async Task<WeatherModel> GetConditions(string city)
  {

    var client = new HttpClient();

    var stringResult = await client.GetStringAsync(
      "http://api.openweathermap.org/data/2.5/weather?" +
      $"q={city}&APPID={myApiKey}&units=imperial");
    var json = JObject.Parse(stringResult);

    var outModel = new WeatherModel()
    {
      Conditions = json["weather"][0]["main"].ToString(),
      TempF = decimal.Parse(json["main"]["temp"].ToString())
    };

    return outModel;

  }

  public class WeatherModel
  {

    public decimal TempF { get; set; }

    public string Conditions { get; set; }

  }

}
```

HttpClient is an API that first appeared in .NET Standard 1.1. You use HttpClient to request data from the openweathermap service. When data is returned from that service, this code parses the appropriate elements from the response into a WeatherModel object with the temperature in Fahrenheit and the current conditions.

You can now add a reference to the new Weather project from your AspTravlerz.csproj file so that you can report the weather in your home location. To do so, add these lines to your AspTravlerz.csproj file to establish the reference from ASPTravlerz to Weather:

```
<ItemGroup>
  <ProjectReference Include="..\Weather\Weather.csproj" />
</ItemGroup>
```

Next, you can adapt the `HomeController` `Index` method to request the weather for your home city. The sample code shown in Listing 24.3 uses Philadelphia as the home city, but you can adapt it as needed.

LISTING 24.3   `HomeController` `Index` **Method with a Call to Fetch Weather for Philadelphia**

```
public async Task<IActionResult> Index()
{
  var weather = await Weather.WeatherProxy.GetConditions("Philadelphia");

  return View(weather);
}
```

You are now passing the temperature and conditions to the view as a model that can be parsed and injected into the page. To properly display this data, you need to define the model on the view and add a short paragraph marker to the Views/Home/Index.cshtml template, as shown in Listing 24.4.

LISTING 24.4   **Updated View to Show the Weather in Philadelphia**

```
@model Weather.WeatherProxy.WeatherModel
@{
    ViewData["Title"] = "Home Page";
}

<p>Current conditions in Philadelphia: @Model.TempF F and @Model.Conditions</p>

<app>Loading...</app>

<script src="~/dist/vendor.js" asp-append-version="true"></script>
@section scripts {
    <script src="~/dist/main-client.js" asp-append-version="true"></script>
}
```

Now when you browse to your application, you see the current weather in your home location—in this case Philadelphia—when you're thinking about your travel plans.

Modularize the Call for Weather

The call for weather information is very simple with your new .NET Standard weather client. Follow these steps to wrap that object into a tag helper to simplify how you report weather:

1. Create a new class in your project called `WeatherTagHelper` that inherits from the `TagHelper` class.

2. Add a string property called `City` to the class.

3. Override the `ProcessAsync` method to make the same calls to the `WeatherProxy`. `GetConditions` method shown in Listing 24.3, but this time pass in the city name stored in the `City` property.

4. Use the `TagHelperOutput` output parameter to append HTML with a similar weather report used in the view in Listing 24.4.

5. Remove the calls in the `HomeController` and Index.cshtml for the model and `WeatherProxy`.

6. Insert in the Index.cshtml view a weather tag with a `city` attribute for your city:

```
<weather city="Seattle"></weather>
```

Future Updates for ASP.NET Core

The future is very bright for ASP.NET Core, as more features are constantly being developed for the World Wide Web as a whole and the Microsoft team is engaged to deliver framework features to support development to accommodate those new web features. You can always find the ASP.NET Core team's current roadmap on its GitHub repository, at https://github.com/aspnet/home/wiki/roadmap. The following are some of the upcoming features being built:

▶ Simplified process startup and reduced configuration for the common scenarios with a `DefaultWebBuilder` construct that eliminates most of the configuration in Program.cs

▶ Simplified reference of all ASP.NET Core packages, allowing you to reference a single All package to get all the Microsoft-supported packages

▶ Simplified use of ViewComponents so that they can be referenced as though they were tag helpers

▶ A new UI paradigm called Razor Pages that allows you to write Razor templates without the need for an entire MVC architecture

▶ An improved publish process that excludes from the publish destination packages that are not used in your application

▶ Tight integration with Azure Application Insights so that you can monitor your application's processor use, memory usage, and logs easily when they are running on Azure

▶ Support for the SignalR framework so that you can push content to visitors of your application by using WebSocket protocols

Staying Connected with the ASP.NET Core Community

The ASP.NET Core community is a living community that is constantly growing and changing. You can observe the speed and growth of projects by visiting https://github.com/aspnet/home. From this repository, you can jump off to any of the child ASP.NET Core projects on GitHub. The team also provides links to preview versions of the framework that you can download and test on your workstation if you are interested in trying the "bleeding edge" features. You can also find the source and discussion for .NET Core on GitHub, at https://github.com/dotnet.

Microsoft provides a vast collection of documents for ASP.NET Core and other development technologies at https://docs.microsoft.com. The documentation is live as well, meaning that you can submit changes to those documents if you think they could be improved. If you do submit updates and the team accepts them, you will have your name and profile picture listed as a contributor to the official documentation.

As the frameworks grow and change, Microsoft makes announcements about Visual Studio, the .NET Framework, and ASP.NET on these blogs:

▶ **Visual Studio blog:** https://blogs.msdn.microsoft.com/visualstudio

▶ **.NET blog:** https://blogs.msdn.microsoft.com/dotnet

▶ **ASP.NET blog:** https://blogs.msdn.microsoft.com/webdev

Finally, the ASP.NET Core program managers are running their project using Agile techniques. This means developers who are using the framework are stakeholders, and stakeholders are entitled to participate in standup meetings. The ASP.NET Core team hosts a weekly standup as a streaming video, typically on Tuesdays, at https://live.asp.net. You can find a complete history of every video standup on that site as well.

Summary

You have many options for enhancing your applications further by building libraries with .NET Standard that will then be "future-proofed" and can be used by any .NET Framework, .NET Core, or Xamarin project in the future. ASP.NET Core continues to evolve, and there are lots of ways for you to engage the ASP.NET Core team to learn more about the present state as well as the future of the product. The team welcomes feedback on its blogs and during its standup calls.

Q&A

Q. Do I need to build class libraries with .NET Standard, or can I still use .NET Framework 4.6+ or .NET Core to build libraries?

A. .NET Standard is another option for building reusable libraries. You are welcome to use any framework you wish to build your project, but by using .NET Standard, you get reuse across multiple .NET Framework types.

Q. I have an existing library written for .NET Framework 2.0. Can I use that in .NET Standard?

A. The upcoming .NET Core 2.0 framework and .NET Standard 2.0 specification provide for a compatibility feature that will allow all .NET Framework-managed code to just work under the .NET Standard 2.0 capabilities. The compatibility feature will do its best to match your library to the appropriate APIs of .NET Core 2.0.

Q. Can I package and deploy my .NET Standard project as a NuGet package?

A. Yes! Using NuGet packages is the preferred way to deliver this functionality, and you can easily generate a package by using the `dotnet pack` command.

Q. I think I found a bug in how .NET Standard/.NET Core/ASP.NET Core works. How do I report that to Microsoft?

A. For these open source frameworks and tools, you should identify the appropriate repository on GitHub under either aspnet or dotnet and use the Issues tab there to report your problem. The engineers working on the project will review and respond to your issue.

Q. I have an idea for a future ASP.NET Core feature. How do I suggest it and start building it?

A. It's great that you have a new feature idea. Open an issue in the appropriate repository on GitHub under either aspnet or dotnet and use the Issues tab but make it clear that you are suggesting a new feature. After you suggest the feature, the team will triage your proposal, and you can then start working on it by cloning the source code and making changes. You should then submit a pull-request that the Microsoft team will review to determine whether to accept your change.

Workshop

The workshop contains quiz questions and exercises to help you solidify your understanding of the material covered. Try to answer all questions before looking at the "Answers" that follow.

Quiz

1. What type of projects can you build that target .NET Standard?

2. What is the minimum .NET Standard version of a project that you can build and consume in a .NET Framework 4.6 project?

3. `HttpClient` is an API that first appeared in which version of .NET Standard?

4. What tag is used in a csproj file to reference the output of another project?

5. How frequently does the ASP.NET Core team host standup video meetings for the public to attend?

Answers

1. .NET Standard supports only the Class Library project type.

2. .NET Framework 4.6 is supported starting with .NET Standard 1.3.

3. .NET Standard 1.1 is the first version to support the `HttpClient` API.

4. The `ProjectReference` tag is used to reference the output of other projects.

5. The ASP.NET Core team hosts standup meetings once a week, usually on Tuesdays, at https://live.asp.net.

Exercise

Now that you have a .NET Standard client that can fetch weather information for a given destination, extend the `Trip` object to include a Primary Destination field. With this additional field populated, add a Current Weather Conditions column to the list of upcoming trips by using `WeatherTagHelper` and the Primary Destination value for each trip.

Index

X-Y-Z

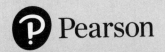